ARCHAEOLOGY, HISTORY, AND SOCIETY IN GALILEE

ARCHAEOLOGY, HISTORY, AND SOCIETY IN GALILEE

The Social Context of Jesus and the Rabbis

RICHARD A. HORSLEY

TRINITY PRESS INTERNATIONAL
Valley Forge, Pennsylvania

Trinity Press International, P.O. Box 851, Valley Forge, PA 19482-0851
Trinity Press International is a division of the Morehouse Publishing Group

Library of Congress Cataloging-in-Publication Data

Horsley, Richard A.
    Archaeology, history, and society in Galilee : the social context
of Jesus and the rabbis / Richard A. Horsley.
        p.   cm.
    Includes bibliographical references and index.
    ISBN 1-56338-182-6 (alk. paper)
    1. Galilee (Israel) – History. 2. Galilee (Israel) – Antiquities.
3. Jews – History – 586 B.C.-70 A.D. 4. Galilee (Israel) – Social life
and customs. 5. Judaism – History – Post-exilic period, 586 B.C.-210
A.D. 6. Jesus Christ – Biography. 7. Jews – Politics and government –
To 70 A.D. 8. Excavations (Archaeology) – Israel – Galilee.
I. Title.
DS110.G2H619 1996
933–dc20   96-42950
                                                             CIP

Printed in the United States of America

96   97   98   99   10   9   8   7   6   5   4   3   2   1

CONTENTS

PREFACE AND
ACKNOWLEDGMENTS

Three major factors (along with several lesser ones) have led me into this project. First, when I was working on popular movements in Jewish Palestine and on Jesus as spearheading a renewal of Israel ten to twenty years ago, it had not yet occurred to me that there were particular reasons to focus specifically on Galilee. Meanwhile, of course, twenty-five years ago archaeologists Eric Meyers and Jim Strange focused their investigations on Galilee, even on villages in Upper Galilee. Yet at the time no one else among either archaeologists or textual scholars understood why Galilee might be important. For example, Sean Freyne's dominant argument in *Galilee from Alexander the Great to Hadrian* (1980), the first major study to focus specifically on the area, was that Galilean Judaism was no different from that in Judea and Jerusalem. Not until about ten years ago, in probing discussions with Burton Mack, did I come to recognize that there might well have been significant regional differences between Galilee and Judea, as well as class differences between ordinary people (Galileans and Judeans) and the Herodian and high-priestly elite in Jerusalem. The first probe of the possible issues was a set of SBL Seminar Papers for the "Historical Jesus" section at the 1988 annual meeting by Douglas Edwards, Anthony Saldarini, Andrew Overman, and myself.

Second, there has been a tendency in studies of Jesus and the Gospels to draw — however critically or uncritically — on rabbinic literature to fill in gaps in our sources for knowledge of the first century, as well as for information on the Pharisees as the principal "opponents" of Jesus, yet largely to ignore the later Jewish history in which the rabbis emerged to prominence. It has become increasingly evident that New Testament scholars must understand the historical context and development of rabbinic circles in order to use rabbinic literature critically as evidence for life in Jewish Palestine, particularly if we are to make projections back into late second-temple times.

Third, I had devoted a great deal of time and energy attempting to tease reliable information about ordinary people in Jewish Palestine out of (primarily) literary sources. Nearly all literary sources, however, express the viewpoint and interests of the literate and ruling elite and focus on political events at the highest level, the interaction between the Hasmonean, Herodian, and high-priestly rulers of Judea and the Romans. Indeed, the only occasions on which sources such as Josephus's histories mention Judean or Galilean villagers or ordinary Jerusalemites was when they disrupted the dominant order. That meant that the only justifiable focus for study of ordinary people in Palestine was their protests and movements (although such were relatively plentiful in late second-temple times). When archaeologists began to dig up village sites as well as cities, it opened up a whole new source of information about ordinary people, particularly about their ordinary lives. I (and others working on the historical Jesus and/or popular movements) had been slow to take seriously into account the material culture that was being investigated by archaeologists.

Because of previous commitments I finally managed to read systematically through archaeological reports particularly on village sites only during the last five years. I was able to bring archaeological materials into the larger study of *Galilee: History, Politics, People* (1995) only to a limited extent. However, the Historical Jesus and the Archaeology of the New Testament sections of the SBL did accept and develop my proposal for a major joint session on "The Historical Jesus and Archaeology of the Galilee" for the 1994 annual meeting. In preparation for that joint session, I read more critically through most of the archaeological reports on Galilean sites now published and wrote a lengthy SBL seminar paper. That reading and paper form the archaeological basis for this book and an earlier article in *BASOR*. Moreover, the papers from that joint session will be published in a forthcoming volume from Trinity Press International (edited by Andrew Overman and myself).

This book could not have been written ten or perhaps even four or five years ago. The archaeological profiles of Galilee have become steadily clearer if still debated. Important critical studies of rabbinic literature and the development of rabbinic circles have emerged very recently. And the distinctive character of Galilee as a region and of regions within Galilee have only recently come into focus. Hopefully, it is now possible to bring the implications of these new developments together toward a fuller understanding of Galilee. In this book (like the earlier *Archaeology, Jesus, and the Rabbis* by Meyers and Strange), I hope to have entered into dialogues and encouraged conversations across related but different fields of study. The respective methods and goals of the fields are different and they are unlikely very soon to come into close contact and collaboration. I am certainly not pretending to be either an archaeologist or learned in rabbinic literature. Much of what I have laid out may be incomplete and provisional and some of it may turn out to be off-base. But I am convinced that it is important for New Testament specialists to become far more conversant with the work of these related fields.

Recent reading of analyses of rabbinic literature has only increased my respect for the sophistication and intricacies of rabbinic scholarship, particularly for the difficulties of using rabbinic rulings as sources for social history. From talking with archaeologists about their excavations, reading their reports, and visiting some of the sites, I have developed great respect and deep admiration for the painstaking work they go through to raise funding, obtain permissions, design their digs, organize the requisite team of specialists, critically formulate typologies and stratigraphy, sift through soil and debris, and even diplomatically handle harassments to produce the evidence that people like me simply appropriate in comfortable libraries. I take seriously comments to the effect that it takes ten years of excavation and teams of several dozen people working in close cooperation to understand a single site.

I thus want to express deep appreciation for the important productive labor of colleagues in these related fields. I acknowledge a special indebtedness particularly to Shaye Cohen, Lee Levine, and Martin Goodman for their critical studies of rabbinic materials and history; to Eric Meyers and Jim Strange for their groundbreaking and innovative archaeological excavations and interpretations in

Galilee; and to Sean Freyne for his magisterial historical study of Galilee.

I would like to express particular gratitude to Tom Longstaff and Neil Silberman for tutoring in archaeology; to Tom for criticism of my first written probes into archaeological reports; to Dom Crossan and Andy Overman for setting up the joint SBL session on "The Historical Jesus and Archaeology of the Galilee" as well as for the general stimulation of their own scholarly work; to Eric Meyers for his generous response to my attempt at dialogue with archaeology in *BASOR;* to Moti Aviam for a guided tour through many sites in Galilee and his unusual archaeological and historical knowledge and "savvy" of the area; and to Kathleen Corley, Randy Huntsberry, Andy Overman, and Marianne Sawicki for criticism of and suggestions about the chapters of this book.

Special thanks also to Laura Whitney and the circulation staff at Andover-Harvard Theological Library and to Gail Pershouse and the circulation staff at Episcopal Divinity School/Weston School of Theology Libraries and to my research assistants, Marcus Aurin, Heather Kapplow, and Jane McIntosh at the University of Massachusetts–Boston.

ABBREVIATIONS

ABD	D. N. Freeman, ed., *Anchor Bible Dictionary*
AJP	*American Journal of Philology*
AJSRev	*American Jewish Studies Review*
ANET	J. B. Pritchard, ed., *Ancient Near Eastern Texts*
ANRW	W. Haase, ed., *Aufstieg und Niedergang der römischen Welt*
AOS	American Oriental Series
ASOR DissS	American Schools of Oriental Research Dissertation Series
ATR	*Anglican Theological Review*
BA	*Biblical Archaeologist*
BAR	*Biblical Archaeologist Review*
BASOR	*Bulletin of the American Schools of Oriental Research*
BJS	Brown Judaic Studies
CBQ	Catholic Biblical Quarterly
CRINT	Compendia Rerum Iudaicarum ad Novum Testamentum
EA	El Amarna
EAEHL	*Encyclopedia of Archaeological Explorations in the Holy Land*
HTR	*Harvard Theological Review*

HUCA	*Hebrew Union College Annual*
IDB Suppl	Supplementary volume to G. A. Buttrick, ed., *Interpreters Dictionary of the Bible*
IEJ	*Israel Exploration Journal*
JBL	*Journal of Biblical Literature*
JESHO	*Journal of the Economic and Social History of the Orient*
JJS	*Journal of Jewish Studies*
JSJ	*Journal of the Study of Judaism in the Persian, Hellenistic, and Roman Period*
JSOT	*Journal for the Study of the Old Testament*
JSOT SS	*Journal for the Study of the Old Testament Supplement Series*
JTS	*Journal of Theological Studies*
NEAEHL	*New Encyclopedia of Archaeological Explorations in the Holy Land*
NTS	*New Testament Studies*
NovT	*Novum Testamentum*
NovTSup	Novum Testamentum Supplements
SBL	Society of Biblical Literature
TDNT	G. Kittel and G. Friedrich, eds., *Theological Dictionary of the New Testament*

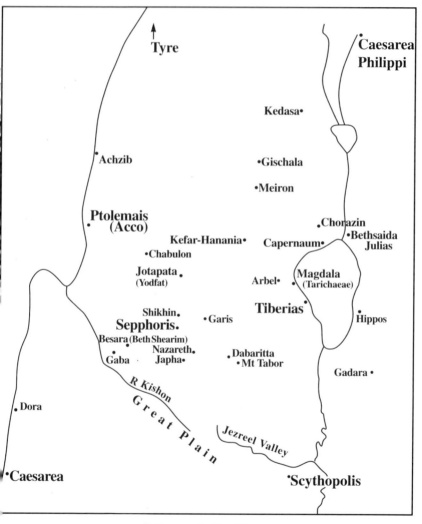

Map of Galilee

INTRODUCTION

In the former time he brought into contempt the land of Zebulun and the land of Naphtali, but in the latter time he will make glorious the way of the sea, the land beyond the Jordan, Galilee of the nations.

— ISA. 9:1

Archaeological discoveries in the Holy Land catch the attention of the press. That gives them the power to shape images of the past. Recent studies of the historical Jesus have seized upon certain archaeologists' claims about the "urbanization" of Galilee in Roman times and used those views to de-Judaize Jesus and place him into a more cosmopolitan cultural context.[1] Even Galilean peasants, it seems, were conversant in popular Hellenistic philosophies. Christians had always been bothered by the Jewishness of Jesus. Sobered by the Holocaust about the implications of Christian anti-Judaism, many scholars reaffirmed that indeed Jesus was Jewish. If Galilee already hosted a cosmopolitan urbanized ethos,[2] however, Jesus could be Jewish without all the supposedly problematic particularism of Judaism.

That such a conclusion about Jesus is by no means necessary or obvious, however, can be seen in the very different conclusion that Jewish scholars draw about the rabbis, particularly Judah the Prince, two centuries later. By that time the city of Sepphoris was more thoroughly Hellenized, with a theater and elaborate Dionysiac mosaics.[3] Yet it was precisely in this culturally cosmopolitan city that Rabbi Judah the Prince, friend of Roman emperors and wielder of influence throughout the Hellenistic-Jewish diaspora communities, presided over the compilation of the Mishnah, the foundation of rabbinic Judaism.

Something seems wrong when these conclusions about cosmopolitan ethos and Hellenistic influences in Galilee are juxta-

I

posed. Certain Christian scholars conclude that Hellenistic influences stemming from Sepphoris had created a cosmopolitan ethos to which villagers such as Jesus responded positively at the very beginning of the period of Romanization. Jewish rabbinic scholars, on the other hand, conclude that the more fully developed cosmopolitan atmosphere of the city provided the context in which the urbane Judah the Prince consolidated indigenous Jewish scribal traditions in Hebrew.[4] The arguments about influence would clearly be more credible if Jesus were the later figure in the more fully cosmopolitan city and Judah the villager at the very beginning of the "urbanization" of Galilee!

These two statements of relationship between supposedly cosmopolitan influence and Jewish responses are particularly salient examples of how even seemingly interrelated fields proceed more or less independently of one another in the academic division of labor. The findings of archaeological excavations in Galilee would be of considerable usefulness both to study of Jesus and the Gospel tradition and to study of rabbinic Judaism. Yet since neither field has been appropriating archaeological reports into its ongoing investigations on a regular basis, when they suddenly do take note of a particular archaeological finding, no conceptual apparatus is readily available for appropriate consideration of its implications.

Surely one of the main reasons why these three fields have proceeded without attending regularly to their close cousins is that each one has focused on its own exciting new questions and innovations. The most recent "quest for the historical Jesus" is itself a development of the last decade. Like others in the New Testament field, Jesus-scholars are working their way out of an old "paradigm" now being recognized as inappropriate to the historical realities it pretended to account for. No longer can they think in the old nineteenth-century European theological terms of the origins of the true universal religion, "Christianity," from the particularist and overly political Palestinian "Judaism," focused on keeping the Law. A necessary first step was to break with the standard Lutheran-Protestant framing of the theological issues at stake in Jesus' ministry.[5] Then, also, Albert Schweitzer's and Rudolf Bultmann's portrayal of Jesus as an apocalyptic preacher proclaiming an imminent cosmic catastrophe no longer seemed to match the sayings that experts judged most authentic; instead, those sayings resembled wisdom teaching.[6] Some began to use sociological and anthropological methods to study Jesus in social context, and attention turned to class analysis and social history.[7] Only in the last few years have interpreters of Jesus begun to consider the implications of archaeological excavations.

Rabbinic studies have been similarly preoccupied with new developments, which helps to explain why little attention has been paid to archaeology in that field as well. Leading rabbinic scholars introduced critical principles for the dating and interpretation of traditions and for the evaluation of overall compilations such as the Mishnah.[8] That ferment in the field has led to attempts to sort out which kinds of materials within rabbinic documents can be used as historical sources, in order then to sketch the historical social context of those rabbis.[9]

Only within the last two decades have archaeologists focused specifically on Galilee. They have necessarily focused on their own research strategies, including the establishment of a pottery typology to guide chronological stratification of sites and innovative regional explorations.[10] While drawing on textual sources in their reports and interpretations, Galilean archaeologists have not been able to appropriate developments in critical analysis of those texts.[11]

Thus just as the newly developed archaeology of Galilee offers much of value both to Jesus studies and to rabbinic studies, such textual studies have much to offer archaeology as well, given their increasing sophistication in critical analysis of texts as historical sources. With the recent resurgence of interest in the social contexts of texts, there are a number of ways in which these three fields of study may be mutually beneficial in coming to a fuller understanding of Galilee as the context both of Jesus and his movement and of the rabbis.

1. Since attention in these fields has only recently focused specifically on Galilee, interpretation generally continues within the standard paradigm of "Judaism," "Jewish Palestine," or "Eretz Israel," within which information from or about Galilee was previously understood. Few distinctions of any sort were made, whether geographical or social. Texts and artifacts that happened to come from Galilee were simply assimilated as evidence for an essential "Judaism." In effect, Galilee was rendered almost

invisible in historical and archaeological interpretation. Some significant older studies dealt with affairs and towns in Galilee during
rabbinic times,[12] and a few Gospel studies noted that Galilee
had a particular theological significance,[13] but none led to fuller
investigation of the distinctive history of Galilee.[14]

Textual study of both the Gospels and rabbinic material have
been heavily oriented toward literary and religious/theological interpretation of the sacred texts. Particular "historical" questions
were asked but within the paradigm of the essence or origin of
a religion, Judaism or Christianity. Interest focused on the very elementary matters mentioned in the sacred texts, such as names,
dates, or the Jewish "sects." Such matters were treated one by one
as part of the "background" to a Gospel, or Jesus, or a doctrine,
or a rabbinic tradition. Often extrabiblical and extrarabbinic references (such as Josephus) were assumed to be directly transparent
to historical realities. The resurgence of critical analysis of sources
such as Josephus's histories is a recent development.

Except for isolated examination of sites of particular interest,
such as Nazareth, Capernaum, and a number of synagogue buildings, more systematic archaeological explorations began with the
expeditions to Meiron and nearby villages and then the excavations at Sepphoris.[15] Yet even after the discernment of differences
between regions within Galilee, findings from Galilee were still
grouped with data from elsewhere in Jewish Palestine for interpretation by topic.[16] Galilee was still subsumed under "Judaism" in
accordance with the standard paradigm. Thus neither archaeology
nor textual studies have given much attention to how particular
pieces of information from Galilee might fit together in a picture
of Galilee as a distinctive area. The fields of rabbinic studies, Jesus
studies, and archaeology should provide a great deal of stimulation
for each other as various aspects of Galilee come more precisely
into focus and a fuller picture of ancient life in the area comes
into view.

2. In the face of an acute lack or imbalance of sources for particular periods in Galilee, these interrelated fields have a certain
complementarity of materials. For the Middle and Late Roman
periods, rabbinic texts and more plentiful material remains are
available. For Galilee in late second-temple times, far fewer material remains have been found. Yet literary evidence is available

through critical analysis of the Gospels and Josephus's histories for important events and movements in the earlier period. Of course, archaeologists may yet uncover important material for the Early Roman period. It is thus conceivable that archaeologists, prodded by revived interest in the historical social context of Jesus and his movement, may in the future design excavations that could provide further knowledge, including a fuller sense of village life patterns and how those patterns may have changed during Roman times.

3. In order for us to explain their seemingly sudden emergence, Jesus and the Jesus movement(s) must be placed in the wider historical perspective that only a broader grasp of earlier and subsequent history of Galilee can provide. Materials and information generated by archaeology and rabbinic studies will be two of the principal sources of such historical perspective.

4. In return, archaeology can glean a particular benefit from textual studies. Like archaeologists working on historical societies elsewhere in the world, archaeologists focused on ancient Galilee can draw upon literary as well as material remains. On the basis of archaeological determination of the layers evident at excavated sites, only a very broad chronology of strata or periods can be distinguished. For more precise chronological determinations in certain connections, however, archaeologists working on Galilee may be able to use the results of critical analysis of literary remains from the related fields.

In these and other connections, Jesus studies, rabbinic studies, and archaeology can now stimulate and assist one another as they seek fuller understanding of Galilee as the historical social context of both Jesus and the rabbis. This book draws upon developments in the three interrelated fields in an attempt to discern some of the implications for several important facets of life in Galilee during Roman times. It focuses not directly on the Gospel traditions of Jesus and his movement and rabbinic texts, but on the broad historical context in which they emerged and to which they responded. It may be useful to reflect briefly on some of the principal problems as well as the prospects of dialogue across the three fields that are now focusing on Galilee in anticipation of the historical analysis and reconstruction attempted in the chapters below.

Problems

Many of the problems posed by previous work on Galilee are shared by textual studies and archaeology, partly because of the common academic heritage of these fields engaged in study of the origins of Judaism and Christianity.

1. In the modern academic division of labor, the fields of biblical studies, rabbinic studies, and to a considerable degree even (biblical) archaeology focus primarily on religion or on texts and other matters understood as religious. In accordance with the modern separation between religious and political and economic institutions (such as church and state), moreover, the standard assumption is that religion is separate from the political and economic aspects of life. Closely related to this modern separation is the Western tendency to understand religion in narrow terms as primarily individual religious faith.[17] In the Roman empire and among its subject cities and peoples, however, religion was usually inseparable from and often embedded in political-economic life and situations.[18] The emergence of a separate religious sphere of individual and social life was a hotly contested issue precisely under the Roman empire, in which the empire had a religious dimension of its own and some subject peoples clung to their traditional way of life, in which religion and politics were inseparable. To understand religion in ancient Galilee and Judea, we must attend to how it is embedded with social life generally, whether at the level of the temple-state based in Jerusalem or at the level of a village community.

2. Rabbinic studies, Jesus studies, and archaeology all practice decontextualization of the often already fragmentary textual or material remains — ironically often for the purpose of recontextualizing the information thus identified. The decontextualization is often in all of three dimensions: (a) Jesus sayings and rabbinic rulings are removed from their current (final) literary context in order to track them through their transmission to another, earlier, perhaps more original context. Archaeologists remove artifacts from their current spatial context, although careful note is taken of their chronological position in well-defined strata. In currently prevailing procedures, removal from literary or spatial context also entails both (b) social and (c) historical decontextualization.

This decontextualization may be most visible in archaeology, but it also occurs in textual analysis. Continuing in the practice of classical and biblical archaeology, artifacts unearthed are regrouped by such categories as pottery, fine wares, lamps, coins, tools, inscriptions, and decorational motifs, or even houses, synagogue buildings, and temples.[19] Some of these items are then re-placed in reconstructed discrete spaces, such as tools in a courtyard or pottery in a house or decor in a building. Most of them, however, remain grouped by category, as if, or actually, in a museum case. Depending on the purposes and manner of decontextualization, clues about their position and function in a wider social context or about their historical significance with relation to previous and subsequent circumstances may be lost in the removal from their (current) spatial context. Something similar happens to the aphorisms of Jesus or the rulings of rabbis. They are regrouped according to categories of type or topic, such as sapiential or prophetic, kingdom or meal, purity or festival. Although form-criticism claimed to be searching for the function of sayings in social context, criticism often stopped short of considering genuinely social connections and implications. In the case of both textual and material artifacts thus freed from their contexts, their recontextualization then becomes totally dependent on the textual or archaeological interpreters, their knowledge, perspective, and interests.

3. It is becoming evident that when interpreters (in all three fields) come to construct a new context for the resulting decontextualized data on Galilee, many of the building blocks they have to work with consist of false knowledge. We are discovering that we don't know what we thought we knew about Galilee in particular and "Judaism" in general. Some of these "discoveries" resulted directly from archaeological and/or textual investigations. The more significant discoveries require serious revision of our previously standard generalizations and assumptions. For example, the failure to find evidence of synagogue buildings in Galilee earlier than the second or third century has led investigators to suspect that such buildings were not being constructed in the first century. This lack of discovery would thus require serious revision of our general understanding of Judaism, as well as of Jesus and the Gospels: for example, in Mark's Gospel Jesus was teaching and healing in village assemblies, not in buildings (see chapter 6 below). In other

cases our knowledge is shifting. Although we may now have some confidence about the social location and role of the Pharisees (as scribal retainers),[20] we have precious little source material for what the Pharisees taught, and virtually the only portrayal of them as active on a regular basis in Galilee lies in the Christian Gospels.

4. Closely related to the problem of false knowledge is that of essentialist concepts. The fields of biblical studies, Jewish history, and archaeology of Palestine share with many other disciplines a tendency toward essentialism that is deeply rooted in modern Western academic constructions.[21] Often the principal conceptual categories of a field are paired in dichotomies, such as "Jewish" versus "Hellenistic" or "Jewish" versus "pagan" (or "Christian"). Artifacts or ideas or words, assumed to be manifestations and examples of a social-cultural essence, are categorized accordingly. Since social life generally is often assumed to have fallen neatly into such categories, moreover, generalizations are drawn from the discovery of a few artifacts in order to categorize as "Jewish" or "Hellenistic" a household, the whole site, or even the whole area, or from the occurrence of a word to the whole document.[22] Unfortunately, such essentialist categories may obscure rather than elucidate the structure and dynamics of concrete social life.[23]

5. Particularly in the United States and Britain we think in (structural-functionalist) terms of social cohesion and encompassing cultural unities, whose structure or "symbol system" we can discern and articulate. But this is surely an overemphasis on the efficacy of symbols, as if the system of symbols was guided by some magnetic telos in a constant movement toward integration. Surely this view is skewed by the modern experience of unifying nationalism (a phenomenon basically of only the last 200 years).[24] The national unification of people, moreover, is now made all the more effective by standardized schooling and other forms of socialization of the young, and by the atomizing and homogenizing mass media. Like all empires, the Roman empire was not a unitary "society," but a combination of many "societies."[25] An anthropologist of the last generation even suggested that "all societies are, in a radical sense, plural societies."[26] Historically, any appreciable degree of integration was achieved only through the exercise of various kinds of power.[27]

Particular "plural" societies did indeed have unifying institutions, such as the Temple in ancient Judea. The Temple, however, was always a contested and negotiated institution, whether at the time of Solomon (built by forced labor against which most of the tribes eventually rebelled; 1 Kings 5, 12), or at the time of its rebuilding in the late sixth century and under the sponsorship of the Persian empire (Haggai, Malachi, Isaiah 56–66, Ezra, Nehemiah) or in the late third–early second century B.C.E. crisis (1 Enoch 92–104; Hellenizing Reform, Maccabean Revolt, Qumran community/Dead Sea Scrolls), or in Herod's massive rebuilding of the Temple in grand Hellenistic-Roman style, or in the great revolt of 66–70. Institutions such as the Jerusalem Temple were contested, negotiated results of continuing compromise by an imperially dominated people.

Procedures and Prospects

In drawing appropriately on the results of recent archaeological excavations as well as critical reading of textual sources for a picture of ancient Galilee, our approach must be more historically precise, more critically comprehensive in terms of the overarching imperial situation, and more relational in terms of the political-economic power relations between cities and villages.

1. It has become common to speak of the considerable diversity in Judaism during Roman times. Concepts and terms used to refer to particular or types of Jewish groups or communities, however, often lack precision with regard to geographical and social location. Our primary sources are often more specific than their scholarly treatment. The Gospel of Mark almost never refers to "the Jews" (only the parenthetical 7:3, where it is likely the more specific "Judeans") although scholarly studies of Mark assume "the Jews" to be a determinative factor in the Gospel.[28] Although Josephus does at points refer to *hoi ioudaioi* in rather indefinite general ways, he is usually fairly precise with regard to "the Galileans" or "the Idumeans" in places where his interpreters substitute "the Jews." Divisions within a "society" tend to become more visible during crises. Josephus's accounts of the great revolt of 66–70 allow us glimpses of particular and fairly distinctive groups that emerged in the countryside and then in succession moved into rival positions in Jerusalem:[29] After the Jerusalemite crowd chased the Sicarii out

of the city, a junta of high priests and leading Pharisees formed a sort of provisional government. Then bands of refugees, who had been forced out of their villages in northwestern Judea by the devastations of the Roman advance, coalesced in the city as "the Zealots" (proper) and attacked wealthy Herodians. After the high-priestly junta summoned the Idumeans to help fight the Zealots, the movement from southern Judea and Idumea headed by the popular king Simon Bar Giora entered the city, where they rivaled the Zealots, but later the two groups fought shoulder to shoulder against the Roman siege. Josephus's accounts also enable us to discern similar regional variations and movements in Galilee during the revolt as well as distinctive types of popular movements at the death of Herod, at mid-first century, and during the great revolt.[30] Taking cues from our literary sources, we can become much more precise in referring to groups and movements by geographical area and date where such information is available.

2. From literary sources such as Josephus and the rabbis and from a number of archaeological excavations, we have a fairly clear sense of the *fundamental social forms* in Galilee. One obvious principle of organizing social and historical analysis would thus be according to such forms and the relations between them within the wider structure of society: families or households, villages (comprised of a number of households) and cities (headed by the ruling or most prominent families). These fundamental social forms, village and city, are the organizing principles of chapters 2, 4, 5, and 6.

3. The key question for understanding the origins, pattern, and effects of a social movement such as that headed by Jesus or the early rabbinic circles concerns the (political-economic-cultural) structural or *power relations and dynamics* between the village communities and their rulers, or between indigenous rulers and imperial rulers.[31] To illustrate the point: the claim of Sepphoris's cosmopolitan influence on villagers mentioned at the outset was made without considering the political-economic relations between ruling city and subject villages. Moreover, it flies in the face of literary evidence for hostile reaction rather than receptive response by Galilean villagers to Sepphoris. Josephus indicates that roughly a generation before and a generation after Jesus' ministry Galileans in the surrounding villages took hostile actions against the city of Sepphoris, and then suffered devastating disruption of their

lives by Roman military forces in retaliation. Galilean peasants do not appear to have welcomed influences coming from the cities at least during the first century C.E. The relations between Jerusalem and the village communities of Galilee involved regional as well as class differences. It is important, therefore, to ask about their degree and manner of cohesion or — under pressure or taxation or war — disintegration, as well as to investigate the dynamics of social conflict (both covert and overt) between rulers and ruled.[32] The political-economic (and to a degree the cultural) relations between cities and villages will be the focus of chapter 3, although they will figure in other chapters as well, particularly chapter 5.

4. Far from pretending that ancient Galilee or Jewish Palestine or Judaism was self-contained and can be treated independently, it is important to give special attention to the *imperial situation* that determined the conditions of the people's lives in key connections. Domination by outside rulers was particularly important in Galilee, which never evolved an aristocracy or ruling class of its own. During the Roman period, decisions in Rome repeatedly had major impact on people's life and work in Galilee. The emperor's decision to divide Herod's realm among his sons was particularly fateful for the immediate and longer-range history of Galilee. With Herod Antipas, the ruler of Galilee established his court and administrative apparatus directly in the area for the first time, building one completely new city and rebuilding another. The impact on traditional life in Galilee would likely have been sudden and dramatic, cultural as well as economic. The "royal" cities of Sepphoris and Tiberias a century later provided the Romans with a basis for the "urbanization" of all of Lower Galilee, placing all the villages of the area under the administration of one or another of these cities. Both the Gospels, focused on the ministry of Jesus, and the Mishnah are literatures of colonized peoples, produced in both accommodation and resistance to the incursions of Roman imperial power into their lives. Because the imperial situation determined other aspects of life in Galilee, the history of successive outside rulers and their treatment of Galilee will be the subject of chapter 1.[33]

5. Both life in a village or urban community and the structural or power relations between ruler communities and ruled also involves an all-important *historical dimension.* Membership (the family

components) in villages and cities was usually transgenerational. The basic structure of relations between ruling group/city and ruled villagers might remain basically the same when one set of rulers replaced another. In early Roman times, however, there were suddenly multiple layers of rulers making demands on the productive peasantry. And one ruler, Herod Antipas, instead of ruling from a distance as had previous rulers, imposed his governing and taxing apparatus directly onto Galilee in the form of newly built or rebuilt cities. Such major changes in the structure of ruler/ruled relations may have placed unusual pressure on village communities and their constituent families.[34] Or, for another illustration, following the consensus that the rabbis (and others) moved from Judea to Galilee following the Bar Kokhba Revolt of 132–135, the historical regional and class differences would have made necessary some degree of adjustment between them and the indigenous Galileans. The construction of synchronic pictures by archaeologists or social scientists (e.g., of the "urbanization" of Galilee) may not elucidate and may even obscure the origins of particular movements. In order to explain the rise and significance of movements, it is important to determine as precisely as possible the dating and sequence of built spaces and artifacts as well as the occupation of sites and movement of people. Significant historical forces, events, and changes will be considered in all of the chapters below.

6. Since Thomas S. Kuhn's main argument in *Structure of Scientific Revolutions* was picked up even by students of the humanities, there has been much discussion about how any field of inquiry and interpretation operates by "paradigms" that define the legitimate issues and questions of study and the parameters in which solutions and statements of significance are articulated. Different, but closely related, are the *models* according to which any historian or social scientist discerns and explains social relations. Social scientists may spend a great deal of time constructing and criticizing such models. Yet all investigators and interpreters work with some model. The only question is how flexibly, reflectively, and self-critically they proceed in analyzing and (re)constructing social relations according to their model. The central question appears to be how the prevailing political-economic power relations are structured in a given historical situation. Less reflective treatments of biblical history and archaeology tend to project the "market"

model familiar from modern Western societies back onto the ancient Mediterranean and Near East. Since the work of Karl Marx, Max Weber, and more recently Karl Polanyi, however, historians can be aware of the different types or forms of political-economic relations in historical societies.[35]

Given the lack of evidence for many crucial areas and aspects of ancient Galilee and Judea, or the Roman empire in general, however, we should not imagine that the models or "ideal types" developed from cross-cultural studies by the sociologist Gerhard Lenski and the political scientist John Kautsky are directly and immediately applicable.[36] These important general studies are valuable mainly in enabling us to pose questions for ancient Galilee and Judea in the context of the Roman empire on the basis of comparable "societies" in other times and places.[37] Archaeologists of Galilee are beginning to recognize the importance of models in reconstructing the social world of ancient Galilee.[38] Chapter 3 will focus specifically on what seems to have been the structure of political-economic relations prevailing in Roman Galilee.

7. More widely developed in the general field of archaeology than in the archaeology of Galilee or in Jesus studies or rabbinic-studies is a critical awareness of the ideology and interests involved in all historical research and interpretation. "Postprocessual" (also "postmodern" and "poststructural") archaeology, in reaction against the scientific pretensions of the so-called New Archaeology that dominated the field — particularly in the United States — during the 1960s, in addition to including issues of power-relations and social conflict in its agenda, has generated a heightened critical awareness of the ways in which archaeology has been framed and used. In Gospel and Jesus studies, such critical perspective is being developed primarily by feminist scholars.[39] In a tone set by Bruce Trigger's germinal essay, archaeologists now discern various interests and ideologies in their field.[40] "Nationalist" archaeology, emphasizing the decisive role of presumed ancestors of modern nations or ethnic groups, has glorified a national past to mitigate modern class conflict.[41] "Colonialist" archaeology, usually practiced in and on lands colonized by Europeans in modern history, tends to denigrate the role and importance of displaced indigenous peoples, thus justifying the European displacement.[42] "Imperialist" archaeology,

developed out of a few national traditions that spread under the aegis of military or economic power, presumes that it has a special understanding of world historical change.[43]

Fields such as New Testament and Jewish history, including Jesus studies and rabbinic studies, of course, have similar or parallel ideologies, interests, and uses. The appropriate response to heightened awareness of the interests and ideologies in which we are pursuing our inquiries and interpretations is self-criticism and acknowledgment of our own positions. This need not mean simply giving up on historical inquiry, however, as if any and all historical reconstructions are purely the constructions and artifice of the investigator-interpreter. Other peoples, known only through their literary and material remains, must be allowed their independent existence and must be allowed to stand over against the interested interpreters. The interpreters can rather criticize and take responsibility for their interpretations. And the more multistranded the fabric of investigation and interpretation, the more compelling will be the construction of the past in which we are interested.[44]

For many the principal reason for focusing specifically on the archaeology, history, and society of Galilee is to better understand the context of Jesus and/or the rabbis. We have come to recognize that the old way in which textual interpreters tended to appropriate "background" information — picking up bits of data piecemeal to apply to particular text-fragments, terms, or place-names — provided no larger context and perspective at all in which to understand texts and the communities or movements that produced them. Thus even if we aim to understand Galilee primarily as a context for Jesus and/or the rabbis, we must take our focus off the latter and adjust it carefully to Galilean history and society. The principal division of the investigation below, therefore, is in terms of the structure and dynamics of Galilean society. Since the primary interest for many is in Galilee as context, however, an attempt is made, usually at the outset or conclusion of the chapters, to indicate the implications of the Galilean realities for certain issues in the study of Jesus and/or the rabbis, as well as to pose questions and issues in the archaeological and historical construction of Galilee.

Chapter 1

GALILEE, CROSSROAD
OF EMPIRES

*The mountains are as a rule a world apart from civilizations, which
are an urban and lowland achievement. Their history is to have none,
to remain almost always on the fringe of the great waves of civilization, even the longest and most persistent, which may spread over great
distances in the horizontal plane but are powerless to move vertically
when faced with an obstacle of a few hundred meters. To these hilltop
worlds, out of touch with the towns, even Rome itself, in all its years
of power, can have meant very little, except perhaps through the military camps that the empire established for security reasons in various
places on the edges of unconquered mountain lands.*

— FERNAND BRAUDEL

Both Hebrew biblical traditions and later Jewish literature represent the people of Galilee as fiercely independent. They needed
to be, for one outside ruler after another took control of the area
and determined its life and landscape. The Judean general and historian Josephus, whose efforts to control the area on behalf of
the provisional high priestly government in Jerusalem met with
considerable resistance, wrote that the Galileans "had always been
numerous and warlike" (*B.J.* 3.41–43). He attributed this to their
energetic devotion to agriculture. He does not even mention that
much of the countryside was so mountainous or rocky that it
resisted cultivation. The Galileans must have been tough and persistent to maintain their independent spirit through a seemingly
never-ending series of outside rulers, from the early Canaanite
cities to the Roman empire.

Independence of the Israelite Tribes in Galilee

The earliest literary evidence for Israelite tribes in Galilee also represents them fighting for their independence from (would-be) outside rulers.

> To the sound of the musicians at the watering places, there they repeat the triumphs of the LORD, the triumphs of his peasantry in Israel.... The people of the LORD marched down against the mighty. The chiefs of Issachar came with Deborah.... Zebulun is a people that scorned death; Naphtali too, on the heights of the field. (Judg. 5:11, 13, 15, 18)

The Galileans' principal ally in resistance to outside rulers was the terrain. The political geography was to a considerable degree determined by the topography. In the series of broad valleys and sharp ridges ascending gradually from the coastal plain that constituted western Lower (southern) Galilee, imperial regimes could establish administrative towns from which to extract taxes and tribute. The land conveniently provided abruptly rising hills on which to locate fortress towns such as Sepphoris, to keep the countryside under surveillance, as well as the fertile valleys such as the Beth Netopha, on which the villagers could grow taxable crops. In the basin that drops quickly from the escarpment at the height of those valleys and ridges into the "Sea" of Galilee, the terrain is steep, with a few flatter fertile areas. The sub-sealevel weather is warm and both travel and fishing are easy on the water. By contrast, communication and transportation are difficult in the mountainous Upper (northern) Galilee, which forms a rugged barrier between Tyre on the west and the rich Huleh Valley north of the lake to the east.

The people of Israel originated in a prolonged period of rebellion and withdrawal from the Canaanite city-states and their Egyptian overlords who had dominated the area in the "Amarna" age. The diplomatic correspondence from a number of Canaanite rulers found in the Egyptian imperial archives at El Amarna indicates that several fortified cities encircled Galilee. Megiddo and Taanach may have impinged somewhat on Galilee from the Great Plain to the south. Acco and Tyre on the Mediterranean coast surely made demands on the produce of western and Upper Galilean villages, while the cities of Dan and particularly Hazor in the Huleh Valley north of the Sea of Galilee pressed in from the northeast. That Abimilki, ruler of Tyre, objected to interference by the "king" of Hazor indicates that both cities had established spheres of control in Upper Galilee (EA 148). Conceivably, even the name "Galilee," short for *galil ha-goyim*, "circle of the peoples" (Isa. 9:1/8:23, cited in Matt. 4:15), may refer in some way to the area being encircled geographically and politically by these cities.[1] Towns in Galilee itself, such as Hannathon in the Beth Netopha Valley (the only town in Galilee itself to be mentioned in the Amarna archives) and the fortified town of Qarney Hittin further east toward the lake, may have been "administrative" outposts of one or another of those cities.

The Canaanite cities' efforts to establish control of Galilean territory, however, did not go uncontested. Particularly intriguing are the *hapiru* in the hill country or the frontier area between the territories controlled by the cities. The city rulers complained of these fierce bands of fighters who raided their areas, whether independently or supposedly instigated by a rival ruler. Recent studies of these *hapiru* discern people of different ethnic origins formed into sizable groups, much larger than the usual brigand-bands, who stood outside the basic structure of villages dominated by city-based rulers, like the Cossacks on the southern frontiers of medieval Russia.[2] When we consider that Hazor was apparently destroyed as early as the mid-thirteenth century B.C.E.,[3] it is not difficult to construct a likely scenario of how the Galileans asserted independence from outside domination in the Early Iron Age.

Comparison with reconstructions of similar turmoil further south based on investigations of patterns of settlement in the central hill country is suggestive. Around 1700 B.C.E., supposedly the time of Abraham and Sarah, the hill country of Canaan was thickly settled with villages and fortified towns. During the Late Bronze Age (1550–1200 B.C.E.) the number of settlements declined dramatically (by as much as 90%), while the large cities along the coast and in the major valleys continued to flourish. Apparently many people of the hill country gradually abandoned their villages and shifted into herding further eastward. Archaeologists have found evidence of about 250 Early Iron Age herders' enclosures, hilltop hamlets, and unfortified villages, whose architecture and artifacts were much simpler than those of Canaanite cities of the preceding Late Bronze Age.[4] When the Canaanite city-state system finally broke down completely in the upheavals of the thirteenth century, those peoples apparently moved back westward. Careful surveys have detected evidence of a gradual population movement from the eastern desert edge into the interior valleys and finally to the western hills during the Early Iron Age, progressively adapting from herding to intensive terrace agriculture.[5]

Evidence of the shifting settlements is consistent with the theory of a sustained resistance to and withdrawal from the dominant political-economic order in Canaanite city-states during the Late Bronze Age.[6] Decline of Egyptian imperial power in the area led to intercity struggles for regional dominance, resulting in turmoil as well as intensified economic demands on subject villages in the hill country. In response to their worsening situation, the people simply withdrew from the villages over which the rulers' military forces held sway and eked out an existence on more marginal land, the desert fringe of the central hill country in the south and the rugged terrain of the interior mountain ranges in Galilee.[7] This is likely the first archaeological glimpse we catch of the people of Israel.[8]

The first literary references to historical action by the tribes of Israel in Galilee fits just such a scenario. Inspired by the prophetess Deborah, the tribes of Issachar, Zebulun, and Naphtali descend from hills and ridges to fight the horses and chariots of the kings of Megiddo and Taanach. The archaic victory hymn called the "Song of Deborah" (Judges 5) also reveals other important dimensions of early Israel in Galilee. As suggested by archaeological explorations, the "heights of the field" (*meromai sadeh*, Judg. 5:18) must refer to the terracing of the steep hillsides by the clans of Naphtali for agricultural subsistence in the mountains far from potential threat by would-be urban rulers.[9] Also, the northernmost tribes do not fight alone, but in close collaboration with some of the other tribes of Israel (Ephraim, Machir [Manasseh?], and Benjamin). Indeed, the covenantal bond by which they are mutually obligated to come to the aid of any tribe that is threatened is evident in the cursing of the units or tribes who failed to respond (Reuben, Gilead, Dan, Asher, and Meroz; Judg. 5:15, 17, 23). All the tribes were apparently expected to stand in solidarity in resistance to attack or domination of any member by an outside ruler. Naphtali and Zebulun again joined with other tribes in struggles against the Midianites led by Gideon, of the tribe of Manasseh (Judges 6–8). The stories of Gideon also illustrate that the early Israelites resisted having any king of their own on the principle that their God Yahweh was literally their king.

Jerusalem Rule: The First Phase

After the history of Israel took its decisive turn toward monarchy, however, the Galilean tribes may not have been so eager to cooperate. Biblical historians and archaeologists often write in glowing terms of the "united monarchy" centered in Jerusalem, its architect David, prototype of the Messiah, and the wise Solomon, builder of the glorious Temple, as if they represented all Israel. That charitable reconstruction then becomes the basis for the assumption that Galileans at the time of Jesus were unquestioningly loyal to Jerusalem, its Temple and its Torah. Biblical literature itself, however, leaves no such illusions about these matters.

According to the histories of the monarchy written or edited by royal scribes, the representative "elders" of all the tribes participated in the popular acclamation or "anointing" (*messiah*) of David as king over all Israel (2 Sam. 5:1–3). There may be some question, however, about whether the threat of Philistine encroachment, concentrated in the south, involved the vital interests of the Galilean tribes. It is clear from the biblical narrative that David continued his shrewd moves toward increasing consolidation of monarchic power. Most ominous initially — and of great significance for subsequent history — was his establishment of his capital in the non-Israelite city of Jerusalem. He captured this Jebusite stronghold not with an Israelite people's militia but with his own mercenaries acquired from his days as a lieutenant of the Philistines (2 Sam. 5:6–10). Israel came quickly to regret having recognized the charismatic David as its messiah. Two widespread rebellions against David erupted, one after the other, the first led by his own son Absalom and centered near Jerusalem (2 Samuel 15–19). David thus had to reestablish his monarchy over the Israelites by conquering them with his own army of foreign mercenaries. The second revolt, led by the Benjaminite Sheba son of Bichri, brought David's professional troops on a search-and-destroy mission all way through Galilee up to the district town of Abel of Beth-maacah in northernmost Naphtali (2 Samuel 20).

David presumably incorporated the Canaanite cities he conquered into his kingdom. Solomon utilized them as military bases for his chariot forces and administrative bases for tax collection. Solomon not only restored the fortress city of Megiddo to its old role in the domination and exploitation of the Great Plain and Lower Galilee, but he also constructed other such fortresses to control the people. Indeed, he divided the kingdom into administrative districts that did not necessarily recognize the old tribal distinctions (1 Kings 4). Among the three "provinces" in Galilee, Zebulun does not appear. Does that mean that the clans of Zebulun were simply divided up and assigned to other districts for administrative purposes? Surface surveys claim that the number of settlements in Lower Galilee increased dramatically during the tenth century. But in what way were the Galileans "flourishing"? The discovery of fifteen fortress towns among the new settlements suggests that the monarchy had a considerable "administrative" role in this sudden new "development" of Galilee.[10]

Solomon became most famous, of course, for building the Temple in Jerusalem. In the ancient Near East, kings built temples and temples legitimated kings, as indicated in the new royal "covenant" that grounded the Davidic dynasty (2 Samuel 7; Psalm 132). Construction of such a sacred edifice — not to mention construction of Solomon's palace twice the size of God's "house" and the many other palaces and fortresses in Jerusalem and elsewhere — required a huge outlay of labor and wealth. In a traditional agrarian society, the only source of either was the subject peasantry. In order to construct the Temple and other buildings, Solomon instituted forced labor among the Israelite tribes as well as among the conquered Canaanite peoples. Galilee, however, was even more dramatically affected than other parts of Israel. When his tax revenues proved insufficient to pay for the timber and technological expertise he bought from Hiram, king of Tyre, Solomon simply ceded to Hiram "twenty cities in the land of Galilee," along with their people, of course.

It is not surprising, therefore, that the ten northern tribes of Israel rose in revolt against the Davidic monarchy at the death of Solomon. The forced labor had made their situation feel like bondage under the Egyptian Pharaoh all over again. That revolt against Jerusalem rule was the beginning of more than eight centuries in which Galilean history diverged from Judean history. Those divergences must be taken into account in any investigation of Galilee, particularly insofar as those centuries were highly creative and significant for Jerusalem and Judeans, with the construction of the Second Temple, the formation of the Torah, and the militant reassertion of the traditional Judean way of life in the Maccabean Revolt against Hellenistic imperial forces.

Galilee under Samaria, Assyria, Persia, Ptolemies, and Seleucids

For the first three generations of their independence of Jerusalem rule, the Galileans and other northern Israelites managed to keep their kings from successfully setting up dynasty over them. Omri finally succeeded in establishing at least a short dynasty. The bands of popular prophets led by Elijah and Elisha, however, steadfastly resisted the oppressive rule of Ahab, Omri's son and successor. Their struggles left vivid memories deeply etched in the popular tradition of their acts of power and their attempts to resist oppressive rule and foreign cultural influences and to renew the Mosaic covenantal ways (cf. 1 Kings 17–19, 21; 2 Kings 1–2, 9).[11]

In the history of the northern kingdom of Israel, the Galilean tribes must always have been peripheral. Omri and Ahab established their newly constructed capital at Samaria in the central hill country. Galilee was useful to the Israelite monarchy, as it had been to Solomon, as a source of tax revenues. Judging from items such as a metal bowl found at Megiddo, a major military base housing chariot forces, and an ivory fragment found at Samaria itself, the ruling elite traded agricultural products obtained through taxation to Phoenician cities such as Tyre for luxury goods.[12] In a continuation of the perpetually changing jurisdictions of rulers over the "circle of the peoples," the Syrian regime in Damascus periodically wrested control of parts of Galilee from the kingdom of Israel (1 Kgs. 15:16–21; 2 Kgs. 10:32–33; 13:3, 7, 22, 25; 14:25, 28). In fact, apparently before the Assyrian empire finally conquered Samaria, Damascus had already taken control of much of Galilee.

An adequate understanding of the Assyrian conquest of Galilee in 733–732 B.C.E. and Samaria in 722–721 B.C.E. is of central importance to the subsequent history of Galilee (and its relation to Jerusalem). The key question is whether King Tiglath-pileser deported virtually the whole population or only a portion of it, leaving the majority of the Israelite peasantry on the land. If the latter, then there was some continuity of Israelite population into Persian, Hellenistic, and Roman times, with a sizable portion of the Galileans at the time of Jesus and the rabbis being descendants of the former Israelites, but not necessarily Judeans. If all or most of the Israelite population was deported by the Assyrians, then we could account for the strong presence of Israelite traditions in Galilee at the time of Jesus and the rabbis either by settlement of Judeans such as Hasmonean soldiers and surplus Judean population and/or, more ominously, by the supposed "forced conversion" imposed on the population by the Hasmoneans after they conquered the area in 104 B.C.E. After the Assyrian conquest there is precious little evidence available on the question, which makes interpretation of the biblical references, Assyrian inscriptions, and surface surveys all the more important.

Neither the Deuteronomistic history in 2 Kings (15:29; 17:6, 23) nor the official Assyrian annals (*ANET* 284) can be taken at face value, that is, that Tiglath-pileser carried "the people" or "the Israelites" or "all [Omri-land's] inhabitants" captive to Assyria. The latter phrase is used of Assyrian treatment of Samaria in 732, yet the context makes it clear that not even all the people of the capital city of Samaria were meant, since sufficient officials and military, as well as a productive peasantry on the soil, were left to produce the huge tribute demanded by the Assyrian regime. Assyrian annals indicate that the regime regularly assimilated skilled dependents of the conquered rulers for its own purposes, often integrating professional chariot warriors or scribes or artisans and builders into its own army, bureaucracy, and skilled servants.[13] Thus the 27,290 prisoners taken from Samaria (*ANET* 284–85) must have been primarily the ruling elite, their military and scribal retainers, and their artisans. Moreover, since Damascus had apparently already taken control of Galilee before the Assyrian invasion, the "people" deported from Galilee were likely not the administrative officers of the Israelite regime in Samaria but those of the

Syrian regime in Damascus.[14] Among the 13,520 recorded as deported from Galilee in 732 were the numbers of 625 or 650 from what were almost certainly administrative towns such as Hannathon, Yotba, Kana, Aruna, and Merom (*ANET* 283), that is, administrative officers and others. In any case, that the Assyrians established a province in Galilee and the Great Plain with their own administrative officials to keep order and gather tax revenues indicates that they must have left most of the peasantry on the land.[15]

On the other hand, surface surveys of Lower Galilee that claim to find a dramatic gap in settlements until Persian times have been used to argue for a total devastation of the land and deportation of the population.[16] Such surveys, of course, cannot detect all sites, must rely only on fragments of pottery on the surface, and lack the carefully controlled stratigraphy of systematic excavations. The archaeologists who conduct such surface surveys also admit that they provide a superficial basis for drawing any conclusions, in the absence of other indications. Thus, since critical interpretation of Assyrian records clearly suggests that the deportations were mainly of officials and skilled personnel, we must conclude that much of the Israelite population of Galilee must have remained in their villages or perhaps withdrew into the rugged interior. Continuity of the Israelite population into later times therefore seems the most likely historical conclusion.

For the next six centuries after the Assyrian conquest, Galilee came under an imperial administrative arrangement separate from that of Judea and, usually, Samaria, coming successively under the Babylonian, Persian, Ptolemaic, and Seleucid empires. During the brief interlude between the Assyrian and Babylonian domination, Josiah attempted to reassert Davidic rule over the northern Israelites. If he pursued the same policies in the north as in Judah itself, destroying local centers of loyalty in order to centralize revenues and power in the Temple and monarchy in Jerusalem, the "reform" would hardly have elicited support. Whatever Josiah's program in the north may have entailed, a mere two decades later the Babylonians conquered Jerusalem, deported the ruling class, and destroyed the Temple.

A major difference between the historical development of Galilee and that of Judea and Samaria emerged from the combination of previous history and Persian imperial policy. Implementing a policy of restoring local aristocracies previously deported by the Babylonians, the Persians sent the exiled Judean royal and priestly aristocracy to rebuild the Temple in Jerusalem[17] and restored the Samaritan aristocracy in the district to the north.[18] Because Galilee had always been subject to one outside regime after another, however, an indigenous aristocracy had never evolved. Thus instead of being headed by a "native" priestly or royal aristocracy, the Galileans were simply ruled and taxed by imperial officers based usually in Megiddo. One of the principal results of this arrangement was that in Judea the priestly aristocracy, and perhaps their Persian overlords as well, sponsored the development of a written and carefully cultivated "great" or official tradition that drew on, paralleled, and influenced the "little" or popular tradition cultivated in the Judean village communities. In Galilee, on the other hand, presumably only the popular Israelite traditions continued to guide life in the village communities, without much interest or interference from the imperial authorities, who left the villages alone as long as the expected revenues were forthcoming.[19]

Yet another major divergence in the historical experiences of Galilee and Judea lies in the different ways they were influenced by and reacted to Hellenistic cultural imperialism. Several Hellenistic cities were founded in the lands bordering on Galilee. Yet not only did they have no political jurisdiction over any part of Galilee, so far as we know, but they also had little cultural influence on Galilean village life.[20] Galileans thus had no experience comparable to the crisis of sudden forced Hellenization in Judea under the Seleucid emperor Antiochus Epiphanes and the long guerrilla struggles of the Maccabean Revolt. Thus the Galileans experienced no sudden threat to their traditional way of life and had no central Temple around which they might rally. They also had no occasion to develop coalitions across class lines in a struggle against foreign domination and did not experience the vindication of having successfully resisted foreign oppression and defended their traditional way of life. Because of the same divergences in historical development, however, the Galileans had no centralized institutional basis and expansive ideological surge from which to expand their own sphere of influence in the ensuing imperial vacuum.

Jerusalem Rule: The Second Phase

Galilee came back under Jerusalem rule again after eight centuries in one of the major steps by which the Hasmoneans extended their rule over most of Palestine. The Hasmonean brothers of Judah the Maccabee, hero of the Judean struggle against the attempt at forcible Hellenization of Judean society, successfully maneuvered between rival Seleucid factions to obtain appointment to the high priesthood of the Judean temple-state. In succeeding generations, John Hyrcanus and his sons extended Hasmonean rule over the Samaritans to the north, the Idumeans to the south, and finally, in 104 B.C.E., over the Galileans. Just how the Hasmonean takeover of Galilee is to be understood has been intensely debated.[21] The evidence consists of the briefest of accounts by the Jewish historian Josephus. Thus much depends on how we read that account. Similarly much depends upon who the inhabitants of Galilee are thought to have been.

Josephus writes that John Hyrcanus's son, the king–high priest Aristobulus, "made war on the Itureans and acquired a good deal of their territory for Judea and compelled the inhabitants, if they wished to remain in the country, to be circumcised and to live in accordance with the laws of the Judeans" (*Ant.* 13.318). It may be helpful to compare his earlier account of how Hyrcanus "after subduing all the Idumeans, permitted them to remain in their country so long as they had themselves circumcised and were willing to observe the laws of the Judeans" (*Ant.* 13.257). The concept of religious "conversion," with its clear emphasis on a transformative experience of the individual, seems singularly inappropriate to "undergoing circumcision and living in accordance with the laws of the Judeans."[22] The phrase "laws of the Judeans" was a standard way of referring to the *politeia* or the constitution and way of life of a particular state or people, in this case of the Judean temple-state.[23] And according to age-old tradition, the rite of circumcision was the means by which people were incorporated into the body politic. So both the Idumeans and the Galileans were being incorporated into the Judean temple-state, agreeing to abide by the state policy and laws, surely including certain tithes and offerings and other dues rendered to the Temple and high priests.

But were the Galileans conquered? The Itureans, based further north in the interior of Lebanon, had taken control of Galilee in the demise of Seleucid imperial power in Palestine. In contrast to his account of the Idumeans, who were both conquered and underwent submission to circumcision and the Judean laws, Josephus distinguishes between the Itureans, whom the Hasmonean ruler defeated, and the inhabitants of Galilee, who submitted to circumcision and the Judean laws. It would seem that the Galileans were not conquered in the same way as were the Idumeans. That the Idumeans had been self-governing, whereas Galilee had been dominated by the Itureans, is a partial explanation. Yet the expectation that the Galileans would somehow be open to Jerusalem rule may have been a factor as well. But what about the parallel submission to circumcision and the laws of the Judeans? If we imagine that the Galileans were Judeans, then the Hasmonean requirement of the inhabitants was pointless.[24] If we imagine that the Galileans were non-Israelite, then the adjustment would have been major. If, as argued above, the Galileans were descendants of the former northern Israelites, then insofar as they shared certain Mosaic and other traditions of early Israel with the Jerusalem temple-state and their long-lost cousins, the Judean peasantry, the adjustment would have been easier because of their common heritage.

In attempting to understand just what the Hasmonean takeover of Galilee meant for the inhabitants we are not left entirely to speculation about the meaning of certain phrases in Josephus. The Hasmoneans may not have conquered the Galileans, but they surely established a military presence in the area. Josephus mentions over twenty-five greater or lesser fortresses that the Hasmoneans used to control or administer the different parts of their realm (*Ant.* 13.416–29). It stands to reason that a half-dozen of these were in Galilee, including the "old citadel" in Sepphoris[25] and the fortresses in both Gush Halav and Yodfat mentioned in rabbinic literature (*m. Arachin* 9:6).[26] This is surely the connection in which the hundreds of coins of Alexander Janneus (Hasmonean king–high priest 103–76) found in the villages of Upper Galilee must be interpreted. No more than the later coins of Tyre are they evidence of a thriving trade with Jerusalem.[27] Nor do these Hasmonean coins mean that these villages had suddenly become distinctively "Jewish" (i.e., Judean). Instead, they attest the Hasmonean military presence in Upper Galilee, along the frontier with Tyre and the Itureans. Yet that does not mean that the Hasmoneans had suddenly succeeded in effectively integrating Galilean villagers into the Judean temple-state.[28]

Alexander Janneus and his successors placed their own trusted officers (their "friends," *Ant.* 13.422) in charge of administrative centers such as Sepphoris and fortress towns such as Gush Halav or Yodfat. We can appreciate the importance of these fortresses and garrisons for Hasmonean rule of Galilee by another comparison with Idumea. There the Hasmoneans — and then Herod himself — controlled the people through alliances with and cooptation of the indigenous aristocracy (such as the family of Herod). Alexander Janneus appointed Herod's grandfather Antipas military governor of Idumea, and then his father Antipater became the "prime minister" of Hyrcanus II (*Ant.* 14.10; *B.J.* 1.123), the last Hasmonean high priest before the rise of Herod. Herod pursued the same practice, making Costobar, scion of the distinguished Idumean priestly family, the military governor in his own country (*Ant.* 15.253–54). In Galilee, by contrast, where no indigenous aristocracy ever evolved, the Hasmoneans placed their own Judean officers in charge of pacification and taxation.

The Hasmonean subjection of the Galileans and the Idumeans to the Jerusalem-based temple-state and the "laws of the Judeans" did not mean that they were integrated into the Judean *ethnos* (nation/people). Outsiders, such as Greek writers and Roman officials, frequently refer to the whole of Palestine under Hasmonean or Herodian rule as Judea. At points, Josephus reverts to this usage as well. Ordinarily, however, Josephus makes clear distinctions between the Galileans and Idumeans and Judeans as separate *ethnoi* or peoples. If most or many of the Galileans were of Israelite heritage, the latter would have provided at least some common basis on which they could be incorporated under the Jerusalem temple-state. Presumably they worshipped the same God and shared certain early Israelite traditions such as the exodus and passover celebration, the Mosaic covenant, circumcision, and legends of common ancestors such as Abraham and Sarah. Even popular traditions of resistance to the Israelite monarchy, in particular the Elijah-Elisha stories, had been taken into the official history of the Jerusalem temple-state.

Nevertheless, because of eight centuries of separate regional histories as well as the structural differences between rulers and ruled, the Galileans would have found the "laws of the Judeans" significantly different from their own traditions and customs. The "laws of the Judeans" articulated the interests of the temple-state, including demands for tithes, offerings, and other dues to sustain the central institutions of Temple and priesthood. Galilean customs and traditions expressed and guided the life of village communities, with emphasis on local reciprocity and the preservation of all families on their ancestral inheritance of land that formed the basis of their subsistence and place in the village community. There can be no question of any effective integration of the Galileans into the Judean temple-community. Ancient societies had no institutionalized means of the "secondary socialization" or "resocialization," such as public schools and mass media, which would have been necessary. The Hasmonean regime, moreover, was seriously preoccupied with further conquests and virtual civil war under Alexander Janneus and at the time of the Roman conquest. We can only imagine that under Alexandra Salome, who repaired the Hasmonean alliance with the Pharisees that her husband and predecessor(s) had broken, these scribal retainers of the regime devoted some attention to the representation of Jerusalem's interests in Galilee, perhaps pressing upon the population the importance of observing the "laws of the Judeans."

Roman Conquest, Client Kingships, and Reconquests

Galileans paid dearly for being subject to the Hasmoneans — as well as for their stubborn resistance to outside rule — when the Romans took control of the eastern Mediterranean. Treatment of the Galileans was usually the spinoff effect of the grand designs of the empire from Rome and/or of the way Rome was handling the Hasmonean regime in Jerusalem and its rival factions. Galilee was, literally and figuratively, in the way.

The Roman general Pompey's initial takeover in 63 B.C.E. was not a military conquest at all, until he stormed the Temple precincts to overcome the impetuous resistance by one of the rival Hasmoneans in Jerusalem itself. In accordance with their policy of ruling indirectly through native aristocracies, the Romans confirmed the Hasmonean dynasty in power, only "liberating" the Hellenistic cities from their control. After a brief interlude in which Gabinius (proconsul 57–55 B.C.E.) set up five regional councils, one based in the fortress town of Sepphoris in Galilee (*Ant.* 14.91; *B.J.* 1.170), the Romans reverted to indirect rule through the Hasmonean regime.

Roman devastation and slaughter in Galilee resulted from the ensuing struggle between rival Hasmonean factions and the empire-wide Roman civil war, as well as certain Roman generals' arrogant striving for fame and fortune. In the last major battle in Gabinius's campaign to put down a serious rebellion by a Hasmonean faction the Romans killed thousands of rebels at Mount Tabor in southern Galilee, and surely devastated the surrounding countryside as well (*Ant.* 14.102; *B.J.* 1.177–78). A few years later (53–52) Cassius, in an expedition to check the rival Hasmonean pretender, "fell upon Tarichaeae (Magdala)...and enslaved some thirty thousand men" (*Ant.* 14.120; *B.J.* 1.180). The numbers are exaggerated as usual and some of those may have been forces of the rebel Hasmonean, but the devastation and enslavement must have denuded the area of its population.

Ten years later, after the assassination of Caesar escalated the empire-wide Roman civil war, the same Cassius imposed an extraordinary levy of tribute on greater Judea and the cities in the area. The energetic young Herod, having been appointed military governor of Galilee by his father Antipater, prime minister of the Hasmonean Hyrcanus II, quickly extorted a huge 100-talent allotment from the Galileans. The periodic warfare back and forth across the country and the extra economic burden placed on the peasantry by the Roman tribute and special levies of taxes over and above the dues already paid to the Hasmoneans had a seriously disruptive effect on the Galilean villagers. It is not surprising that Josephus mentions brigand groups in several Galilean locations. Indeed, in another aggressive action as military governor of Galilee, Herod captured and killed "the brigand-chieftain Ezekias [who] was ravaging the district on the Syrian frontier with a large troop" (*Ant.* 14.159; *B.J.* 1.204). The Galileans thus became the first of Herod's later subjects to become acquainted with the typical strong-arm tactics of their future king. All of this devastation, enslavement, and taxation seems to have provoked a certain level of anti-Roman, anti-Herod feeling among the Galileans.

It should not be surprising, therefore, that when the Romans appointed Herod in 40 B.C.E. as their client-"king" to bring order to greater Judea, he met with more sustained resistance in Galilee than elsewhere. Galilean opposition to Herod and the protracted three years of campaigns necessary for him finally to assert control of the area were complicated by the efforts of Antigonus, the last Hasmonean rival, in alliance with the Parthians, to seize power in Judea. With Roman troops in addition to his own forces, Herod quickly took control of the Hasmonean fortresses, including Sepphoris. The garrisons of Antigonus offered only temporary resistance (*Ant.* 14.413, 417, 427). When Josephus says that "all Galilee" had gone over to Herod (*Ant.* 14.295) he must have meant, from his aristocratic viewpoint, all those who counted (i.e., those connected with the declining Hasmonean regime) quickly went over to Herod.[29] As soon as Herod returned to his main campaign against Antigonus, however, "the usual promoters of disturbance in Galilee" slew the military officer he had left in charge (*Ant.* 14.432–33). In another widespread popular insurrection some time later, "the Galileans rebelled against the power-holders in their country and drowned those who were partisans of Herod in the lake" (*Ant.* 14.450; cf. *B.J.* 1.326).

Once he beat down the recurrent popular resistance, Herod would surely have garrisoned all the fortresses with his own troops headed by trusted officers. He became famous for the tight control he maintained on his entire realm, adding massive fortresses such as Masada and Herodium to those he took over from the Hasmoneans. Sepphoris became his principal fortress town from which to rule and tax Galilee. Beyond that Josephus and other sources tell us very little about Herod's rule in Galilee in particular. We can only reason from what Herod did elsewhere to its effect on Galileans.

While retaining the high priesthood, he made it an instrument of his own policies, eventually suppressing all Hasmoneans and appointing to the high office men from high-priestly families in Egypt and Babylon. The new high-priestly families, of course, built themselves luxurious mansions in the New City overlooking the temple complex. Such moves would not have enhanced the legitimacy of the office in Judea proper and may have only further discredited it in the outlying district of Galilee. In one of his most famous projects, Herod had the temple complex vastly expanded and the Temple completely rebuilt in grand Hellenistic-Roman style (*Ant.* 15.380–402).[30] Correspondingly he lavished munificent favors on cities around the eastern Mediterranean where there were large Jewish diaspora communities, posing as their protector and fostering their attention — and pilgrimage — to his glorious Temple. On the other hand, the Temple must have seemed remote in cultural and class terms to the Galilean peasantry who were peripheral at best — so long as their revenues were forthcoming — to Herod's grand kingship that more and more was attempting to rival that of David and Solomon.

Herod also mounted a massive building program of monuments to Augustus Caesar and Roman-style theaters and amphitheaters. In addition to the two cities dedicated to Caesar, the newly constructed seaport of Caesarea, which featured a temple and huge statue and other monuments to the emperor and the rebuilt city of Sebaste ("August"), was the temple of white marble dedicated to Caesar at Paneion, near the site of ancient Dan, which later became Caesarea Philippi. There is no record of such building by Herod, however, in Galilee. Herod maintained intense pressure for taxes in order to fund such projects along with his lavish court life and munificence to Hellenistic cities.

The Pharisees presumably continued in their traditional role as experts in interpretation of the laws of the Judeans, which Herod left intact along with the Temple and high priesthood as the governing infrastructure of the realm. Yet if they were active beyond Jerusalem, where Josephus mentioned them hovering around Herod's court, there remains no evidence of it. Herod himself surely observed the laws of the Judeans in the breach — to the point that Judeans objected to his violation of traditional customs. Far from sponsoring enforcement of the "laws of the Judeans," the effect of Herod's programs and other administration would have been to undermine them. That meant that peoples in the outlying districts must have been left to pursue their own local and regional customs. Herod's own Idumean appointee as military governor of Idumea is a telling example. Being the scion of a family of priests of the Idumean god Coze, Costobar both cultivated the Idumean customs and helped the Idumeans resist conforming their life to the laws of the Judeans. Under Herod it seems that the cause of neither Temple nor Torah would have been advanced in Galilee.

When Herod died in 4 B.C.E., while Jerusalemites protested his policies, large groups of peasants in every major district of his realm asserted their independence. The insurrection in Galilee was led by the son of that brigand-chieftain Hezekiah whom Herod had hunted down decades before: "Judas got together a large number of desperate men at Sepphoris, . . . made an assault on the royal fortress/palace, and made off with all the goods that had been seized there" (*Ant.* 17.271). Josephus's parallel account, that "he attacked other aspirants to power" (*B.J.* 2.56) may indicate that the rebellion in Galilee was fairly widespread. That the popular insurrections in Judea and Perea, as well as in Galilee, took the same social form of popular messianic movements which were focused on a leader acclaimed as "king" by his followers like Saul or David of old suggests that after experiencing the oppressive kingship of Herod, the people were more than ready to have a king from their own ranks who would act in the interests of the people.[31]

The Romans retaliated brutally in their reconquest first of Galilee and then of the rest of greater Judea. Assembling a massive army, they proceeded first against Galilee, as had become the pattern in invasions of greater Judea. A detachment of troops proceeded against "the Galileans who inhabit[ed] the region adjoining Ptolemais." Then, says Josephus, the Roman army captured and burned Sepphoris and enslaved the people (*Ant.* 17.288–89). The recent excavations in Sepphoris have, as yet, unearthed no clear evidence of massive destruction in the Early Roman period.[32] Since the Romans would unfailingly have retaliated against any insurrection, however, and since the rebels had evidently been peasants, the Roman attack may have been directed against villages around Sepphoris. In any case, in the villages around Sepphoris such as Nazareth the people would have had vivid memories both of the outburst of rebellion against Herod and the Romans and of the devastation of their villages and the enslavement of their friends and relatives.

After suppressing the popular insurrections after Herod's death, the Romans divided his realm among his sons. Judea proper and

Samaria were given to Archelaus, Galilee and Perea were set under Antipas (ruled 4 B.C.E.–39 C.E.), who received the title of Tetrarch. Thus after having been under Jerusalem rule for exactly a century, Galilee was now set under separate political-economic jurisdiction, and, with the exception of a short period under Agrippa I (41–44), some or all of Galilee remained under separate administration for the rest of the first century. It is important to distinguish between these events and affairs that were distinctive to Galilee and events that pertain to Judea and/or Jerusalem, only some of which may have influenced affairs in Galilee. For example, only Judea and not Galilee was affected by the deposition of Archelaus and imposition of direct Roman rule, including the census, in 6 C.E. Perhaps the name of one of the leaders of the resistance to payment of Roman tribute, "Judas of Galilee/Gaulanitis" has been misleading in this regard. The name, however, indicates that he was *from* (not active in) Galilee or Gaulanitis. Similarly, the Roman governors such as Pontius Pilate watched after affairs in Judea and Samaria, but not in Galilee. Jesus and other Galileans had to journey into Samaria or Judea to come under the Roman governor's jurisdiction.

That Galilee was no longer under the political jurisdiction of the Temple and high priesthood in Jerusalem raises the question of just what influence the latter may have retained over the Galileans and what sort of relationship continued between Galileans and Jerusalem. Since virtually no information exists on the issue, we should be cautious about making assumptions. For example, studies of pilgrimage to festivals in the Temple such as Passover have grossly overestimated the number of pilgrims in general and the number from Galilee in particular. There is literary evidence for *some* pilgrims from Galilee, but the numbers were likely small.[33] The claim that Galileans were generally "loyal" to both Temple and Torah has to be argued against the evidence adduced.[34] The many centuries of separate historical experience, followed by a century of Galilean subjection to the Jerusalem temple-state, suggest that the historical regional differences and different class interests may have outweighed whatever bonds may have been established during the century of troubled Jerusalem rule in Galilee. The Christian Gospels are the only sources that portray the scribes and Pharisees active in Galilee during the early first century as representatives of the Jerusalem authorities. The historical credibility of such stories will depend upon complicated historical reasoning that considers a variety of circumstances and factors. Given the institutional political-economic-religious structure in first-century Palestine, if there was any representation of Jerusalem interests in Galilee, scribal retainers of the temple-state such as the Pharisees would have been the obvious candidates.

In the new Roman arrangement for Galilee, the priestly aristocracy in Jerusalem and the Tetrarch Antipas were in fact now competing for influence and particularly revenues from the Galilean peasantry. With political jurisdiction Antipas had the advantage, and he was desperately in need of those revenues. Soon after taking over his territory, Antipas set about rebuilding the fortress town of Sepphoris as his capital, "the ornament of all Galilee" and "Imperial City," says Josephus (*Ant.* 18.27). Within two decades, however, he began construction of a completely new capital on the shore of the lake (*Ant.* 18.37–38), named Tiberias after the new emperor Tiberius (14–37). Since these cities will be the focus of chapter 2 below, suffice it to make two points here by anticipation. First, these building programs required huge amounts of resources that had to be extracted from his only economic base, the Galilean and Perean peasant producers. Second, suddenly, within two decades of Antipas's takeover, most Galileans, who had been ruled from distant capitals before, now experienced one of these "royal" capitals as an immediate presence, within view and only a half-day's walk away. These cities of the Roman client-"king" were suddenly both an immediate and pressing cultural and political-economic presence in the Galileans' lives.

No more than his father Herod did Antipas observe the traditional customs and laws of the Judeans, at least to hear the wealthy Jerusalem priest and historian Josephus tell it. On his coins he was careful not to cause offense.[35] On the other hand he built the new city of Tiberias on a graveyard and decorated his royal palace there with representation of animals in a style forbidden by "the laws" (*Ant.* 18.38; *Life* 65) — and presumably offensive to his Galilean subjects who were committed to basic covenantal commandments. Later in his reign he married his brother's wife Herodias in violation of Judean law (*Ant.* 18.136; cf. Lev. 18:16; 20:21). His conflict with John the Baptist indicates that Antipas drew opposition from both his own subjects and from Judean officials or retainers. John apparently preached sharp prophetic indictments against Antipas as part of his message of covenantal renewal. Antipas arrested and executed John. Then when Antipas's whole army was destroyed by the Arab king Aretas (in retaliation for Antipas divorcing his daughter in order to marry Herodias), "some Judeans" interpreted it as divine vengeance for the execution of John (*Ant.* 18.109–19).

Far from having developed any relationship with his Galilean subjects living in the villages near his two capitals — other than collection of taxes, that is — Antipas cultivated the Roman-Hellenistic urban political-culture of a client-ruler who had been raised and educated in Rome. As portrayed in the legendary story of "Herod" Antipas's birthday banquet in Mark 6, the "leading figures of Galilee" (*hoi protoi tes Galilaias;* Mark 6:21) in attendance were not Galilean village heads, but the principal officials and councillors of the royal administration. A generation later "the leading figures" (*hoi protoi*) of Tiberias were clearly the officials in Agrippa II's administration, probably men in the next generation of the same families of "Herodians" (*Life* 64, 67; cf. *Ant.* 18.273; Dan. 5:23). The story's terms for the military officers betray the Roman-Hellenistic character (and limited size) of Antipas's regime: *chiliarchos* was standard in the eastern empire for a "commander of a thousand," and the Latin loan word *speculator* is best attested in reference to the imperial guard at Rome. If the names mentioned by Josephus in Tiberias in 66 are any indication — Justus son of Pistus, Compsus son of Compsus and his brother Crispus (*Life* 33–36) — the Herodian administration of Antipas was already heavy with Latin names (adopted by Greek or Judean Herodians?).

After deposing Antipas in 39, the emperor Gaius (Caligula) bestowed Galilee and Perea along with the title "king" upon (Herod) Agrippa I. King Agrippa then received Judea and Samaria as well from the emperor Claudius in 41. Thus for a brief period, 41–44, Herod's realm was reunited under his grandson. Having been raised "with the circle of Claudius" in Rome, Agrippa was more interested in playing a role in imperial political affairs, in particular as the patron and protector of Jewish diaspora communities, than in the mundane affairs of the remote district of Galilee. While his coins from Jerusalem bear no images, those minted elsewhere bear the image of Caesar and even of Agrippa himself. Like

Herod the Great, Agrippa lavished gifts on Hellenistic cities, and he sponsored games in honor of the emperor. Yet he also took an aggressive role in the politics of the Temple and high priesthood, making visits to Jerusalem for festivals from his preferred residence in Caesarea, as the Roman governors before and after him had done. In his absence, Galilee was managed by his royal administration in Tiberias headed by his brother Aristobulus and "other powerful members of the [Herodian] house" (*Ant.* 18.273; *Life* 37).

The crisis touched off when Gaius ordered Petronius, Legate of Syria, to erect his statue in the Jerusalem Temple reveals much about the dynamics of Herodian rule in Galilee. A massive popular protest begun apparently in Judea spread to Galilee. The peasants refused to plant their crops on which the Herodian revenues as well as the Roman tribute depended. Before long the Herodian officials, worried lest the emperor's intransigence touch off a "harvest of banditry" in place of the harvest that supplied their revenues and timely payment of the tribute, attempted to mediate with Petronius. Although on issues such as this there were disagreements between the different layers of rulers on how to handle a restive populace, the basic political-economic (and religious) division was between the people on the one hand and the rulers of all levels on the other.

An Interlude of Independence; Roman Reconquest and Urbanization

By establishing royal capitals at Sepphoris and Tiberias that bore down heavily on the people both visibly and materially, Antipas intensified the structural political-economic conflict in Galilee. Resentment must have festered among the villagers for much of the first century, under Antipas, Agrippa I, and then under the Roman governors and Agrippa II. A severe drought in the late 40s further exacerbated conditions for the peasantry. The escalating banditry reported by Josephus in the 50s and 60s may be an index of the resulting economic hardship and social disintegration. Once the widespread revolt erupted in Galilee as well as Judea in the summer of 66 the previously latent conflict between rulers and ruled became manifest.

While a more dramatic faceoff between the people and their rulers (Roman, Herodian, high priestly) erupted in Jerusalem in the summer of 66, the Roman-Herodian order simply disintegrated in Galilee. In one respect the escalating banditry became epidemic and flowed imperceptibly into peasant revolt, a rare development even during serious crises in traditional agrarian societies. Large bands of brigands, however, are not necessarily revolutionary. In the absence of occupying Roman troops or an adequate garrison for its own security, the city of Sepphoris resorted to hiring a horde of bandits, headed by a certain Jesus, as mercenaries to protect itself from the hostile Galileans in the surrounding villages. Elsewhere the brigands did form the nucleus of revolt, or simply of local independence movements, as in Gush Halav and other villages of Upper Galilee where their leader John came to prominence (see, e.g., *Life* 105; *B.J.* 2.511, 587–89).

In Galilee in 66–67, the "great revolt" took the form of a number of separate local independence movements that were neither coordinated by the rebel leaders themselves nor controllable by the provisional high-priestly government in Jerusalem.[36] No sooner had the high priests (who remained in the city) and the "leading Pharisees" formed a "council" to attempt to control the nascent revolt (i.e., by pretending to go along, as Josephus says in both of his histories!) then they delegated "generals" to each district. It is a significant indication that the Jerusalem high priests still considered themselves as the rightful authorities over Galilee that they sent three "generals" to that district, including Josephus himself. Once we cut through Josephus's portrayal of himself as a great general and worthy opponent to the illustrious Roman general Vespasian (who of course became emperor in the middle of putting down the revolt), it is possible to discern how divided and anarchic the situation was in Galilee.

The Roman general Cestius Gallus had made an initial incursion into Galilee to put down the revolt, slaughtering many and supposedly suppressing the unrest. Probably that only fanned the fires of resistance and generated bands of rebels from the villages thus disrupted or destroyed, as it did in northwest Judea in the late summer of 67. Josephus attempted to control the brushfires of insurrection one by one and bring them under his own authority.

To enhance that "authority," of course, he brought along his own mercenary forces from Jerusalem. In Tarichaeae he seems to have had some success. Tiberias, on the other hand, was sharply divided between the wealthy and powerful Herodian leading men and the party of the poor headed by Jesus son of Sapphias. Both sides steadfastly resisted Josephus's designs. His principal rival for influence and leadership around Galilee was John of Gischala (Gush Halav), who apparently did have ambitions of leadership beyond the villages of Upper Galilee.

Josephus claims to have had at least some success with the general peasantry in Lower Galilee, those he calls "the Galileans." A key stratagem was to persuade them to give him resources, which he would then use to "hire" some of the bands of brigands (themselves fugitive villagers) to "protect" the Galilean villages. He could only manipulate but not control the "Galileans," however. They were eager to attack Sepphoris, which, as the Roman administrative city in western Galilee, remained steadfastly loyal to Rome. In eastern Galilee similarly, the Galilean villagers hostile to their Roman client-ruler Agrippa II and his officers made common cause with the "party of the poor" in Tiberias itself in attacks against the royal palace as well as against "the leading men" of Tiberias, that is, the Herodian officials (*Life* 30, 39, 273–80, 390–92).

When the Romans finally launched their massive expedition to reconquer greater Judea in 67, starting as usual with Galilee, they met with little resistance. For all of the pages the great general Josephus writes about his own supposedly brilliant preparations for and strategy in battle against the Romans, he cites precious few incidents of actually engaging in combat. The one major exception is Jotapata. Of all the sites he claims to have fortified, this one now has at least some credibility. It has finally been excavated.[37] The Romans did indeed besiege and destroy this town, although the scale of the conflict was nowhere near what Josephus claims. In the midst of the battle, of course, Josephus found a way of deserting to the Romans and thereafter assisted the enemy in reconquering the land and people. The other principal resistance came in Upper Galilee, at the refortified village of Gischala. The Romans, however, rode roughshod over the villages and towns, regardless of any resistance, and in their retaliatory "forceful suasion" slaughtered or enslaved tens of thousands (*B.J.* 3.304–6, 336–39, 540–41).

After the Roman reconquest, western Galilee remained under direct Roman administration. The area around the lake was returned to Agrippa II, then came under direct Roman administration at the outset of the second century. Galilee should probably not be lumped with Judea in discussions of the Roman disposition of the land following the reconquest. In either case, the territory was evidently not taken as imperial land after the revolt. Recent critical analysis suggests that only rebels' lands were confiscated.[38] Early rabbinic literature indicates that Galilean households still farmed their own family inheritance, and were not largely tenants on imperial land. The destruction of the Temple and high priesthood in Jerusalem eliminated the institutional base for enforcement of tithes to priests and offerings to the Temple. But the Romans added a *tributum capitis* (poll tax), which was felt to be burdensome and, as a punitive measure, a special two-drachma tax on all Judeans in replacement of the Temple tax.

In late first- and second-century Palestine, the Romans implemented a process of "urbanization," as they phased out their reliance on client-rulers such as the Herodians. Villages previously organized in toparchies were placed under the jurisdiction of cities for taxes and other administration. Although evidence is sparse for Galilee, it appears that all of Lower Galilee was placed under (either) Sepphoris or Tiberias by the time of Hadrian, remaining in that status through the late Roman period. Sepphoris, reconstituted as Diocaesarea, and Tiberias thus came to dominate political-economic relations in Lower Galilee even more than they had as the seat of the administration of Antipas. Only Upper Galilee was left outside the city system, as a *tetracomia* under a representative of the provincial governor.

No texts, coins, or archaeological excavations indicate that Galilee was involved in the second great Judean revolt against Roman rule, the Bar Kokhba Revolt of 132–135. The extensive disruption and devastation were confined to Judea. Following the first revolt, however, Roman military presence increased in the area, as did the economic burdens that entailed. After the second revolt, the Romans stationed two full legions plus auxiliaries in the province of Judea, one of them located in Legio just south of Gali-

lee. At Sepphoris and Tiberias cohorts manned the fortresses. With
the military presence in and around Galilee, however, came demands for *annona*, exactions of goods, and *angariae*, "service to the
state," which gradually evolved into new forms of regular taxation. As early rabbinic texts indicate, the Roman soldiers could not
only press animals into service, but could draft gangs of workers
as needed (*m. B. Meṣ.* 6:3; *m. B. Bat.* 9:4).[39]

Although it was not involved in the second revolt, the massive
Roman destruction in suppressing the two great revolts in Judea
had a dramatic long-range historical impact on Galilee. After ruling Galilee for a hundred years and then exerting considerable
influence on life there for another six decades, the Temple and
high priesthood were completely destroyed. The immediate impact on Galilee was surely nothing comparable to its effect on
Judea. Yet the destruction of the institutions that had attempted to
hold the Galileans together with the Judeans under one political-
economic-religious system would have had some effect on social
religious life. The major impact of the Roman destruction of
Jerusalem and Judea came after the Bar Kokhba Revolt with the
migration of prominent Judean families to Galilee and the resulting development of rabbinic academies in Sepphoris and Tiberias.
Indeed, by late antiquity, Galilee and Tiberias in particular had
become perhaps the most important centers of nascent rabbinic
Judaism, with influence reaching far and wide in the Roman
empire and into the Babylonian Jewish communities.

After the Romans destroyed Jerusalem and the Temple, they resettled many prominent Jerusalem and Judean families in Yavneh,
Azotus, and Lydda, a fertile area near the Mediterranean coast that
had traditionally been royal-imperial land. The Judeans resettled
there included prominent scribes and Pharisees, who established
an academy at Yavneh under the leadership of Yohanan ben Zakkai,
according to the later foundational legend.

After the further Roman devastation of Judea in suppressing
the Bar Kokhba Revolt, many of the sages moved to Galilee, establishing academies first in Usha and Beth Shearim and then in
Sepphoris. The claim of a massive migration of Judeans north-
ward to Galilee appears to be based on the assumptions according
to which the fragmentary indirect evidence is interpreted.[40] The
literary evidence claimed for mass migration actually pertains only

to the rabbinic schools at Usha and Beth Shearim (*Gen. Rab.* 97; *b. Roš Haš.* 31a–b).

Recent critical analyses of the development of rabbinic academies conclude that, contrary to previous claims, there is no evidence to suggest that the rabbis had any official recognition from the Romans of their political authority in Judea and Galilee.[41] That they became more influential by the end of the third century was apparently due to their association with the Patriarchate, based at first in Sepphoris and later in Tiberias. Suddenly in sources for the early third century the person of Judah the Prince emerges with considerable power and influence in Galilee and beyond. The Christian theologian Origen commented that "he differs in no way from the king of a nation" (*Ep. ad Afric.* 20, 14). The principal basis of his power in Galilee and his authority in the Jewish diaspora was the friendship he cultivated with the emperor and imperial house. Judah managed to extract from this friendship grants of land for himself, increased civic rights for Tiberias, and considerable influence for himself and his associates.

In Galilee itself Judah the Prince built up his extensive influence in social-economic and cultural affairs by cultivation and intermarriage with the wealthy families. He managed to influence the appointment of local judges, although some villages, such as Simonias, west of Nazareth, protested or dismissed his candidates.[42] Judah and his successors employed what was in effect a private police force, and they engaged in certain kinds of fundraising, including collection of tithes. It is unlikely, however, that Judah had any official role sanctioned by the Romans, for example, in the collection of taxes, which would have been handled by the city officials of Diocaesarea and Tiberias.[43] However strong the influence of Judah and the Patriarchate he established may have become, the cities of Diocaesarea and Tiberias still held official jurisdiction over the territory of Lower Galilee in the structure of Roman imperial rule.

Even in late antiquity, Galileans had not lost their passion for independence of outside rule. In 351 or 352 a revolt broke out under Gallus, the vice-emperor in the East. As in 4 B.C.E. after the death of Herod, the insurrection focused on Sepphoris, where rebels seized arms from the Roman fortress. Archaeological evidence now suggests that Upper Galilean villagers were also involved in the revolt.[44] The social form taken by the revolt also seems familiar from 4 B.C.E. According to the earliest pagan source for the revolt, "the Jews raised up Patricius in some sort of kingdom."[45] And again in a familiar historical pattern of Roman imperial rule, the Roman army burned many villages and took punitive measures against Sepphoris/Diocaesarea, as evident from archaeological excavations as well as literary sources.[46] The "Gallus Revolt" of late antiquity thus indicates that after four centuries of Roman rule, the Galilean people still retained their independent spirit.

Chapter 2

Sepphoris and Tiberias, Monuments of Urbanization

The theater was regularly situated at a central or easily accessible site, its soaring facade, clad in marble and richly ornamented, towering over the surroundings. As in Rome, seating was by social status, so that the cavea, when full with spectators, presented a vivid reflection of the carefully structured social hierarchy within each city. The Augustan theater was surely no place to go to forget politics and lose oneself in a spontaneous, Dionysiac entertainment.

— Paul Zanker

The Tetrarch Herod [Antipas], inasmuch as he had gained a high place among the friends of Tiberius, had a city built, named after him Tiberias, which he established in the best region of Galilee on Lake Gennesaritis. . . . This settlement was contrary to the law and tradition of the Jews because Tiberias was built on the site of tombs.

— Josephus, *Antiquities* 18.36–38

By the mid-third century Tiberias had emerged as the center of Palestinian and, to an extent, of Imperial, Jewish life.

— Lee I. Levine

Well into the 1980s ancient Galilee appeared from the modern scholarly distance to have been a rural backwater: "Literary and archaeological sources combine to confirm a picture of an essentially rural Galilee, whose inhabitants are committed to the peasant way of life and live in villages, though surrounded by a circle of

Greek-style cities on the periphery."[1] A widely read handbook on archaeology in relation to the rabbis and early Christianity does not even mention the city of Sepphoris/Diocaesarea. It mentions Tiberias, the other major city that ruled Galilee, only briefly in connection with synagogue art and reburial in late antiquity. The irregular topography and outside influences suffice to explain the cultural differences within Galilee.[2]

The archaeological explorations of Sepphoris that began in the mid 1980s, however, touched off a pendulum-like reaction against what appeared as an idyllic picture of a rural Galilee. As often happens, the reaction became an overreaction. Suddenly Sepphoris and Tiberias grew into some of the most populous and cosmopolitan cities of antiquity, and Galilee became as urbanized as anywhere in the Roman empire. With Lower Galilee in particular so heavily urbanized, Magdala/Tarichaeae and Capernaum (literally "Nahum's Village") also became cities, with populations of 15,000 or even 25,000. And if the population of such cities and towns was so large and they were in such proximity to such long-standing Hellenistic cities as Ptolemais on the Mediterranean to the west and Scythopolis in the plain to the southeast, surely the Galilee where Jesus ministered also had a cosmopolitan culture. After all, Sepphoris, Tiberias, Tarichaeae, and other Galilean sites boasted most of the typical Hellenistic-Roman urban institutions that made a city a *polis:* courts, theater, palace, colonnaded streets, city walls, markets, archives, bank, amphitheater, aqueduct, stadium.[3] Despite the provisional character of such archaeological interpretations, some Jesus scholars took them as support for sketches of a relatively urbane Cynic-like Jesus.[4]

There are serious problems with this picture and with the procedure by which it was produced. Institutions from different sites and from different times were lumped together into a synchronic synthesis. Most influential in its impact, the population of the cities and towns was grossly overestimated (reminiscent of exaggerated population figures offered by the ancient Judean historian Josephus). Criteria for critical estimation were not formulated. For example, no one thought to ask about the "carrying capacity" of the land. Initial explorations in calculating the carrying capacity of the land in Galilee suggest that a population of 25,000 in Sepphoris alone would have required not only the produce of the valley around the city itself, but the entire agricultural produce of the two large valleys under the city's jurisdiction as well, leaving nothing for the peasant producers themselves to live on.[5] That means either that Sepphoris had some other source of support or, more realistically, that the population was nowhere near that large.

Estimations of population are notoriously precarious. They usually depend upon two factors: a critical measurement of the area of a site and an estimation of the density of its population, which in turn is dependent on what is known about critically chosen comparative sites. A survey of the population of Palestine in the Late Roman–Byzantine period, one of maximum density, estimates Diocaesarea (Sepphoris) and Tiberias in Galilee at 60 and 40 hectares, respectively, compared with Caesarea on the Sea at 95 and Aelia Capitolina (previously Jerusalem) at 120.[6] If the density of the Galilean cities was more comparable to that of Pompeii, at 125–56 per hectare, than that of Ostia, at 435,[7] then the population of Sepphoris and Tiberias would have been under 10,000 each. Assuming the areas of those cities were smaller at their (re)building early in the first century than at maximum size in the Late Roman period, then the population would have been correspondingly less. Given Broshi's still generous calculations for all of Western Palestine, a million at most in the Late Roman–Byzantine height of population, the population of Galilee as a whole would probably have been under 150,000 at the time of Herod Antipas and Jesus, even if it was one of the more densely populated districts. Given the comparative sociological generalization that a traditional agrarian society requires ten people cultivating the soil for every non-agrarian producer, that estimate of the overall population of Galilee corresponds with the above estimate of the combined population of Sepphoris and Tiberias at roughly 15,000.

Similar problems have attended recent discussions of ancient Sepphoris based on the continuing archaeological excavations there. Much of this discussion focuses on essentialist issues such as the ethnic-religious identity and cultural character of artifacts and residents of the city, or measures archaeological findings by vaguely defined synthetic concepts.

Reflection on the problems of recent archaeological discussions increases our awareness of certain procedural pitfalls in analysis of the cities in Galilee. Instead of combining artifacts and institutions found in various sites into a synthetic picture of the culture of Galilee in general then projected back onto a given site, we must analyze each site in its own integrity. Instead of conglomerating artifacts and institutions into a synchronic picture of "the cities" of Galilee, we must distinguish between different archaeological strata and historical periods in order to discern significant changes and developments. Given the limitations of archaeology to broad strata that span several generations, textual sources (where available) become relatively more important in attaining anything close to precise historical distinctions. Unusual caution is necessary for periods for which very little archaeological or textual data are available. Instead of classifying artifacts, terms, and ideas according to essentialist categories in order to prove or disprove the presence of a certain culture, religion, or people, data must be questioned — indeed generated — in terms of a complex network of political-economic-religious power relations.

If we broaden our approach to include a full range of social relations, a different set of questions seeks answers from the combination of material and literary remains. The crucial question for the cities of ancient Galilee, which were subject to imperial rule through most of their history, is what political-economic-cultural function the cities served in the broader imperial order. In the case of Sepphoris and Tiberias, archaeological findings as well as literary references confirm what we might deduce from historical sociological studies of agrarian empires. Sepphoris appears to have been the principal administrative town through which Galilee was ruled and taxed by a series of imperial regimes, from the Persian to the Roman empire. Tiberias, of course, was founded by Herod Antipas as his capital, and remained an administrative city throughout the Roman era. Thus even if Sepphoris had not been located in such proximity to Nazareth, Jesus' "home town," and even if Tiberias had not been situated directly across the lake from Capernaum, the "headquarters" of Jesus' ministry, these cities would still have had a major impact on the Galilee of Jesus' ministry and movement. And even if a prominent rabbinic academy had not been established in Diocaesarea and the Mishnah (probably) compiled there, and even if the most prominent rabbis and their academies had not located in Tiberias, these cities would have played a key role in the emergence of rabbinic Judaism simply as the urban centers from which Galilee was ruled.

Sepphoris Under the Hasmoneans and Herod

The very topography of Sepphoris, rising sharply 300 feet above the plain, along with evidence of its fortress from several periods, suggest its function as the administrative town of rulers. The substantial quantities of Iron Age II potsherds uncovered at Sepphoris indicate that it was settled by the seventh-sixth centuries B.C.E. and occupied in the Persian period (fifth-fourth centuries).[8] After the conquest by Alexander the Great, first the Ptolemaic regime in Egypt and later the Seleucid regime in Syria must have used Sepphoris as an administrative center, for the Hasmonean high-priestly regime in Jerusalem inherited it as an already defensible fortress when they took over Galilee in the late second century B.C.E. Josephus reports that Ptolemy Lathyrus was unable to take the town from Alexander Janneus shortly after the latter became king–high priest in 104 B.C.E. (*Ant.* 13.388).

The recent excavations have found numerous Hasmonean coins along with other late Hellenistic artifacts and traces of late Hellenistic architecture at the site. These finds support indications in Josephus that the Hasmonean regime in Jerusalem stationed some officers and a garrison in Sepphoris as well as in certain other strongholds in Galilee, presumably to maintain order and assure the payment of taxes (*Ant.* 14.413–14; *B.J.* 1.303). The Hasmonean regime controlled Sepphoris for only two generations before the Romans took control of Palestine and then installed Herod as their client-ruler. The Roman general Gabinius based one of five regional governing councils (*synhedria*) there, indicating its importance as the principal town in Galilee at the end of the Hasmonean period. That Sepphoris was the key to control of Galilee is indicated in Josephus's report that Herod's first move in conquering his Rome-bestowed kingdom was to take the fortress there (*Ant.* 413–14). Josephus's only other reference to Sepphoris during Herod's reign (37–4 B.C.E.), in particular "the royal fortress" along with the arms and goods stored there, indicates that Herod continued to use the town as his principal administrative base in Galilee (*Ant.* 17.271; *B.J.* 2.56).[9]

The political function of a town like Sepphoris, symbolized in its prominent fortress, would have determined its culture. Each successive regime that used Sepphoris as an administrative base would have influenced the ethos of the town in some way, if only through the principal administrative officers it stationed there during its period of domination. Since the Seleucid administration of Galilee had been based there, one would therefore presume that Sepphoris was a Greek-speaking Hellenistic town when the Hasmoneans took it over. Would the Hasmonean regime have replaced all the Greek-speaking Hellenistic inhabitants with Judeans? At the very least they would have installed trusted Jerusalemites or Judeans as the officers or aristocracy at the head of the administrative apparatus there. In this connection, it would be helpful to know more about the "Greek words in Hebrew letters in Sepphoris as early as the Hasmonean period," which apparently "refer to titles or data that may be associated with officials or official functions of the city."[10] The Hasmonean regime was otherwise characterized by increasing Hellenistic influence, particularly under Alexander Janneus. These Greek words for administrative officers and functions in Hebrew letters suggest that while Hebrew may have become the official administrative language of the city, Greek terms and culture continued to thrive in the town. Since the Hasmoneans were preoccupied for much of this time with further expansion of their rule and virtual civil war first with their subjects and then between rival factions, however, they seem unlikely to have devoted much energy to the thorough implantation of Judean culture in a recently secured district administrative town such as Sepphoris.

Herod would likely have rooted out any remaining Hasmonean "aristocracy" in Sepphoris just as he eliminated Hasmonean family and high officers in the rest of his realm. Given his practices elsewhere of sponsoring Hellenistic-style building projects and administration, it seems unlikely that he would have fostered a distinctively Judean administration and culture in Sepphoris.[11] Perhaps he left Galilee more or less the way it was. Despite his extensive building projects elsewhere, including huge palatial fortresses and monuments to Caesar Augustus, we hear of no building in Galilee. Josephus mentions only "the royal [fortress-palace]" in Sepphoris (*Ant.* 17.271; *B.J.* 2.56). Despite the circumstances of the Hasmoneans during their brief control of Sepphoris and the characteristic Hellenistic-Roman orientation of Herod, it seems possible that a certain degree of Judean culture could have become established during the hundred years of Jerusalem's control of the town. It would be most significant, therefore, were some clear indications of Judean culture to be found in further excavations at Sepphoris. Meanwhile, Josephus's account of the popular insurrections that erupted after the death of the hated tyrant Herod indicates the political-economic function of the town (control and taxation) and the fundamental conflict between the town and the surrounding villagers: "Judas son of the brigand-chief Ezekias . . . when he had organized a large number of desperate men around Sepphoris in Galilee raided the royal fortress; having seized all the weapons stored there, he armed all his followers and made off with all the goods that had been seized there" (*Ant.* 17.271).[12]

Sepphoris and Tiberias as Rival Royal Capitals

What happened after the death of Herod the Great is of considerable importance for interpretation of Jesus, whether in terms of the direct impact of events there on people in nearby villages or in terms of longer range political-economic and cultural impact on Galilean villagers generally. The literary evidence has been well known for some time: Josephus writes that, in retaliation for the insurrection led by Judas son of Ezekias, Varus, Legate of Syria, "burned the city and enslaved its inhabitants" (*Ant.* 17.289; *B.J.* 2.69). Herod's son Antipas, having been entrusted with rule of Galilee and Perea (from 4 B.C.E. to 39 C.E.) by the Romans, then "fortified Sepphoris to be the ornament [*proschema*] of all Galilee, and called it Autocratoris" ("Imperial/Capital City"; *Ant.* 18.27).

Thanks to the industrious and painstaking efforts of the major ongoing archaeological expeditions at the site, we have an ever-increasing amount of material evidence for Sepphoris as well. With regard to events after the death of Herod, however, there is very little by way of material remains and some disagreement about interpretation between leaders of two of the major expeditions. "The Joint Expedition has found no trace of violent destruction in the Herodian period [but rather] a great degree of continuity between the Late Hellenistic and early Roman (Herodian) structures."[13] In excavations of building after building, however, the University of South Florida expedition discovered their foundations on bedrock in the early Roman period. That would seem to confirm Josephus's report that Antipas rebuilt the city as his first capital (*Ant.* 18.27).[14] The respective dating of the Roman theater at Sepphoris reflects these different "readings" of the site. One team dates it at the end of the first century C.E. or later,[15] while the other team finds construction by Antipas to be more credible.[16]

Josephus, of course, does not say that the Romans destroyed the town.[17] But he does suggest that Antipas did some rebuilding, at least of fortifications. Depending on the dating of the building of his new capital city of Tiberias and how long we estimate the construction to have taken, Antipas would have established a capital suitable for his status as a Roman client-"king" as soon as possible following his appointment, with the administrative town of Sepphoris being the obvious site. Perhaps further assessment of current findings at Sepphoris and/or future finds will provide further clarity regarding the rebuilding of Sepphoris as a Roman city, including whether this was done by Antipas soon after 4 B.C.E. or later in the first century C.E.

In the middle of his long reign, around 18 C.E., Antipas founded Tiberias near the town of Hammas, known for its "hot baths," along the southwest coast of the Sea of Galilee. Josephus views the original inhabitants with disdain. Besides the officers of Antipas's regime, they consisted of Galileans and other "poor" and perhaps (debt-) slaves drafted from the territory subject to Antipas (*Ant.* 18. 36–38). Presumably the royal palace, stadium, and "prayer-house" with which Josephus himself claims to be very familiar were built at the founding of the city. Compared with Sepphoris, little archaeological excavation has been done on Tiberias. Apparently the city was not walled and fortified until much later (around 200 C.E.). Of Antipas's original city, only the southern gate set between two columns mounted on pedestals and the corresponding street into the city, paved in Roman style, have been unearthed. The large open space between this gate and the original area of buildings suggest an initially sparsely settled city with room to grow.

Tiberias thus replaced Sepphoris as Antipas's capital, and apparently remained the locus of the court and administrative apparatus such as the archives and "royal" bank under Agrippa I, whom the Romans appointed ruler of Galilee (39–44 C.E.) prior to naming him king of greater Judea as well (41–44). After Antipas was deposed (39 C.E.) and again after Agrippa I died (44 C.E.) Galilee was placed under direct Roman rule. In 54 the emperor Nero placed the Galilean "toparchies" of Tiberias and Tarichaeae under Agrippa II, leaving the rest of Galilee under direct Roman rule, centered in Sepphoris. In the course of these shifts of jurisdiction and capital, an intense rivalry apparently developed between the two cities for status and power in the territory (Josephus, *Life* 36–39). As in Sepphoris under earlier regimes, so in both Sepphoris and Tiberias under Antipas, the Agrippas, and the Romans, their function as cities from which Galilee was governed determined their ethos.

The Political Culture of Roman Client-Rulers

Two of the teams currently excavating at Sepphoris have dramatically different interpretations of the character of the city during the first century C.E. One team envisages a Sepphoris in late second-temple times in which "virtually all of the inhabitants...were Jewish," including "many priests, some of whom even served as high priests in the Jerusalem temple," the city having become culturally more mixed and cosmopolitan only after 70.[18] Another team suggests that "Herod Antipas' reconstruction of Sepphoris marked its transition from a Greek city to a Roman one."[19] This divergence of interpretation requires some critical review of the archaeological and literary evidence — which suggests that essentialist interpretive categories may not be appropriate.

In the absence of pertinent archaeological data, a review of the literary evidence for Sepphoris under a sequence of outside rulers suggests that the city would not have been completely Judean in the first century C.E. Because Sepphoris was an administrative center for regimes based in Jerusalem for a century prior to Antipas, one would have to assume that an appreciable number of its residents at the end of the first century B.C.E. were from Jerusalem or Judea. Herod, however, was noted for using non-Judeans in his administration. Judging from the Roman names of the powerful Herodian figures in Tiberias during the great revolt in 66–67

(Crispus and others mentioned in the *Life*), it would appear that Antipas also had utilized non-Judeans (or Judeans with Roman or Hellenistic names) in his administration, probably at Sepphoris as at Tiberias. There were a number of "Greeks" in Tiberias at the outbreak of the revolt in 66 (*Vita* 67). Since Sepphoris had by then been a city of direct Roman administration for nearly thirty years, remaining staunchly pro-Roman during the great revolt, we would expect there to have been more "Greeks" or "Romans" (at least non-Judeans and non-Galileans) at Sepphoris than at Tiberias. More to the point, however, the cultural ethos of both Sepphoris and Tiberias was surely set by their political-economic function as cities of the Roman client regime of Antipas and the Agrippas, and essentialist dichotomies (such as "Jewish" vs. "Hellenistic") do not particularly apply to the leading Herodian officers who set the political-cultural tone in both cities, some probably Judeans with Roman or Greek names.[20]

There appears to be no real evidence, literary or material, to support the assertion that "Sepphoris was apparently the home town of many priests, some of whom even served as high priests in the Jerusalem Temple."[21] Given Stuart Miller's critical analysis[22] of the references in Josephus and rabbinic texts that were previously taken synthetically as a basis for such speculation, it can no longer be imagined that the high priest Matthias (end of Herod's reign) was from Galilee, let alone that Joseph ben Ellim was a "priestly aristocratic landowner in Sepphoris."[23] Rabbinic awareness of priestly presence in Sepphoris can be dated to the latter half of the second century C.E. at the earliest.[24] We may speculate that some of the Hasmonean officers stationed in Sepphoris would likely have been priests, but they may not have survived Herod's purges. Perhaps we simply cannot know, on the basis of current evidence, whether there was much of a distinctively Judean or priestly presence at Sepphoris during the century of Jerusalem rule of Galilee through Sepphoris.

On the premise that rulers, as rebuilders or founders of cities, determined their cultural ethos as well, it seems more likely that Sepphoris as well as Tiberias would have been more Roman-Hellenistic than Judean in cultural orientation, whatever the ethnic background of its inhabitants. Thus the alternative recent archaeological view that under Antipas and subsequent Roman administrations Sepphoris changed from a Greek to a Roman city seems more appropriate to material remains such as the theater and colonnaded streets. Strange claims broadly that the Roman client-ruler Antipas superimposed on indigenous "Jewish" culture a "Roman urban overlay." This "urban overlay" would have brought into Sepphoris (and other cities) the major institutions and symbols of Roman culture, such as "baths, hippodromes, theaters, amphitheaters or circuses, odeons, nymphaea, figured wall paintings, statues, triumphal monuments, and temples (sometimes on a co-opted Hellenistic base)."[25]

At first glance, Strange's hypothesis of "Roman urban overlay" would appear to have considerable promise for interpretation of both Sepphoris and Tiberias. Continuing disagreement about the date of the theater in Sepphoris does not prevent us from realizing that a Roman client-ruler would have been eager to design his capitals in accordance with the imperial Roman ideology. Herod the Great had set the tone with his building projects, including temples, stadia, hippodromes, and newly founded cities at key locations in his realm. Antipas is often described in New Testament studies as a "Jewish king," perhaps because of his aniconic (imageless) coins. It seems doubtful that the stricter Judeans such as the Pharisees in Jerusalem would have viewed him so. Certainly the priestly aristocrat Josephus and the priestly provisional government in Jerusalem at the beginning of the great revolt of 66 did not view him as particularly loyal to the "laws of the Judeans" (to use Josephus's phrase). In building Tiberias, he had both desecrated a cemetery and decorated his royal palace in violation of the law and ancestral tradition of the Judeans, which the Jerusalem priestly government now wanted destroyed (*Ant.* 18.38; *Vita* 64–65). It would seem rather that Antipas would have established a Roman-Hellenistic–style capital at both Sepphoris and Tiberias, befitting the background and position of a Roman client-ruler in the East. After all, he had been raised and "educated" in Rome. And as Tetrarch of Galilee and Perea he both socialized and competed with other such Roman client-rulers.[26]

Moreover, the Roman character of the cities would have continued after Antipas's death. Sepphoris served as the Roman administrative city in (at least western) Galilee, and again received the official archives and bank from the rival administrative center in Tiberias. Tiberias continued as an administrative city of Agrippa II. The persistent pro-Roman stance of Sepphoris and of the Herodian elite of Tiberias during the revolt of 66–67 was consistent with their function and ethos as Roman administrative cities. Both cities very likely symbolized Roman dominion in Galilee. In Sepphoris, at least, the theater by itself announced "Rome!" Nevertheless, the evidence is insufficient to argue that Antipas and his Herodian successors made Sepphoris and Tiberias into heavily Romanized cities. One had a palace and a stadium, the other perhaps a theater. Yet excavators have not yet found the other principal "symbols" of the Roman overlay, such as a gymnasium, an odeon, a nymphaeum, or a hippodrome at either of the sites. As of the first century, these newly (re)built cities can be seen only as fitting into a general pattern of "Roman urban overlay" because of the prominence of so many of those "symbols" elsewhere in Herodian Palestine.

Judging from its problematic presentation, however, the concept "Roman urban overlay" requires considerable refinement in order to be appropriate to an imperial situation such as Roman Galilee. If our purpose is a better understanding of the Galilean social world, then particular cultural forms, imposed or indigenous, cannot be considered out of the context of the dynamics of the history of political-economic domination and subordination in Palestine under Roman rule.[27] Some parts of Palestine, such as Scythopolis, just south of Galilee, were indeed already urbanized from Hellenistic times and seemingly acquiescent in Roman imperial rule. Herod, of course, had completed a grand building program of Romanization, the outstanding examples being perhaps Sebaste ("August") in Samaria and Caesarea on the Sea, the handsome seaport and new capital of the Roman province of Judea after his death.[28] To say that the culture was already urban as well as rural and therefore prepared for Roman dominance[29] is untrue both of Galilee and of Judea proper. In fact, such a generalization flies in the face of the history of Palestine during what archaeologists call the "Early Roman" period (Pompey through Bar Kokhba). In late second-temple Judea proper the only city was Jerusalem itself. Prior to Antipas, with only the administrative town of Sepphoris (the size of which at the time is still unclear), Galilee was hardly urbanized. The popular rebellions against the Roman conquerors and/or their client-rulers in 40–37 B.C.E., 4 B.C.E., and 66–70 C.E., as well as several ad hoc protests and resistance movements among both Judeans and Galileans in the Early Roman period hardly indicates a people prepared for Roman domination and favorable to urbanization.

Similarly, it would be historically untrue to suggest that the indigenous local "Jewish" culture "bore its own institutions, ideas, and symbols" without much disruption by the overlay.[30] The latter appears to ignore striking examples of how the very "Jewish symbols" mentioned had already been dramatically affected by the influences of Hellenistic-Roman culture and political domination. The most obvious example is the Temple, which Herod had massively rebuilt and in which there were prayers and sacrifices for Rome and the emperor, which were led by high priests who were the creatures of the Romans' client-king or resident governors. Synagogue buildings, of course, did not exist yet in the first century (see chapter 6), unless we mean a *proseuche* ("prayer-house") such as the one in Tiberias, a city built as another prime example of the "Roman urban overlay." As Strange himself comments, "Jewish architecture is difficult to pinpoint in the first century."[31] That would presumably be because rulers determined major building projects, and they were pressing precisely "the urban overlay." Strange leaves unaddressed what characterized indigenous Judean or Galilean culture, which is precisely what many are hoping archaeology might be able to illuminate from its findings at various sites.

That "the idea 'city'" was not a foreign idea but "expressed what the locals had in mind" as they planned, built, and lived in the city[32] assumes that we already know both the character of the city and the background of the inhabitants, and that they determined the building. As noted above, however, we have no decisive evidence about who the initial inhabitants of Antipas's "ornament" would have been, much less if they were "locals" (whether that means Judeans or Galileans). If they were Herodian officers from Caesarea or Sebaste, Strange would have a point. If they were Jerusalemites or previous residents of Sepphoris, Antipas's "Roman urban overlay" would likely have seemed at least odd. In any case, city-building was sponsored by the Roman client-rulers and designed by their officers. In the case of Tiberias, of course, we have Josephus's account that the new population forced into the city had virtually nothing to do with the planning, let alone the conception of the newly founded city. What resulted both in Sepphoris and (even more) in Tiberias was surely a mix (but not yet a "synthesis") of "foreign" Roman elements of "urban overlay" and of local traditions and styles. What blocks further understanding of the relations between the overlay and the indigenous culture, however, is the lack of evidence for just what the indigenous culture may have been in and around Sepphoris and Tiberias.

The political-culture of Roman client-kingship that Antipas imposed on Galilee in the building of Tiberias and the further Romanization under Roman administration in Sepphoris later in the first century are best symbolized in the royal palace at Tiberias and the theater at Sepphoris. The lavishly constructed and furnished palace at Tiberias was decorated with representations of animals that symbolize the cultural transition and conflict inherent in the projects of Herodian client-kingship. As soon as they regained control in Jerusalem following the eruption of the great revolt in the summer of 66, the high priests and leading Pharisees who formed the provisional government there ordered the demolition of the palace in Tiberias. The Herodian officials in Tiberias, however, found nothing objectionable in the Roman-royal ethos in which they had grown up (assuming they were the sons of Antipas's original officers), and resisted the order (*Life* 64–65).

Patterned after the importance of political-religious celebrations and spectacles in Rome, theaters spread rapidly throughout the early empire, with Augustus encouraging theatrical events. Herod the Great had built theaters both in Jerusalem and at Caesarea by the Sea which were "spectacularly lavish but foreign to Judean customs," as Josephus points out (*Ant.* 15.268, 341). Theater ceremonies and performances usually involved the whole populace of a city.[33] The festivals honoring the gods and/or the emperor, other religious celebrations, public spectacles, as well as public trials and political meetings held in the theaters indicate the integral relationship among politics, religion, and public entertainment.[34] More particularly the theater, with its standard decor that included statues of the emperor and reliefs depicting Dionysus, helped perpetuate the honors and dedication to the emperor. Among the festivals held in the Herodian theaters at Jerusalem and Caesarea were elaborate games in honor of Caesar celebrated every five years. Although undoubtedly an extreme case, the posturing of Agrippa I in the theater at Caesarea in 44 illustrates how a client-king (such as Antipas, if the theater in Sepphoris could be dated that early) could use political-religious ceremonies in the theater in support of his own glorious position within the overall Roman imperial order. At the spectacles celebrating the "salvation" (*soteria*) of Caesar, with all of the royal officers and nobles of his kingdom present, Agrippa made a grand entry into the theater at daybreak dressed in a garment completely woven of silver. The spectators, dazzled by the sun's radiance glittering from Agrippa silver gown hailed him as divine! (*Ant.* 19.343).

The decor on the Herodian royal palace in Tiberias symbolized the alien culture that had suddenly intruded upon the Galilean landscape along with the "in-your-face" city built so visibly from revenues regularly taken from the threshing floors and olive presses of Galilean villages by officers who lived lavishly near that palace. Before Josephus could negotiate with the Herodian elite of Tiberias for a discrete dismantling of the palace in accordance with the order from Jerusalem, however, the Galilean villagers (in collaboration with the riff-raff of Tiberias) assaulted the palace and its lavish decor (*Life* 65–66). The theater in Sepphoris through its festivals, performances, and assemblies served to integrate the ethnically eclectic populace of the newly rebuilt city, officers and artisans alike, into a political-religious ethos of the new imperial order. If the numerous injunctions against theater performances in later rabbinic literature are any indication, stricter Judeans and presumably the more traditional-minded Galileans were extremely suspicious about such an alien political-religious presence in their midst.

The Cosmopolitan Veneer of Newly Built Provincial Cities

That the political culture of first-century Sepphoris and Tiberias were probably dominated by a degree of "Roman urban overlay" does not mean that they were "cosmopolitan." Prior to his reports on the recent excavations that view first-century Sepphoris as predominantly "Jewish," Meyers claimed that Sepphoris and "the other great urban centers" of Lower Galilee were linked with "the pagan, and hence Greek-speaking west, with its more cosmopolitan atmosphere and multilingual population" and the centers of Roman provincial government through which these "dominant cultural tendencies" influenced the villages of Lower Galilee.[35] Recent interpretations of Jesus and Jesus traditions, moreover, have seized upon archaeologists' representation of an "urbanized" Lower Galilee as also "cosmopolitan" in portraying Jesus and his followers as itinerant Cynic-like philosophers. Pending the discovery of further material evidence, we are dependent on a critical review of literary accounts for assessment of this issue.

The literary evidence is relatively more plentiful for Tiberias, although the city would have been in existence for only ten or twelve years by the time of Jesus' "ministry." Although it had some features of a "Roman urban overlay," Tiberias must not have been all that cosmopolitan, judging from Josephus's accounts of his dealings with the city in 66–67. As mentioned above, Antipas had built the city without scruples about violating the cemetery on the site and decorated his royal palace with features objectionable to the later provisional high-priestly regime in Jerusalem. In addition to the royal palace, the other principal civic building was the "stadium," although there was also an apparently sizable *proseuche* ("prayer-house") where a large public political meeting could be held. Among the residents fifty years after the founding were some "Greeks," although not a substantial enough group to hold their own in 66 against the resentful popular party led by Jesus son of Sapphias (*Vita* 66–67). The ten "principal men" (many with Latin names) who dominated the city politically and economically were apparently officers in Agrippa II's administration (of the toparchy centered there or of Agrippa's main court?). Justus, professional intellectual and rival historian to Josephus, was dependent on the patronage of Agrippa II. Perhaps this tiny provincial elite had pretensions to cosmopolitan culture. They resisted the orders of the provisional high-priestly government in Jerusalem to tear down the royal palace because of the objectional representations in its decor (*Vita* 65–66). If those "Greeks" and Herodian officials cultivated a degree of cosmopolitan culture, then it constituted only a thin veneer in Tiberias as a whole. The bulk of the Tiberians, the sailors and the poor, Josephus considered mere riff-raff, whose ancestors were inauspicious people from the surrounding territory forced into the city as colonists (*Ant.* 18.37–38). After the outbreak of the great revolt in 66, they killed the Greeks and, together with "Galileans" from nearby villages, burned and looted the royal palace (*Vita* 66–67). We can surmise whether the motives were political-economic resentment or cultural hostility or both.

Sepphoris probably used Greek as its official administrative language at the time of Jesus. The Hasmoneans continued to use Greek titles for their officers stationed there, and Herod the Great's administration there probably used Greek. As noted just above, it seems that Antipas imposed some features of a "Roman urban overlay" in Sepphoris, advertising Roman power and his own position as Roman client-ruler. Sepphoris, however, was quickly displaced as Antipas's "ornament" by the new capital Tiberias, losing the archives and the royal bank as well as other important patronage of Antipas that might have sponsored "Greek" culture. As at Tiberias, the administrative elite at Sepphoris who may have acquired a modicum of cosmopolitan culture were not likely to have been more than a small percentage of the populace. Given the lack of literary as well as archaeological evidence for the early first century we can only speculate whether through or underneath that elite there were carriers of cosmopolitan culture in the city.

The limited degree of Romanized urbanization and cosmopolitan culture in first-century Sepphoris and Tiberias can be placed in perspective by comparisons with Scythopolis, the largest city in Palestine, and Caesarea, Herod's creation on the Mediterranean coast only decades prior to Antipas's founding of Tiberias. These bustling and populous cities boasted most of the typical institutions of a Hellenistic-Roman city. Most striking is the quality of their buildings and high culture, including numerous imported marble columns and plentiful imperial Greco-Roman artworks. Nothing close to this level of imperial cosmopolitan culture is found at Sepphoris and Tiberias, even after the more intense Romanization following the great revolt and the Bar Kokhba Revolt. There appears to have been only a thin veneer of cosmopolitan culture in the cities of Galilee shortly after they were (re)built by Antipas. That is hardly the sort of cultural atmosphere in which Cynic philosophers would have flourished and somehow influenced or provided models for Galilean villagers.[36]

Although it goes beyond the evidence to say that first-century Sepphoris and Tiberias were centers of cosmopolitan culture, it also seems inappropriate to characterize Sepphoris as a center of "Galilean urban culture."[37] That is an odd phrase particularly when compared with the use of terms by our principal literary source, Josephus, who uses "Galileans" for people from villages precisely over against Sepphoris and the elite in Tiberias. As evident from literary and archaeological evidence together, Roman-Hellenistic urban culture was brought into Galilee precisely in the (re)building of Sepphoris and Tiberias. Josephus writes that in order to obtain enough settlers for Tiberias, Antipas had to coerce people of disgracefully humble origins, most likely Galileans from the immediate area. Is there any indication that Sepphoris and Sepphoreans in the first century included any culture and traditions distinctively Galilean? If there were any Judeans, particularly priests, in first-century Sepphoris, they would likely have been originally from Jerusalem and their culture Jerusalem-priestly in its roots (as still prominent in the Mishnah). It is noteworthy that passages in the Mishnah make clear distinctions between the respective regional customs of Judea, Perea, and Galilee. In the first century, the urban culture of the (recently rebuilt?) "royal" city of Sepphoris must have seemed like a foreign body set down upon Galilean culture of the villages: as a provincial "urban overlay," a cultural mixture dominated by Roman political-cultural features.

There is no question that both Sepphoris and Tiberias had an impact upon Galilean villagers. Given the political-economic structure, it seems likely that reaction and resistance outweighed assimilation and acculturation. This would likely have been the case in the first century as the Galilean villagers felt the initial impact of the sudden construction of cities and a royal administration resident in Galilee rather than at a distance, with gradual adjustments taking place over a longer period of time. For any assessment of the possible cultural influence of the cities on villagers and popular movements, of course, we must keep in mind that the impact of forces in the cities would have been mediated by the structures of political-economic relations between cities and villages — which will form the focus of the next chapter.

The Height of Roman Urbanization and Emergence of the Rabbis

Taken over by the Romans after the death of Agrippa I, Sepphoris would have been even more dominated by Roman administrative and military personnel after the Roman reconquest of Galilee in 67. Symbolic of the increasing Romanization was the reconstitution of the city as Diocaesarea ("city of Zeus-Caesar") under the emperor Hadrian, who had taken the title of Zeus Olympios. A milestone found nearby inscribed with "Diocaesarea" enables us to date this reconstitution of the city around 130, just prior to the Bar Kokhba Revolt in Judea (132–135). A temple to the Capitoline triad was apparently erected.[38] The city's coins soon displayed the title "Diocaesarea" and an image of a temple to Zeus-Jupiter.[39] An aqueduct joined the theater among the typical Roman constructions in Sepphoris, and the Romans directed the construction of roads linking the city with Acco and Tiberias and eventually Legio and Scythopolis.

Tiberias, similarly, was further Romanized in the second century after the completion of Agrippa II's reign. A large temple to Hadrian[40] and the appearance of Zeus and Hygeia on the city's coins suggest the tone now being set in the administration of the city. Indeed, the further Romanization of both Tiberias and Diocaesarea, under which all of Lower Galilee was now subordinated, was part of a general Roman policy of "urbanization" of the administration of Palestine.[41] Even prior to the Bar Kokhba Revolt in Judea (132–135), the Romans stationed two legions in the province of "Judea," one at Legio in the Great Plain. That made the small province of Judea the most heavily garrisoned area in the empire, with half of the troops located just to the south of Galilee.[42] Military units were also stationed at both Diocaesarea and Tiberias.

Whatever the presence of Judeans had been in Sepphoris and Tiberias in the first century C.E., there would appear to have been a significant increase in that presence from mid-second century. Virtually no evidence, literary or archaeological, has been found for a mass migration of Judeans to Galilee after the Roman reconquests of Judea in 70 and 135. Nevertheless, some Judeans did resettle in Galilee and played significant roles there. As noted in chapter 1, many of the most prominent Jerusalem families of scribes and priests settled in the coastal plain near Yavneh following the destruction of Jerusalem in 70, and some of those same families then relocated to Galilee after 135.[43] After locating initially at Usha in western Galilee and at Beth Shearim, the rabbis then established academies in Sepphoris later in the second century and in Tiberias by the early third century. Under the leadership of Judah the Prince, rabbis compiled the Mishnah probably in Sepphoris early in the third century.

At that point, of course, Judeans and their culture and traditions would have been coexisting with the Roman-Hellenistic culture already well established in the two cities. Rabbinic literature mentions a number of "synagogues" (assemblies) in Sepphoris. Excavations have very recently found a synagogue building, but from the Byzantine period. Otherwise in the excavations to date the only possible hints of a Jewish public building from Roman times are some fragments of a mosaic floor with several Hebrew letters and animal figures.[44] Rabbinic literature also refers to a number of "synagogues" at Tiberias. In Tiberias only a sixth-century synagogue building has been located, while just to the south at Hammath, which was eventually included in Tiberias, a fourth-century synagogue building was found. The public building that lay underneath the synagogue, however, was likely a gymnasium, judging from its Doric and Corinthian architectural features. Otherwise in Tiberias the buildings excavated have been those typical of a Roman-Hellenistic city: the *cardo* (colonnaded main street), a bathhouse dating from the fourth century, a basilica from the second century, and a somewhat later large public building with a white mosaic further in from the lake.[45]

Politically, relations between the Romans and the recently relocated Judeans must have been solid, even cordial. Judah the Prince apparently established his power and influence in Galilee, what came to be called the "Patriarchate," by cultivating Roman imperial leaders.[46] A coin from the reign of Caracalla (emperor 211–17) bears the significant legend "Diocaesarea the Holy City, City of Shelter, Autonomous, Loyal, friendship and alliance between the Holy Council and the Senate of the Roman People." Regardless of whether this legend and/or later rabbinic references indicate that the majority of the city council of Diocaesarea were Jewish at the time,[47] it suggests that political affairs were in good order within the city.

The recent archaeological excavations at Sepphoris/Diocaesarea have produced extensive finds from the Middle and Late Roman periods (roughly second to fourth centuries), in contrast to the meager results for the earlier periods. In the western residential area of Diocaesarea, for example, excavators found ceramic incense shovels similar to those used in the Jerusalem Temple, storage jars decorated with menorahs (seven-branched lampstands), and more than twenty installations that they identified as Jewish ritual baths (*miqva'ot*).[48] Yet in this same residential area were found hundreds of second/third-century disc lamps, many decorated with pagan symbols, several bronze figurines with pagan motifs (e.g., Pan and Prometheus).

Further clarification of the archaeological evidence and perhaps some reconceptualization of our categories of interpretation may be necessary in order to assess the implications of such a striking mixture of Greco-Roman and Jewish culture. Clarification is needed, for example, on what criteria are used in determining the particular (ritual?) usage of installations described as ritual baths. Much weight is placed on these bathing installations in the western residential area as being clearly Jewish *miqva'ot*.[49] Yet similar installations have been found in seemingly non-Jewish buildings such as the villa with the Dionysiac mosaic and another villa examined by the South Florida expedition.[50] Much of the categorization and interpretation of findings at Sepphoris has proceeded according to the broad essentialist categories of "Jewish" or "pagan." Subdivisions are then made as necessary between "Torah-true" if the evidence seems unmixed or "Hellenized" and "upper class" (e.g., where lamps with pagan symbols or Greco-Roman figurines are found in the same houses with *miqva'ot*).[51]

Other possibilities, however, can be considered simply by moving away from the standard essentialist categories. It is possible, perhaps even likely, given the long Hellenistic influence in Palestine, that some Jews considered themselves faithful even while they utilized what would be classified as pagan or Greco-Roman symbols as a matter of course in their everyday lives. Certainly the later synagogue buildings display a degree of "syncretism," symbols in their decor being similar to those in pagan temples and other public buildings in Syria. More important yet for future investigations, instead of simply categorizing artifacts by essentialist categories, excavators could look for larger social-relational patterns within a whole section of a site, such as the western residential area of Sepphoris. Presumably a correlation between a mix of cultural motifs, the relative size of the house, and the position of the house within the overall site would indicate the political-economic position of the family. Correlation might be sought between the size of houses (and/or the cultural motifs found) and size and possible function of the underground silos for storage of grain, oil, and wine. Similarly, the significance of the *miqva'ot* could be sought by comparison with the character of sites in which other similar installations were found, such as the Hasmonean winter palace at Jericho and houses of the wealthy in Herodian Jerusalem.

The discovery of an elaborate "Roman villa" or public building (75 x 100 feet) that forms a virtual triangle with the fortress and the theater at the center of the city was clearly the most dramatic indication of Roman-Hellenistic political culture in Late Roman Sepphoris. The main room, the banquet hall (*triclinium*) of this palatial building, featured an elaborate mosaic depicting scenes from the life of Dionysus and the ceremonies that celebrated him in Roman religion. In addition to being the god of wine, of revelry and celebration, and of the theater, Dionysus had become closely associated with the imperial cult by Roman times. The central position of this "Roman villa" in the configuration it forms with the theater and citadel suggests that this may have been the palace of a Roman official or a city-head who also in effect functioned as a Roman official. This mansion and the elaborate and beautiful mosaic celebrating Dionysus in its banquet hall provides a vivid illustration of the cultural diversity and coexistence in Diocaesarea in the third century.

The considerable archaeological evidence now available from second- to fourth-century Sepphoris makes it clear that the Roman-Hellenistic cultural forms in Sepphoris (and likely in Tiberias as well) were by no means merely empty shells left over from Herodian days.[52] "The construction of the villa and its mosaics took place at precisely the time when the Jewish community of Sepphoris, under the leadership of Judah the Prince, was at its zenith."[53] That was the very time during which the leading rabbinic academy was located in Sepphoris and Judah was spearheading the compilation of the Mishnah.

Critical analysis of rabbinic texts has led recently to the conclusion that the rabbis were located primarily in the cities rather than in villages, as previously thought. Among the places where rabbis first established academies, perhaps Usha was a typical Galilean village, but Beth Shearim lay along the frontier of what had traditionally been Galilee. Moreover, it quickly became an unusual center special to international Jewry, a sacred site in which the bones of hundreds of wealthy diaspora Jews were reinterred.[54] By the beginning of the third century rabbinic activity centered in Sepphoris. During the third century the rabbinic academies in Tiberias became even more prominent. Indeed, Tiberias quickly became the most authoritative center of Jewish learning in the world, attracting many Jewish sages from Babylon and elsewhere. If, as was previously thought, the rabbis supported their own scholarly activity by working as artisans,[55] they would most likely have been living in the cities, since village households ordinarily handled most of their own craft needs. Recent critical study of rabbinic texts indicates, however, that many of the sages managed to establish themselves as wealthy landowners in Galilee or enjoyed the patronage of wealthy landowners,[56] and such landowners customarily resided in the cities. That the rabbis had very little interaction with or influence on social-economic life in Galilee, virtually no interest in civil and criminal cases, and no role in local village assemblies — as they themselves regularly remark — also points to their residence in the cities.[57] Their residence primarily in the cities would also help account for the social distance they felt between themselves and "the people of the land" (*am ha-aretz*).[58] Following the leadership of Judah the Prince and the Patriarchate that became the legacy of his consolidation of social-economic power in the network of imperial relations, the rabbis gradually emerged as a new but unofficial social infrastructure in the cities of Galilee.[59] From their social-economic base in Sepphoris and Tiberias, they were attempting to cultivate ancestral Jewish traditions over against the dominant Roman imperial political culture.

Chapter 3

TRADE OR TRIBUTE: THE POLITICAL ECONOMY OF ROMAN GALILEE

Among many of the peoples who are subject to the Romans, it was the city-dwellers' practice to collect and store enough grain for all the next year immediately after the harvest, leaving what remained to the country people.

— GALEN 6.749–50

What is worse, is that the majority sees its goods confiscated by individuals for whom the public collection of tax is a prey they make their own and who make private gain under pretext of fiscal debt.... Is there in fact a town, or a municipium, or a borough where there do not exist as many tyrants as curiales [quot curiales, tot tyranni]? Where is the place where... the chief men of the cities do not devour the entrails of widows and orphans?

— SALVIAN 5.17–19 (a Gallic monk writing between 440 and 450)

Trade plays an important role in scholarly constructs of ancient Galilee. The hypothesis of extensive international trade between Galilee and other areas of the Roman empire supports the claim that Galileans would not have been so isolated and backward economically and culturally as had previously been suggested by outsiders, from the early rabbis to romantic Western European writers such as Renan. Claims of a thriving trade between Galilean cities and villages provides the basis for scholars located in the

modern imperial metropolis to argue for nonexploitative reciprocal urban-rural relations in ancient Galilee. Claims that Galilean
villagers marketed their products in Sepphoris and Tiberias also
provides the instrumental interaction whereby peasants could have
been influenced by the supposedly cosmopolitan atmosphere of
the Lower Galilee cities.

With such an irenic social context in Galilee, there appears to
be no serious political-economic conflict in which Jesus and his
followers or the later rabbis were involved. Far from being con-
strained by the usual difficult circumstances of an overburdened
peasantry they were supposedly free to criticize social conventions
and engage in alternative lifestyles. And, as noted in the previous
chapters, if Galilee was already well on its way to a cosmopolitan
culture in the first century, then Christian scholars have a basis
for imagining Jesus and his movement as solidly rooted in the
more universal and individualistic spirit of Hellenism. A Galilee
characterized by active trading, moreover, would have provided
the network of interaction by which the small circles of rabbis
could have influenced the rest of Galilean society and the network
of international relations by which they communicated with the
diaspora and the Roman empire at large.

Archaeologists have recently based claims of major patterns of
trade on two types of material remains, coins and pottery. In
both cases, however, these constructions appear to be at vari-
ance with the artifactual evidence when it is recontextualized in
a more complex network of political-economic relations. Trade
has also played a major role in more general studies of ancient
Galilean (or wider Jewish Palestinian) society. Again, however, the
historical constructions stand in tension with the mainly textual
references on which they are based. A critical review of the recent
archaeological and historical constructions leads to an alternative
model for understanding political-economic relations in ancient
Galilee.

Coins and Trade in Upper Galilee

The archaeologists who carried out the innovative excavations of
villages in Upper Galilee write that "one of the most basic assumptions and building blocks" governing their work was "that from

the Hellenistic period until the end of the Roman period, the Upper Galilee was oriented toward the Phoenician coast at Tyre, at least economically."[1] They base their building block on the high incidence of coins minted in the city of Tyre found in excavated villages. "The villagers of Upper Galilee were marketing their oil and other products in the direction of Tyre and receiving Tyrian money in return."[2] They claim support for this direct connection between coins and trade from Josephus's portrayals of John of Gischala (*B.J.* 2.591–94) as a typical "businessman" exploiting the law of supply and demand as well as Jewish scruples about using oil from the "Holy Land."[3] They conclude that "the businessmen" of Upper Galilee were involved in a thriving trade with Syria generally and Tyre in particular. This sense of a commercial economy in Upper Galilee in turn influences their assessment of other finds in the villages. The excavators interpret one Middle Roman building at the village of Meiron as a "large domestic-industrial complex" that manufactured barrels for shipment of olive oil to Tyre in exchange for grain and money.[4]

Neither Josephus's report nor the incidence of Tyrian coinage found in Upper Galilean villages, however, provides evidence for such extensive trade. As noted in the introduction, the use of Josephus's histories for historical evidence requires critical assessment of his viewpoint and rhetoric, with careful attention to his parallel accounts.[5] The grand scale in which Josephus portrays the leading characters and events in the *Jewish War* carries over to his portrayal of John, his archrival for control of Galilee in 66–67. He writes vaguely of John gaining a monopoly of the olive-oil crop in Galilee in order to supply "the Judeans in Syria" with oil (*B.J.* 2.591–92). The report in *Life*, however, is far more precise. There "the Judeans living in Caesarea Philippi, having been shut up, at the king's order, by his viceroy Modius, had requested John to supply them with pure oil for their personal use . . . and John sent off all the oil in the place [Gischala]," with Josephus's own reluctant permission (*Vita* 73–74). The scope of the operation appears limited to the town of Gischala in this version.[6] Most problematic for the archaeologists' use of the incident reported by Josephus is that it was an ad hoc, one-time-only arrangement in the midst of the crisis of nascent revolt in 66–67. Thus this incident can hardly be used as evidence for a supposed general practice of marketing Galilean olive oil in Syria by "the businessmen" of Upper Galilee, let alone as the basis for projecting a thriving generalized trade between Upper Galilee and Tyre or Syria more generally.

The direct connection between the high incidence of Tyrian coins found in Upper Galilean villages and trade also seems questionable. Does the presence of coins minted by a particular city or ruler indicate trade with that city or ruler? Several considerations invite doubt about such a simple and direct connection.[7] General numismatic evidence (including evidence of coinage from literary sources) indicates that Tyrian coinage was the most frequently used currency throughout the Eastern Mediterranean, including nearly everywhere in Palestine. It was probably the standard coinage against which others were measured and exchanged, including in the Jerusalem Temple. Indeed, the evidence of a coin horde found at Migdal (74 coins of Tyre, 15 of Acre, 17 of Gadara, and so on) compares interestingly with the third-century coins found at Meiron (25 from Tyre, 2 each from Acco, Petra, Bostra, and so on).[8] The incidence of Tyrian coinage in the Migdal horde may simply indicate that it was the standard currency most in circulation, probably because it was minted in the greatest quantity,[9] not that entrepreneurs of the fishing industry in Migdal were trading with Tyre. If Tyre was a major supplier of money in the Levant, then the incidence of Tyrian coins in Upper Galilee would have been nothing unusual and would not imply trade with Tyre. Indeed, one could imagine a very different (and direct) connection between John's unique "windfall" oil deal and the Tyrian coins found in Gischala: since Tyre was the major supplier of money in the region, the Jews/Judeans in Caesarea Philippi would likely have paid for the oil in Tyrian coinage.

The coinage-based hypothesis of thriving trade with Tyre, in fact, stands in direct contradiction to the otherwise consistent "pattern of factors that are the peculiar features of Upper Galilean economy," an area "tied to the Golan with distinctive features of pottery, an area of architectural conservatism that used local materials for construction, an area of limited goods for export."[10] All of those "peculiar features," however, suggest relatively less interaction with the cosmopolitan culture of Greek-speaking Tyre.[11]

The only material evidence that suggests economic and cultural contact, direct or indirect, is the fine ware found in a few large houses of the third century c.e., that is, trade confined to luxury goods for the well-to-do, as we might expect. However, "the contact required for such trade was limited, as shown by the [limited] quantities involved."[12]

Pottery and Trade in Galilee

More promising than coins as potential evidence for trading patterns in ancient Galilee is pottery. It was a basic item of use in every household, was virtually indestructible in its fragments, placeable and datable in its types (it was usually traded simply from place of production to place of use), and has been recovered in large quantities at every excavated site. The sophisticated new technique of neutron-activation analysis has enabled archaeologists to demonstrate that much of the common cooking ware used throughout Galilee was made at Kefar Hanania, a village between Upper and Lower Galilee.[13] The same technical analysis shows that a large percentage of the storage jars used in Lower Galilee were made at Shikhin, a village near Sepphoris. While the pioneer of this innovative analysis is cautious about the potential implications,[14] others have claimed the distribution of Kefar Hanania pottery as evidence for a widespread trading network in Galilee and beyond.

As with the leap from the incidence of coins to trade, so there are reasons to be skeptical about concluding from the distribution of common pottery that Galilee had a commercial economy. As established in many studies, manufacture and trade in the Roman world were primarily local. "Self-sufficiency in basic products was a fundamental principle of the ancient economy."[15] Given the high cost of overland transport for heavy items such as pottery, trade was even more localized where waterways were not accessible. Only a small percentage of the cooking ware recovered at Ptolemais came from Kefar Hanania, which suggests relatively little trading with that coastal city. The "small proportion of Kefar Hananya ware recovered at the Golan sites, compared with Galilean settlements at a similar distance from Kefar Hananya" may indicate "difficult accessibility" from Galilee.[16] It may also indicate that certain political factors were at play, and not simply pure "trade" — that is, a "political economy" was involved.

A combination of material and literary evidence indicates that pottery was not "marketed" in the early modern mercantile sense or in the modern capitalist sense, either by "merchants" or at "central markets" in the cities. Virtually all the rabbinic references to sale portray the potter selling at the workshop or carrying the pots directly to the buyer in other settlements (e.g., *m. B. Qam.* 5:2, where the potter brings pots into a courtyard).[17] Some passages (e.g., *t. B. Meṣ* 6.3, where the price is determined before the product is finished) suggest that pottery was "ordered" or "procured" from potters by those who needed pots, as was done for many products in preindustrial, precapitalist economies. One rabbinic text (*y. Maʿaś.* 2.3, 49d) seems to portray Kefar Hanania potters as peddlers (*rokhlim*) of their own products, going around to four or five settlements and then returning home by nightfall. A study of all rabbinic references to the term *rokhlim*, however, suggests these were a specific type of itinerants peddling cosmetics and spinning goods to women of outlying settlements. The products they carried in their baskets were all lightweight, small in volume, and of relatively high value. Significantly, *rokhel* is never used in connection with the selling of goods by the producer nor is it used with reference to pottery.[18]

The rabbinic references which are cited as evidence that Tiberias and Sepphoris (both about 25 kilometers from Kefar Hanania) functioned as "central market places" where middlemen sold Kefar Hanania pottery actually pertain not to Tiberias and Sepphoris but to largely gentile cities outside of Galilee.[19] That the relative quantity of Kefar Hanania pottery found at sites varies inversely with the distance from Kefar Hanania itself, the site of production, appears decisive against the claim that Sepphoris and Tiberias were the principal marketing centers for that pottery. Moreover, the fact that Kefar Hanania pottery comprised the majority of the common cooking ware in Sepphoris does not in itself indicate that the villages near Sepphoris were buying their pots at a "central market" in the city. The distribution pattern of Kefar Hanania pottery, taken together with rabbinic references to the transport and selling of pottery and other goods, thus suggests limited social interaction among Galilean villages or between Galilean villages and the two major cities of Sepphoris and Tiberias. The sale of pottery from production sites such as Kefar Hanania or Shikhin (near Sepphoris) apparently entailed interaction primarily between the potters themselves and their customers.

It seems all the more unlikely that we can extrapolate from pottery to a more general system of commercial and cultural interaction. To do that we would need reason to believe that many villages specialized in some product, such as cosmetics, spinning goods, oil, or wine, and then either "marketed" their produce in a "central market" or traded with numerous other villages. But the literary evidence of peddlers and the general evidence of nonspecialization in agricultural crops make this highly unlikely. Because it is dependent on the availability of the right kind of clay, pottery-making would have been specialized in certain locations. The distribution of pottery, therefore, does not appear to be a good indicator of intraregional mobility and cultural interaction, let alone of interregional economic and cultural contact.

Empire-wide studies lend solid support to the conclusion that generalizations cannot be based on the particular case of pottery. "The sheer survival of pottery has sometimes tempted archaeologists and economic historians of the ancient world to exaggerate its importance in the ancient economy."[20] Trade in pottery could possibly be representative of manufactured items of medium value. Yet extrapolation to a generalized commercial economy is utterly unwarranted. Overland transport was very costly, and no network of transport for general trade had developed. "It was [for example] impossible to move large quantities of cereals for long distances overland, unless the transport was organized by the government and the cost imposed on taxpayers."[21] Even in the case of general famine, the government seldom intervened.

Finally, knowing the distribution of pottery from Kefar Hanania and Shikhin does not change the general picture of Galilee as primarily (not exclusively) agrarian or of the exploitation of the Galilean peasantry by the wealthy and powerful resident in Sepphoris, Tiberias, and (earlier) Jerusalem.[22] The recent studies of pottery distribution, however, leave us with a far clearer picture of local trade in one product that is precisely traceable: trade in pottery was relatively unique, it was local, and it involved limited contact primarily between producer-seller and buyer-user.

The Question of a Market Economy

Previous assessments both of the coins found in Upper Galilean villages and of pottery distribution in the Galilee and the Golan generally assume a market model of economics. This is the economic model most frequently assumed and used in scholarly analysis of biblical literature and history, particularly in the previous generation. It is the model most familiar from the history of Western Europe. Its prevalence in biblical studies and biblical archaeology may also be due to the influence of Rostovtseff's monumental works on social and economic history in Mediterranean antiquity.

Although it has been decisively challenged in recent studies of ancient political-economic structures, the market model is still assumed and defended in certain historical and archaeological studies of ancient Galilee. According to these studies, trade was prominent at two levels. There were "large-scale trade patterns between Galilee and surrounding areas," in which "thriving commercial life," "merchants," and "small but successful businesses" "exploited the larger markets."[23] Galileans supposedly marketed their oil "in the bigger city markets on their borders" to earn coin in order to pay Roman taxes and buy luxury goods. The "internal economy" of Galilean villages also operated basically as a market. Food was "the commodity sold most often," supplemented by craftsmen who had "permanent shops" in the market places, "guilds of wool-weavers, bakers," and "service industries" employing moneychangers and scribes.[24] A recent major study even claims that the "economy of Roman Palestine" was a uniquely "open" market system in which, in addition to "active trade between a mother city and its surrounding villages" and "active trade between rural villages and the coastal harbor cities," the villages themselves "had a highly developed level of trade," with a "highly developed level of communal services" and wide range of specialists.[25]

Such studies, however, can offer little evidence, either textual or archaeological, to substantiate their assumption of a market economy in ancient Galilee. The limited archaeological evidence suggests that the principal imports were luxury goods for the wealthy, such as the fine wares found primarily in non-Jewish urban sites and Hasmonean-Herodian governmental sites in late second-temple times and ceramic wares from the mid-third century C.E. found even in villages such as Capernaum and Meiron.[26] In later Roman times, several sources reflect the export of olive oil to Egypt and probably to Tyre.[27] The claim that "most of the oil produced was intended for sale or for export outside the particular town where it was produced and, most likely, outside the local region and the province" rests not on direct evidence but on scholarly reasoning about the relative value of crops.[28] Later rabbinic passages mention markets in Sepphoris and Tiberias in connection with nonagricultural products. Missing are references to "the direct marketing" of villagers' agricultural produce in the city or of city goods in the village. Also missing are indications that villagers depended upon the city's services or trade.[29] Generalizations about different areas of Palestine having specialized in one or another crop in Roman times appear to be rooted in a scholarly habit of reading rabbinic references to the *quality* of a certain town's produce as implying also *quantity* and therefore specialization. A text indicating a crop growing with particular quality in one location does not mean that it was not grown at other places. "Wheat was grown in all regions of Palestine" and, except for times of drought and famine, Galilee in particular and Palestine in general supplied itself with grain as well as wine and oil.[30]

Virtually nothing indicates that towns and villages had established stores or even small markets. No buildings have been found in rural settlements that could be associated with stores or markets. No texts attest the appointment of an *agoranomos* (market inspector or supply officer) in villages.[31] Rabbinic passages adduced for "market days" refer instead to "days of assembly" and court (e.g., *m. Meg* 1:1; 3:6; *m. Ketub.* 1:1; *m. B. Meṣ* 4:6).[32] There would have been no need for a local village market since there was apparently little division of labor in village communities based on agricultural production. "The farmer undertook all stages of production," including the processing of the crops at communal installations such as olive or wine presses and threshing floors.[33] It is only scholarly analysis by topics that obscures the fact that peasant productivity included crafts as well as agricultural labor. Rabbinic and other sources indicate that "the farmer also functioned as an occasional artisan or laborer," that what might otherwise look like "artisans" in the villages were also "farmers."[34] As in agricultural production proper, so in production of clothing and other crafts, the household members undertook most or all stages themselves. The rabbinic ideals of a self-sufficient household and hostility to commerce simply reflect the traditional practices of peasant households and villages attached to their ancestral lands.[35] In this regard, peasants in Galilee were no different from those elsewhere in the Roman empire: "Most produce was consumed by the peasants who produced it; each peasant and his family produced most of what he and his family consumed; the market was not involved."[36] If there was a surplus or if craft-production was for sale, the producers apparently did most of the selling or bartering themselves, as noted in the case of the Kefar Hanania potters above (produce, *m. Ma'aś.* 2:1; utensils, *m. B. Bat.* 2:3; clothing, *m. B. Qam.* 10:9). At times the house functioned not only as "workshop," but as "store" as well (e.g., *m. B. Bat.* 2:3). "Most transactions in the village were between local householders."[37] Far from the village being a market economy, it appears that most village communities as well as their constituent households were relatively self-sufficient.[38]

The cities, on the other hand, most certainly were not economically self-sufficient. Yet there is little or no evidence of either an appreciable volume of trade between cities or of trading relations between city and villages. While there was a minimal level of trade within villages and a larger volume within cities, the model of a market economy is simply inappropriate to ancient Galilee. Most serious is its failure to help us understand urban-rural relations, or, more particularly, how the city could live without enough production by city-dwellers themselves to support itself — which may turn out to be one and the same.

The remaining problem that requires an answer is why a particular village became a center of pottery production when nearly all other villages strove to be more or less self-sufficient in production and consumption. Does the exception prove the rule? Cross-cultural study of pottery production finds that when peasants in a village did not have sufficient crops to feed themselves (after taxes and rents) they had to supplement their "income" through craft production. Where the necessary clay and a sufficient demand were available, such peasants might have turned to pottery production. But pottery-making is a "secondary choice to agriculture resorted to by people with poor quality, insufficient or no land. Pottery making, as an indirect subsistence technique, is the result of population pressure and not a desirable occupation for most farmers."[39] This does not make sense, however, on the assumptions of market theory of economy. How can we explain the pressures that would drive peasants of Kefar Hanania to a means of subsistence considered so undesirable by most peasants? Might the new demand for pottery have something to do with the pressures that drove such villagers to pottery-making?

The Political Economy of Roman Galilee

In assuming a market model for economic relations, recent archaeological studies of Galilee have not paid attention to key developments in the general field of archaeology. Most important in relation to ancient Galilee, perhaps, are two realizations now standard in general archaeology. (1) Following the fundamental procedural principle of attending to the relationships among archaeological sites (as well as to relationships of elements within a site) led to the recognition of political power relations between sites. Certain studies have shown, for example, that irrigation systems in early Mesopotamia tended to expand and collapse in response to political changes, or that changing forms of political-economic organization affected the size and distribution of settlements in the valley of Mexico.[40] It is essential, therefore, to focus on the social organization and the exercise of power or dominance among sites. (2) While archaeological work on prehistoric sites enjoys no such luxury, exploration of historical societies can utilize literary sources to shed light on many questions of such social organization and power relations.[41]

In attempting to follow these two procedural principles it makes sense to draw upon major developments in other related fields of inquiry. Both recent studies of the Roman empire and parallel studies of the ancient Near East (including Israel-Judea) have turned to alternative models of political-economic relations. Other models are readily available, whether from Max Weber's (largely structural-functional) sociological heirs such as Karl Polanyi, Gideon Sjoberg, and Gerhard Lenski or from historical materialist analysis, such as G. E. M. de Ste. Croix.[42] Some theorists, such as T. F. Carney, draw primarily on Roman data,[43] others such as de Ste. Croix's studies are based more broadly on general Greco-Roman data, while both Sjoberg and Lenski make synthetic use of ancient Mediterranean, medieval European, and Asian data. In a significant departure from the previous assumption and imposition of a market model of economic relations, M. Finley and others have taken seriously the reminders of Polanyi that movement of goods in antiquity was not necessarily "trade." Indeed, it now seems generally accepted that "the transport of goods by order of or under the control of the state, 'redistribution,' or 'administered trade,' was of singular importance under the Roman empire."[44] Archaeologists as well as sociologists and anthropologists are now asking more precisely how economic relations should be understood in particular cases: "Interpretation of exchange systems requires consideration of what the likely mechanism may have been: whether reciprocal exchange, redistribution, or market exchange."[45]

Several generally familiar events and/or literary references from biblical or Judean history indicate that political-economic relations in Palestine were part of what has been called "redistributive" or "tributary." Judea was headed by a temple-state, under imperial sponsorship, in which the priestly aristocracy was supported by tithes and offerings from the people, who "were obligated to bring the first-fruits of every tree, year by year, to the house of the Lord...and to bring the Levites the tithes from our ground...in all our rural towns,...and [to bring to] the priest, the son of Aaron, the contributions of grain, wine and oil" (Neh. 10:35–39). One of the functions of the high priesthood, then, was to collect the tribute for its imperial sponsor, successively the Persian, Ptolemaic, and Seleucid regimes. The collection and payment of the tribute was at the center of the late third-century power-struggle between the Oniad high-priestly family and the Tobiads, based in the trans-Jordan, and their imperial patrons, the Seleucids and the Ptolemies, respectively (*Ant.* 12.157–236). The Ptolemies' intensive exploitation of the land and people in Palestine, as in Egypt itself, was not "commercial" but a program administered by the Ptolemaic state and its agents. The Hasmonean regime's extension of its control over most of Palestine under John Hyrcanus, Aristobulus, and Alexander Janneus merely extended Hasmonean

taxation and (probably) the system of tithes and offerings to priesthood and Temple to the villages and towns of Idumea, Galilee, and
other annexed districts.

When the Romans took control of Palestine they simply
adopted the tributary system already in place. They confirmed
the Hasmonean family in their (religiously legitimated) political-
economic power and privileges, as can be seen in the decrees of
Julius Caesar cited by Josephus (*Ant.* 14.194–209):

> Hyrcanus, son of Alexander, and his children shall be Eth-
> narchs of the Judaeans and shall hold the office of High
> Priest of the Judaeans for all time in accordance with
> their ancestral customs [*ta patria ethe*] ... and whatever high-
> priestly rights and [economic] privileges exist in accordance
> with their laws [*tous idious nomous*], these he and his children
> shall possess.... His children shall rule over the Judean na-
> tion and enjoy the fruits of the places given them.... [The
> Judaeans] shall pay tithes to Hyrcanus and his sons, just as
> they paid to their forefathers.

The people, of course, were also "to pay the tribute" to Rome as
well, "one-fourth of the produce" every second year. The same
tributary political-economic system was perpetuated, only in a
more complicated way, when the Roman Senate installed Herod
as their client-king over Judea and the rest of Palestine. The Romans were thus providing an "income" for their client-kings as
well as "indirect rule" over territories along their eastern frontier.[46]
The revenues from Herod's realm must have been around 900 talents yearly, since his sons Antipas and Archelaus received revenues
of 200 and 400 (or even 600) talents, respectively, from the territories of Galilee, plus Perea and Judea, plus Samaria and Idumea
(*Ant.* 18.317–20; *B.J.* 2.94–98). Herod, however, left the Temple and high priesthood intact, still requiring economic support
from tithes and offerings despite its reduced political function.
This meant that the Galileans had gone from one to three layers of rulers in the sixty years from the Hasmonean takeover to
the imposition of Herod, with three layers of payments due, taxes
to Herod and tribute to Rome as well as the tithes and offerings
to Temple and priesthood.

It is likely that the advent of Roman rule over Palestine and the stabilization of the *pax Romana* once Augustus established the empire meant increased commerce, as political-economic affairs previously dominated by the temple-state were somewhat more integrated into the wider Mediterranean economic system. Yet the increase in trade should not be overestimated, for several interrelated reasons.

First, as Josephus indicates, as an almost exclusively agricultural area, greater Judea (including Galilee, and so on) came into the Roman empire virtually undeveloped commercially. What differentiated Judean Palestine from Tyre, Sidon, and the other Phoenician cities along the coast, as well as from the Greeks and Romans, was the lack of historical trading made possible by inexpensive transport around the Mediterranean.

> Ours is not a maritime country; neither commerce nor the intercourse which it promotes with the other peoples has any attraction for us. Our cities are built inland, remote from the Sea; and we devote ourselves to the cultivation of the productive country with which we are blessed. (*Ap.* 1.60)

Second, while the mode by which the cities obtained resources from the agricultural producers was different, the cities of Palestine, like Hellenistic-Roman cities, lived from the production of the countryside. As Finley and others have emphasized recently, with a nod to Weber's earlier insight, "the consumer city" of Hellenistic-Roman antiquity "was primarily a center of consumption, in contrast with the medieval city, which was primarily a center of production."[47] The cities of Western antiquity did not pay for their maintenance with their own products. The urban economy derived its support "on the basis of a legal claim such as taxes or rents without having to deliver return values."[48] The city was both the base of the major landowners, who were also the wealthiest residents, and the center and focus of their expenditures, "which were funded in large part by their rural investments" (in land).[49]

The only difference between Hasmonean-Herodian Jerusalem and its administrative outpost Sepphoris and the usual Hellenistic-Roman cities was that the former depended upon religious dues along with taxes while the latter's "consumption" of goods from the countryside came in the form of rents along with taxes. Correspondingly, the wealthy and powerful in Jerusalem and Sepphoris were Hasmonean or Herodian officers more than landowners in their own right. Of course, given the heavy economic burdens on the Palestinian peasantry, those Herodian officers may well have moved into control of both lands and labor as creditors of indebted peasants.[50]

Third, recent studies of the Roman empire suggest that political-economic relations in the Roman empire were less commercial and more politically managed than previously portrayed. Again, recent studies of political-economic relations in the Roman empire suggest "a more significant role for taxes and requisitions in kind in army supply, lower spending capacity among soldiers, who received little of their pay as cash, lower political horizons among local aristocrats (and therefore less adjustment of their economic behaviour), and in general less penetrating monetarization of local economies."[51] All of the above means, for Galilee and for the Roman empire in general, less trade, local and regional, greater importance of taxation by rulers, and gradually increasing indebtedness to the powerful and wealthy (often officers of the client regime).

Archaeological evidence combined with certain other literary references indicate various aspects of how the tributary political-economic system worked in Galilee. Adequate assessment of literary references as well as archaeological data, however, require a more consistent regional and systematic approach than is common in reports on individual sites.

That Sepphoris was the site of a fortress is usually recognized only in passing, perhaps because the fortress still standing atop the acropolis stems only from medieval times. Josephus's accounts indicate, however, that the most significant installation in the city at the time of Herod was the royal fortress-palace and armory and that Antipas (re)"fortified" Sepphoris as "the ornament of all Galilee" (*B.J.* 2.56; *Ant.* 17.271; 18.28). The fortress at Sepphoris, moreover, was apparently the central administrative installation in a series of fortresses in Galilee. In what appears to be a projection into the time of Joshua of Hasmonean and/or Herodian installations, the Mishnah (*Arachin* 9:6) mentions the "old" castra at Sepphoris in connection with fortresses in Yodfat (Jotapata) and Gush Halav (Gischala). Josephus's reports of his own construction of fortresses in Galilee has long since evoked scholarly suspicion. Thus when he also reports that John of Gischala built up the walls of his native place and that Titus directed his troops to pull down some of the walls at Gischala (*B.J.* 4.117), he is probably referring to the remains of the Hasmonean-Herodian fortifica-.tions at the time of the great revolt. The current excavation at Jotapata has indeed found the remains of a well-fortified town.[52] The Hasmonean regime and/or the Herodian regime must have constructed fortresses (or taken over Hellenistic installations) as the bases from which they administered and taxed the Galilean villages. Recent studies in Hasmonean and Herodian military affairs provide further evidence and historical context for the way in which the Judean temple-state and Herodian regime ruled and taxed its territories through precisely such installations.[53]

The coins found in excavations of Upper Galilean villages should be reassessed precisely in connection with evidence for Hasmonean-Herodian fortresses at sites such as Yodfat or Gush Halav. While more coins were found from the Late Roman period than from all other periods put together, the quantity of Hasmonean coins, especially those of Alexander Janneus, is striking (nearly 200, compared with 34 Tyrian coins from the third century C.E.).[54] The large number of Jannean coins, as well as the 122 coins from Tyre that predate the Hasmonean takeover of Galilee, can be more readily interpreted as evidence for tributary relations than for trade relations. The regional officials and the army of a regime staking out its claim to an area would be obvious carriers of coins. As the ability of the Seleucid regime to control Palestine and western Syria declined, cities such as Tyre stepped into the power vacuum and new regimes such as the Hasmoneans steadily expanded the territories they controlled. The latter took over Galilee from the Itureans just as Janneus came to power, and it would not be surprising if Tyre had expanded its influence into Upper Galilee in the mid-second century B.C.E., before the Itureans took over the area. The seizure and garrisoning of three fortresses in Galilee by Marion, the "tyrant" of Tyre in 42 B.C.E., amid another vacuum of imperial power in the area was surely not unprecedented by a Tyrian regime (*Ant.* 14.297–98). The Hasmonean coins and those of pre-Hasmonean Tyre both must have come into Upper Galilee via the respective Hasmonean and Tyrian officers and army who were sent to "administer" the area, that is, to tax as well as control the villages there.[55]

The most obvious and major evidence that political-economic relations were structured in a basically tributary system is the reconstruction of the city of Sepphoris and the foundation of Tiberias as a new city by Antipas, all within about two decades. Such major building activities and the lavish courtly life of a Roman client-"king" would not have been possible without the substantial annual tax revenues that Antipas received from the villagers of Galilee and Perea. Thus every archaeological discovery of building activity in those cities is further evidence for the tributary political-economy of early Roman Galilee (precisely at the time of Jesus).

Evidence for the tributary or "redistributive" political-economic relations between Rome and the villagers of Galilee, finally, comes from Josephus's accounts. In fact, precisely in the same literary context as the incident used by archaeologists as support for their claim of direct trade between Galilean "businessmen" and Tyre, Josephus mentions "the imperial grain stored in the villages of Upper Galilee [*ton kaisaros siton keimenon en tais tes anothen Galilaias komais*]" which John of Gischala wanted to seize but which Josephus himself intended to reserve for the Romans' or his own use (*Vita* 71–73). These are paralleled by Josephus's account of the grain stores in the village of Besara, in the Great Plain just south of Galilee, an area whose produce the Romans had apparently bestowed on another Herodian ruler, Queen Berenice, sister of Agrippa II.

All of these literary references and archaeological findings provide clear evidence that the centuries- (if not millennia-) old political-economic system of the ancient Near East was still in place in Upper Galilee as elsewhere. Regional and/or imperial rulers claimed a certain percentage of the villagers' crops as taxes or tribute. Depending on the regional circumstances, the crops taken as taxes or tribute were then used by the rulers at different levels for their purposes. The Hasmoneans, Herod, or Antipas would have used their revenues to provide sustenance for the artisans and others who served their needs in the capital cities, such as Jerusalem, Sepphoris, and Tiberias, as well as to support their regime's officers and military garrisons. The Romans may have used their revenues from Upper Galilee, in particular, to help support the needs of a regional city (such as Tyre) which constituted a key component in the imperial system.

The gradual phasing out of client-rulers did not mean an end to the tributary system in Galilee. After the deposition of Antipas in 39 and the death of Agrippa I in 44, Galilee came under direct Roman administration, with only the "toparchies" of Tarichaeae and Tiberias rendering their taxes to Agrippa II after 54 (*Ant.* 20.159) until nearly the end of the first century. Yet early rabbinic texts indicate that the same basic political-economic system continued in the second century, with the city administrations of Sepphoris and Tiberias now collecting the taxes instead of the Herodian officers stationed in the cities.[56]

With this tributary political-economic system in mind, we can take another look at the political-economic relations between the Galilean cities and villages and between Tyre and Galilee.

City-Village Political Economic Relations in Galilee

The recent archaeological investigations of pottery distribution and the way in which pottery moved from producers to users, as summarized above, confirm the impressions we have of Galilean political-economic relations in general from our principal literary sources for ancient Galilee (the rabbis, the Gospels, and Josephus) and comparative studies of traditional agrarian societies — in two important respects.

1. Trade was not a major factor in the economy. Other than the fine wares brought in from outside by the elite of the cities and large villages, trade was primarily local. Moreover, it was confined to a few specialized items such as pottery which could not be produced except where the necessary materials or technology was available. The economy was overwhelmingly agricultural. The basic units of production were also the basic units of consumption, that is, households, which produced most of what they consumed and consumed much of what they produced. Household production included the processing of crops (e.g., the pressing of oil from olives, wine from grapes, the threshing and grinding of grain) and the principal craft needs of the household (e.g., clothing). As noted above, rabbinic references suggest that specialized products such as

pottery were apparently delivered directly by the producers to the buyers. Villagers, therefore, had limited need to either "market" their produce or to buy products in city "market places."

2. Trade, however, is not the only way that the produce of the countryside could end up being consumed in the cities. Some inhabitants of Sepphoris and Tiberias may well have worked the fields near those cities. Many of the inhabitants of the Galilean cities, however, certainly those who were engaged either in administration (such as tax collection) or crafts that served the wealthy and powerful families, did not produce their own necessities. The goods necessary for their sustenance derived (whether directly or indirectly, through rulers or patrons) from households in the towns and villages through the mechanism of taxes, tribute, and tithes. In Hellenistic and Roman cities elsewhere, the principal mechanism of transfer of the "surplus" product of the countryside was apparently rent and interest on debts. Those forms probably became increasingly important in Middle and Late Roman Galilee. In late second-temple times, however, under the temple-state and the Herodian client-rulers, the predominant modes of economic "redistribution" were temple and priestly dues, royal taxation, and tribute, as organized by the well-developed political system of the temple-state and Herodian and imperial administrations.[57] As indicated by Josephus's references to the imperial grain stores or the stored grain belonging to Queen Berenice, tribute and taxation were "in kind," that is, in the form of the produce itself rather than money. Rabbinic references (e.g., *t. Dem.* 6.3; *p. Ma's S.* 4,54d) attest the continued collection of taxes in kind into late antiquity.[58] Again, this parallels the situation elsewhere in the Roman empire, where apparently most taxes were levied in kind — and thus stood outside any "market" relationships.[59] Insofar as tithes and offerings were brought to the Temple in Jerusalem, at a considerable distance from Galilee, dutiful Galileans would have sold some of their produce for money to take to Jerusalem, where the moneychangers would facilitate the acquisition of the appropriate offering. For the "redistribution" of Antipas's and the Agrippas' tax revenues taken in kind from the Galilean villages we must imagine some connection with the "markets" of the administrative cities, Sepphoris and Tiberias. That is, some or much of what passed through the *agora* (city-square or "market-place") in Sepphoris or

Tiberias, as supervised by the *agoranomos* (supply officer or market supervisor) of the respective cities, must have been taxes paid in kind by the household producers in the villages of Galilee.

Again, the recent studies of the distribution of pottery in Galilee provide confirmation of this picture of a politically managed economy. It is surely of significance that the sudden increase in the incidence of pottery from Kefar Hanania coincides with the rise to prominence of Sepphoris and the founding of Tiberias. Not only would increased demand for cooking ware have stimulated an increasing specialization of production of pottery at Kefar Hanania,[60] but the Herodian administration in those cities would have been concerned to assure an adequate supply of such an essential item. It is also pertinent in understanding a redistributive economic system to recognize that a portion of the agricultural products of villagers in Galilee provided, directly or indirectly, the "income" or resources with which the Sepphorites or Tiberians were able to buy pottery from Kefar Hanania.

Political Economic Relations Between Galilee and Tyre

While it is highly doubtful that the port of Tyre was "bustling with merchants, traders, and peasants" from other sections of Palestine such as Upper Galilee,[61] it is likely that products from Upper Galilee were consumed in Tyre. As recent studies of economics in the Roman empire have pointed out, economic relations were mediated by political structures. In the case of political-economic relations between Galilee and Tyre, the portrayal of Tyre in the Book of Ezekiel (27:3–25) from an earlier time may be instructive.[62] Tyre traded mainly in metals, military goods, and luxury goods, all of the sort desired by rulers. Moreover, since Tyre itself would not have used all these goods, the famous seafaring Tyrian merchants must have been "middle men" supplying rulers of various kingdoms and empires. As both Strabo (*Geography* 16.2.23) and Pliny the Elder (*Nat Hist* 5.17.76) make clear, at least in early Roman times, Tyre was known for the highly distinctive luxury products of shellfish and purple dye, which were unlikely to have been in high demand among Galilean villagers.

As at the time of Ezekiel, so also in Hellenistic and Roman times, the principal products of Judea, Samaria, and Galilee available in trade for the military and luxury products carried by Tyrian merchants were agricultural (wheat, olives, figs, honey, oil, balm). The principal "surplus product" of the Galilean or Judean peasantry, however, was under the control of the Herodian or high-priestly rulers and/or the Roman government in the form of taxes, tithes and offerings, and tribute. Trade between Judea or Galilee and Tyre was thus under the control of the very rulers who expropriated the agricultural products of the peasantry and who desired the luxury goods Tyre had to offer — as mediated perhaps by traders working for the Judean or Roman rulers. Tyre, of course, with its shortage of land from which to draw agricultural produce, was dependent particularly on imports from nearby agricultural areas with a "surplus," such as Galilee. The Book of Acts provides an illuminating window onto these trading relations. It was precisely "because their country depended on the king's country for food" that the leaders of Tyre and Sidon sought reconciliation with an angry King Agrippa I, who controlled the Galilean agricultural surplus (Acts 12:20).

Additional transfer of agricultural products from the districts of Galilee most accessible to Tyre, for example, Upper Galilee, would likely have been arranged by the Roman authorities. The latter, like the Seleucid officials before them, were concerned to maintain sufficient food supplies to Tyre, which was commercially important to the overall economy of the empire. We can reasonably surmise that this, along with provisions for the army,[63] would have been one principal function of the "imperial stores of grain in the villages of Upper Galilee" mentioned by Josephus (*Vita* 71–72). The reason why the donkey caravans mentioned in rabbinic literature "did not use or need the services of middlemen" and "did not sell produce to small-scale retailers"[64] was likely because such caravans were transporting grain or other produce under contract from imperial or city officials. Rabbinic traditions that wheat was bought at a government storehouse in Yavneh (*t. Dem.* 1.13) suggest that the imperial and/or city officials at major cities such as Tyre similarly supervised the provision of an adequate supply of grain and other produce.[65]

Two images in particular may help us keep in mind how the political economy of Roman Galilee worked: Roman roads and Roman aqueducts. Archaeologists make much of the system of roads in Galilee, particularly the paved and demarcated Roman roads begun under Hadrian that connected the major urban centers of Galilee with cities on the coast and those in the Great Plain to the south. This system of roads is then (synchronically) transformed into "a highly developed local trade network upon which the citizens of Galilee transported goods and services from village to village, to town, and to cities, and vice-versa."[66] The second-century Roman roads at the center of this system, however, were built by the Romans as a means of political-economic control of the countryside and a way of deploying troops quickly to the frontiers of the empire. The roads bisected, ordered, and controlled, politically as well as visually.

Also symbolic of the economic relationship between the cities and the villages under their "administration" is the aqueduct built to bring a steady flow of water from the countryside to Sepphoris. If we may borrow from a consultation of classical historians and archaeologists: the aqueduct symbolizes the Roman city

> siphoning off . . . the resources of the land into the urban centre, to feed the public baths where the imported water acts as a focus of sociability and as a symbol of the "washed" and civilised way of life that rejects the stench of the countryman. Implicit in the aqueduct is a dynamic of power, flowing between country and town.[67]

Perhaps, as an afterthought, we might also think about the source of the labor used in the construction of the aqueduct that brought the flow of water from the Galilean countryside to Sepphoris.

To understand either Jesus and his movement in the first century or the rabbinic circles in the third and fourth centuries, we would have to situate them appropriately within the dynamics of the political-economic structure in which the Galilean people were required to provide economic support for the cities charged with administering the Galilean *chora*.

Chapter 4

VILLAGES OF UPPER GALILEE

The mountains are forced to be self-sufficient for the essentials of life, to produce everything as best they can, to cultivate vines, wheat, and olives even if the soil and the climate are unsuitable. . . .

There can be no doubt that the lowland, urban civilization penetrated to the highland world very imperfectly and at a very slow rate.

— FERNAND BRAUDEL

Galilee, like Judea and other inland areas of the eastern Roman empire, was a traditional agrarian society.[1] "We devote ourselves to the cultivation of the productive country with which we are blessed," wrote the Jerusalem priest-historian Josephus, who had attempted to control the area during the great revolt of 66–67 (*c. Ap.* 60). Josephus even draws a connection between the rural, agricultural character of Galilee and the people's passion for independence of outside rulers.

> The two Galilees have always resisted any hostile invasion. . . . The land is everywhere so rich in soil and pasturage and produces such variety of trees, that even the most indolent are tempted by these facilities to devote themselves to agriculture. In fact, every inch of the soil has been cultivated by the inhabitants. . . . The towns are thickly distributed, and even the villages, thanks to the fertility of the soil, are all so densely populated that even the smallest of them contains above fifteen thousand inhabitants. In short, Galilee . . . is entirely under cultivation and produces crops from one end to the other. (*B.J.* 3.41–44)

That description involves blatant exaggeration in its glorification of the country and population that the self-styled general had purportedly prepared to defend against the Roman reconquest. Yet when he writes at another point that "there are two hundred and four cities and villages in Galilee" (*Vita* 235), his numbers may not be inflated at all. Since only two settlements would really have qualified as cities, with another few having been towns, that leaves 200 or so villages. Recent surface surveys of the area have identified about the same number of settlements from the late second-temple period.[2]

The vast majority of Galileans were thus members of a village community. Villages consisted of a smaller or larger number of families or households. As the most fundamental social form in a traditional agrarian society, the household was the basic unit of production and consumption. According to the Israelite ideal (similar to that of other peasantries), each family worked and lived from the produce of its ancestral inheritance of land. Each household produced most of what it consumed and consumed much of what it produced.[3] As indicated by both rabbinic texts and archaeological excavations, within the village settlement each family lived in a "house" of a small room or two (3 x 4 m) opening off of a courtyard shared with one or more other families. In the courtyard they shared use of oven, millstone, and cistern. In the village they shared use of a common wine-press and olive-press. Galilean villages, called variously *kefar* or *'ir* in early rabbinic literature, ranged in size from tiny settlements of a few dozen families to towns of a few thousand. The majority of settlements, occupying from two to five acres with roughly 40 to 60 people per acre would have included fewer than 300 people each.[4]

The building and expansion of the cities of Tiberias and Sepphoris did not mean that Galilean villages disappeared — except perhaps for those that were disrupted in the founding of Tiberias. An "agrarian" or "peasant" society in Hellenistic-Roman times included by definition rulers and their supporting scribal retainers, military forces, and artisans resident in cities who lived from part of the produce of the villages. Since they formed the economic base of the cities, village communities remained and presumably expanded in population and production as the expanding cities demanded more in taxes, rents, and interest on debts. From a historical perspective, the most distinctive feature of life for the Galilean people during Roman times was the social-economic impact of the founding and development of Tiberias and Sepphoris. As indicated in the historical survey in chapter 1, decisions made by outside rulers often determined dramatic changes and/or slower but steady pressures in Galilean village life. In exploring the life of ancient Galilean villagers, particularly for late second-temple times (including the time of Jesus) it will be important to keep in mind the frequent changes in political arrangements imposed on Galilee by the Romans.

Until recently, the only evidence for Galilean village life was what was gleaned from the Christian Gospels and rabbinic rulings. Except perhaps for traditions in the Gospels, nearly all of our sources for antiquity come from the literate elite living in cities and expressing urban interests. In the last few decades much more information on peasant village life is becoming available from new archaeological explorations and from social historical analysis of literary sources.[5]

The Hypothesis of Galilean Regionalism

Josephus divided Galilee into two regions, Upper and Lower Galilee (*B.J.* 3.38–40). Rabbinic traditions made a three-way distinction, further dividing Lower Galilee into the western region and the region around the lake.

> In what concerns the law of removal, [Galilee is divided into] upper Galilee, lower Galilee and the valley; from Kefar Hanania upwards, wheresoever sycamores do not grow, is upper Galilee; from Kefar Hanania downwards, wheresoever sycamores grow, is lower Galilee; the region of Tiberias is the valley. (*m. Sev.* 9:2)

The distinguishing characteristics are clearly topographical. The point of the rabbinic distinction is the resulting differences in growing season and time of harvest. Upper Galilee was far more rugged, with mountains near 3000 feet and east-west ridges intersected by other faults. The complex series of ridges, mountains, and basins made communication difficult within the area and even more from outside, especially directly from the south. The villages of Upper Galilee were thus more isolated from the outside world. Western Lower Galilee consists of several basins separated by ridges running west to east which give way to series of plateaus oriented northwest-southeast rising to the escarpment overlooking the great basin around the lake. Within those western basins and plateaus communication was easy, although the ridges between them inhibited interaction. Main routes connected the cities but not many of the villages, which were situated on the ridges or along edges of the basins.[6] The huge basin around the lake, which is below sea level, differs dramatically in climate from the west and Upper Galilee. The terrain varies from open plains to abruptly rising banks around the western shore of the lake.

The archaeologists heading the pioneering excavations of Upper Galilean villages in the 1970s formulated the hypothesis that Upper Galilee had a distinctively different culture from that of Lower Galilee. The rugged topography "had profound influences on the material culture of the north in general if not upon the entire socio-economic and social-religious picture."[7] Inscriptions indicate bilingual Greek and Aramaic-Hebrew in Lower Galilee, whereas Aramaic-Hebrew dominates in Upper Galilee. A number of ceramic types are found only in Upper Galilee and the Golan, and the architecture in Upper Galilee suggests a "regional conservatism in art."[8] Upper Galilee similarly exhibits a conservative religious orientation that must have been traditional in the area. Simply stated, its topographic isolation led to its cultural isolation.

By contrast, the "great urban centers linked to the more pagan and hence Greek-speaking west, with its more cosmopolitan atmosphere," the "very administrative centers of the Roman provincial government," provided dominant cultural influences that villages such as those associated with Jesus (Nazareth, Nain, Cana, Capernaum) could not have escaped.[9] As noted in the introduction, recent studies of the historical Jesus have taken this picture of Hellenistic-Roman cosmopolitan influence on the villages of Lower Galilee as a basis for constructing a Jesus more familiar with Hellenistic culture than previously thought.[10]

There is a serious discrepancy in the presentation of the "Galilean regionalism" hypothesis, however, even as it integrates literary and archaeological materials. The archaeological evidence on the basis of which Upper Galilee is judged to be solidly "Jewish," even "conservative," is almost all "Middle and Late Roman," largely third and fourth century c.e., and from villages.[11] On the other hand, the evidence on which Lower Galilee is judged to · be more cosmopolitan and Roman-Hellenized in culture is either introduced in connection with the city of Sepphoris in the first century or is heavily weighted toward materials from cities or large towns such as Hammat-Tiberias, Magdala-Tarichaeae, and Beth Shearim.[12] The comparison is thus between Upper Galilean villages and Lower Galilean cities, and between upland villages in late antiquity and lowland cities and towns more at the earlier period of the initial impact of the cosmopolitan Roman-Hellenistic culture.

Indeed, upon closer analysis, the material culture of Upper Galilean villages and that of Lower Galilean villages may not be all that different. The inclusion of inscriptions from Beth Shearim, which became the burial place of choice for wealthy diaspora Jews, skewed the comparison between Upper and Lower Galilee. And the remainder of the sample of inscriptions from Lower Galilee were clustered in sites around the lake. The difference between the largely Aramaic-Hebrew inscriptions in the remainder of the Lower Galilean villages and the almost complete lack of Greek inscriptions in Upper Galilean villages is not particularly striking.[13] A significant proportion of the cooking wares in both Lower Galilee and Upper Galilee was produced at the village of Kefar Hanania, on the border between the two regions. The art characterized as "conservative" in Upper Galilee varies little from the art found in Lower Galilee in most of the motifs attested, the only significant variation being with regard to menorahs (55/30% Upper/Lower), animal representations (30/80%), and human representations (12/40%).[14] Different architectural types of synagogue buildings, finally, vary not by region but across and within regions, the broadhouse at Khirbet Shema' situated only a kilometer from the basilica at Meiron.[15]

The basic difference between Upper and Lower Galilee was political as well as topographical.[16] The political difference developed in stages during the first and second centuries. The Hasmoneans and Herod apparently administered Galilee from the fortress town of Sepphoris (and additional smaller fortresses). As noted in chapter 2, Herod Antipas not only rebuilt Sepphoris as "the ornament of all Galilee," but founded Tiberias as a second city in Galilee on the lake. Not until the second century was all of Lower Galilee placed under the jurisdiction of one or another of those cities, as part of the general Roman program of "urbanizing" the administration of Palestine and other areas of the empire. Those cities, moreover, as noted in chapter 2, did not change status from royal (or imperial) administrative centers to independent cities until the turn of the second century. Clearly the Roman imperial administration saw the adoption of Hellenistic-Roman urban culture as desirable. But that was not a prerequisite for "urbanization" of administration.[17] Indeed, the imperial administration seems to have been using "urbanization" as a means of "civilizing" the subject peoples of the East.

The hypothesis that the topographical difference entails a cultural difference between Upper and Lower Galilee requires reexamination and reformulation on a more solid basis in two important respects. The fundamental difference between the regions of Galilee was determined not simply by topography, but by the political structure, which was determined from outside Galilee and changed dramatically during the period we are considering. The more basic differences of culture, moreover, were probably between the cities and the villages, not between Upper Galilean villages and Lower Galilean villages.

Entangled with much of the discussion of the regional differences in Galilee has been the assumption of a massive migration of Judeans to Galilee after the Roman destruction of Jerusalem in 70 C.E. and/or after the Bar Kokhba Revolt in 132–135. Since the general relocations of large numbers of Judeans in Galilee is an important operating assumption for archaeological excavations in the last few decades and is used as an explanatory factor for a number of issues,[18] it merits some critical examination.[19] Rabbinic references to resettlement in (mostly Lower) Galilee usually pertain only to the rabbis themselves, a few hundred people at most. The theory of a mass migration of Judeans to Galilee thus places a great deal of credibility in later Jewish traditions about the locations of the priestly courses in late antiquity.[20] The priestly *mishmarot* and their places of residence were popular themes in the medieval liturgical poems called *piyyutim*.[21] Rabbinic references to the priestly courses and their locations are generally late. As noted in chapter 2, the priests in Sepphoris previously thought to be active in the Temple prior to 70 cannot be located in Sepphoris until the second or third century.[22] The minimal archaeological evidence for migration of the Judean priestly courses to Galilee consists only of an inscription from Caesarea dated to the end of the third or early fourth century with a list of priestly courses and their towns.[23] Assuming that such a relocation of the priestly courses did take place, then it must not have taken place until after the Bar Kokhba Revolt. Moreover, since priestly courses relocated in Lower Galilean cities and villages as well as in Upper Galilean villages, then their presence cannot be used as a factor in the supposedly distinctively "conservative Jewish" culture of Upper Galilee.

The question of a migration of Judeans to Galilee after the Bar Kokhba Revolt raises a prior historical question of crucial importance for understanding the social dynamics of Galilee: the background of the Galilean people. Continuing use of the term "Jews" (even if a synonym for "Israelite") with reference to the inhabitants of Galilee, particularly in late second-temple times, simply blocks recognition of the historical regional differences and diversity. Outsiders such as Roman rulers and Hellenistic historians referred to nearly all of those subject to Herod and the Jerusalem temple-state as *ioudaioi*, "Judeans." Yet, as explained in chapter 1, despite the lack of direct evidence, it seems highly likely that most of the inhabitants of Galilee in late second-temple times were descendants of the northernmost Israelite tribes, and not "Gentiles/pagans" or Judeans.[24]

For a hundred years after the Hasmonean high-priestly regime took control of the area, Galilee was ruled from Jerusalem. That the Hasmoneans required the inhabitants of Galilee to live according to the "laws of the Judeans" (according to Josephus) suggests further that they incorporated the Galileans under the Jerusalem temple-state, which was ruled according to the "laws of the Judeans."

That does not mean, however, that the Galileans would have been quickly integrated into the Judean temple community,[25] much less that Galileans suddenly began to conduct local village affairs according to the "laws of the Judeans." In most traditional agrarian societies or "aristocratic empires," peasant villages are semiautonomous communities. As descendants of Israelites, Galilean villagers would have shared many traditions with the Jerusalem temple-state, as well as with Judean villagers. During their eight centuries of divergent historical experience, distinctive Judean-Jerusalem institutions such as the temple-state and the Torah had been developed after the return from exile by the Judean ruling aristocracy in the late sixth century B.C.E. Meanwhile Israelite traditions such as the Mosaic covenant would have undergone separate development in the Galilean villages. In Galilee, local village affairs would have been conducted according to what anthropologists call the "little tradition" or popular customs, while the Jerusalem temple-state was legitimated by and ruled by the "great tradition" or official laws of the state.[26]

Following the death of Herod, Galilee was ruled first by Antipas and then by a series of Roman officials and later Herodian client-kings. We simply do not know much about how representatives of the Jerusalem high-priestly regime may have attempted to continue influencing life in Galilee during the last seventy years of the Second Temple. The rabbis did not relocate to Galilee until after the Bar Kokhba Revolt, and most of them quickly established themselves in the cities. Thus it is difficult to know just what the presence of Judeans and Judean influence may have been in Galilean villages of any region in the first and second centuries.[27]

Upper Galilean Villages Under the Hasmoneans and Herodians

In the 1970s a team of innovative young American archaeologists launched a project of considerable importance for subsequent understanding of Galilee. Instead of concentrating, as usual, on the monumental remains of a Jerusalem or Caesarea, they conducted several excavations in some remote villages of Upper Galilee: Gush Halav, Meiron, Khirbet Shema', and Nabratein. Finally some archaeologists were focusing not on another city where the political and cultural elite lived in relative luxury, but on some of the hundreds of sites where the vast majority of people lived in a traditional agrarian society such as Galilee.

The villages of Upper Galilee also appear in literary sources, both in Josephus and the rabbis. According to Josephus, the most energetic and sustained rebellion and resistance during the great revolt in Galilee in 66–67 came from these villages. Rabbinic legends associate certain sages with Meiron and Khirbet Shemaʿ. Josephus, of course, must be read with a critical eye on the chaotic Galilee he attempted to control in 66–67. Rabbinic sources, similarly, must be read critically for the dating and functions or particular traditions. Just as archaeologists have begun a regional approach to the material remains they excavate, so we should take a "regional" approach to literary sources. The information on social relationships that Josephus ties to one village may well be pertinent to other villages as well. Although the evidence is unevenly spaced across sites and centuries, the combination of literary evidence for the first century and archaeological evidence for the second to the fourth centuries enables us to sketch a more complete profile of the social world of Upper Galilee than we are yet able to do elsewhere in Galilee.

Our first step must be a critically reflective formulation of a strategy for "reading" the archaeological and literary evidence in the appropriate contexts and connections. Neither text-fragments nor material artifacts can be adequately assessed if torn from critically established context. As explained in the introduction, most important is a critical awareness of the several interrelated levels of societal relations that determined the patterns of village life, from household to village community to the political-economic-religious structure of the whole region. Such critical reflection on strategy and operative models leads to revisions and shifts in the previous concepts and generalizations regarding the social world of Galilean villages which were rooted in a theologically or religiously determined paradigm that may now seem inappropriate.

The villages in which limited excavations were conducted in the 1970s and 1980s are located in the center of Upper Galilee just to the northeast of the long ridge of Mount Meiron (ca. 750 m). In antiquity they would have been close to the frontier of the area controlled by the Hellenistic city of Tyre. More extensive excavations were carried out at Meiron, and the results and interpretation well published. The excavators also reported and interpreted their more limited explorations at Khirbet Shemaʿ, Gush Halav, and Nabratein. Because of the more abundant archaeological materials available on Meiron and the literary references to Gush Halav (Gischala) by Josephus, the discussion below focuses more on those two villages.

With regard to claims of the importance of Meiron or Gush Halav in antiquity, it would be well to maintain a broader regional and comparative perspective when evaluating the villages of Upper Galilee. Recent investigations into the ancient Roman road system constructed mainly from the second century on indicate that the main military and trade route across Palestine went through the Great Plain. Herod's construction of Caesarea on the Sea, which became the western terminus of the main east-west road, decreased the importance of Acco-Ptolemais immediately to the west of Galilee. The principal route across Galilee itself lay between Sepphoris and Tiberias, with the principal north-south route being from Scythopolis (Beth Shean) through Tiberias to Caesarea Philippi — that is, roads connecting the principal cities. By comparison, the minor routes through Meiron or Gush Halav and links with other villages were unimportant either for Roman administration or for interregional trade.[28] They were apparently routes primarily for local intervillage communication.[29]

Gush Halav must have been a well-established settlement for centuries before the Hasmonean high priests took over Galilee at the very end of the second century B.C.E. "Significant quantities of Chalcolithic, Early Bronze and Middle Bronze pottery,... significant quantities of Iron II material,... several nearly complete bowls [from the Persian period]," and Hellenistic and Hasmonean coins and ceramics were found there.[30] We may surmise that, if there had been continuous settlement from the eighth century through Persian times into the Hellenistic period, the villagers were descendants of the ancient Israelites. That the material remains at Meiron begin in late Hellenistic times may indicate that the village was begun or expanded at about the time the Hasmoneans secured the area. There must have been some turmoil in the region as the Seleucid empire weakened and the Itureans dominated temporarily before being pushed out by the Hasmoneans.

Three kinds of evidence indicate that the Hasmoneans and/or Herod the Great must have maintained a fortress and garrison at Gush Halav, which was probably one of the northernmost villages they controlled. In a projection from rabbinic times back into the time of Joshua, *m. Arachin* 9:6 refers to the "old" fortresses as Gush Halav as well as at Yodfat and Sepphoris, that is, the Hasmonean and Herodian structures that were three centuries "old" by the end of the second century c.e. The large number of Hasmonean coins found at Gush Halav and nearby villages, particularly those minted by Alexander Janneus, who took over the high priesthood just as Galilee came under Hasmonean control, also points to a military presence in the area. As explained in the previous chapter, the high incidence of coins minted at Tyre probably does not indicate trade. Similarly, the Hasmonean coins should not suggest trade but a military presence to defend against rival powers with designs on the area, such as Tyre, garrisons that were most likely supported by the tax revenues they collected from the Upper Galilean villages. The third indication of a Hasmonean and Herodian fortress and garrison at Gush Halav comes from Josephus's reports. He recounts that when Herod took over his kingdom he had to reconquer some of the fortresses of Galilee from Marion, the ruler of Tyre, who had taken them during the chaotic period of Roman civil war and struggles between rival Hasmonean rulers. Most likely those fortresses were at sites along the frontier with Tyre, such as Gush Halav. Apparently some of the fortifications at Gush Halav remained through the time of the great revolt. We must be skeptical of Josephus's claim to have fortified Gush Halav and other sites. It is far more credible that the local strong man, John of Gischala, Josephus's rival for control elsewhere in Galilee, rebuilt the walls of the town. Josephus also reports that the Roman general Titus directed his troops to pull down some of the walls after the village surrendered in 67 (*B.J.* 4.117).[31]

This evidence for a Hasmonean military fortress at Gush Halav points to the concrete realities of the relations between the villagers of Galilee and the Hasmonean regime. The literary and numismatic evidence for a fortress at Gush Halav makes clear that the Hasmoneans, like Herod later, were the rulers of Galilee and that their rule involved military garrisons and administration in the area. The principal concerns of these outside rulers would have been the maintenance of their own control of the area and the collection of tax revenues. Since villages remained semi-independent communities running their own local affairs, there is no reason to believe that the interaction of the garrison and the villagers would have entailed conforming local community life to the "laws of the Judeans" or that the villagers would have been eager to become more fully integrated into the Judean temple-state.

Little material evidence and no literary references are yet available for Meiron, Gush Halav, and nearby villages for the time between Hasmonean rule and the great revolt, that is, for the reigns of Herod and Antipas in Galilee. More complete probes into wider samples of the sites would appear to be necessary before concluding that Meiron was "smallish" yet "expanding" or that Gush Halav underwent "growth" just after the great revolt. It seems highly unlikely that coins, even "rare numatic specimens," necessarily indicate "economic vitality" in a village. Nor, given the sharp structural divisions between rulers and ruled, would coins of the Romans' client-king Agrippa II, much less coins of the emperor Nero, indicate "involvement in the national life of the Jewish population of Palestine."[32]

The excavators conclude that there is "virtually no archaeological evidence for Meiron or its environs being involved" in the great revolt of 66–67.[33] Of course there was a "bronze finger ring engraved 'DOMITILA' in Greek" found at Gush Halav.[34] Josephus, however, provides repeated and extensive indications that the most active and insistent insurrection and resistance against Roman and Herodian rule was centered in Upper Galilee, particularly at Gush Halav. In reading Josephus's accounts about the revolt in Galilee, we must be completely skeptical about both his portrayal of himself as the great general organizing massive resistance to Roman reconquest and about his repeated attempts to defame John of Gischala (Gush Halav), his principal rival. In Galilee the revolt was never a unified or organized rebellion motivated by "nationalism" but a patchwork of local or regional conflicts, of villagers against their rulers. In the villages of Upper Galilee long-standing tension along the frontier with Tyre was a complicating factor. We may doubt that the people of Meiron, Gush Halav, and other villages were involved in the attack Josephus reports on Kedasa at the eruption of hostilities in the summer of 66. On the other hand, he also reports, in a far less schematic account, an attack on Gischala and a defensive or retaliatory strike by John and his forces from Gischala (*Vita* 44–45) and, more generally, that Kedasa was "always at war" with the Galileans (*B.J.* 4.104–5). Moreover, he indicates that the large numbers of refugees from along the frontier with Tyre were a major factor in the continuing insurrection in Gush Halav and Upper Galilee generally (*B.J.* 2.588, 625; *Vita* 372).

Josephus's very attempts to denigrate John of Gischala suggest not only that he was an energetic and capable leader, but that he had a substantial and loyal following, else he would have been no threat to the wealthy Jerusalem priest's efforts to control Galilee himself. He may well have gotten his start as a brigand chief, as Josephus charges. It is also likely that his "force" included numbers of those fugitives from the Tyrian frontier along with other Gischalans (*B.J.* 2.587–88).[35] John and his followers, not Josephus, rebuilt the fortifications of the town (*Vita* 45, 89; cf. *B.J.* 2.575, 590). Although Josephus himself had designs on it, John and his force seized control of the imperial grain stores in the villages of Upper Galilee (*Vita* 70–73). To take (back) the grain that the Roman officials had taken as part of the tribute to Caesar was an act of blatant rebellion.

At that early point in the revolt, John was apparently still cooperating with Josephus, having asked permission before seizing the grain. With his own solid support of Gischalan refugees and others in Upper Galilee, however, John began to rival and oppose Josephus's efforts to control Galilee as representative of the provisional government in Jerusalem. Under the leadership of John of Gischala peasants apparently formed an alliance and made common cause with the party of the poor in Tiberias and even began cooperating with a rival delegation from the provisional government in Jerusalem composed basically of leading Pharisees (*B.J.* 2.614–25; *Vita* 368–72, 204).

The Gischalans and other villagers were apparently not naive about the might of the Roman army, having heard reports from Lower Galilee about their scorched earth practices and brutal slaughter and enslavement of the people elsewhere. Thus Josephus's report seems highly credible that they offered little resistance to the Roman attack on Gischala, while many fled to Jerusalem to continue their resistance (*B.J.* 4.106–16).[36] The Roman reconquest of Gush Halav, including the destruction of fortifications, provides an appropriate context for the one coin from the great revolt of 66–67 recovered at Meiron. It also provides a context for the bronze ring engraved with "DOMITILA" in Greek found at Gush Halav.[37] There had been three generations of "Domitilas" in the Flavian family, with the "granddaughter" born prior to Vespasian becoming emperor in 69. Thus the name would have been significant to Vespasian's son Titus and his army that retook Gush Halav in 67. The minor disruption found by the excavators of Gush Halav in their limited probes to the sides of the lower synagogue building, finally, can be explained by this Roman military action and need not be taken as an indication of a gap in occupation.[38]

Upper Galilean Villages from the Second to the Fourth Centuries

Virtually no information exists for the villages of Upper Galilee in the generations following the great revolt. Evidence increases dramatically after the Bar Kokhba Revolt in Judea (132–135), in what archaeologists call the Middle and Late Roman periods (135–250, 250–365).[39]

The excavators of Meiron argue that numbers of Judeans, particularly the priestly clan of Yehoiariv, relocated in this village after the destruction of the Temple in 70 C.E.[40] As noted above, evidence for such a relocation by Judean priests is late and shaky. The earliest rabbinic passage linking the Yehoiariv clan with Meiron (*y. Ta'an.* 4,68d) cites Rabbi Levi, who was active in the second half of the third century, and Rabbi Berakhiah, who was active in the fourth century. The excavators of Meiron also cite "neutron-activation analysis of certain Meiron and related materials." Such analysis can indicate the location in which pottery was made, if a control group of pottery or wasters is available. Thus it could be established that some of the pottery found at Meiron was made at a place in Judea. That still leaves the question of how it came to Meiron. One of the principal practitioners of neutron-activation analysis concludes that the distribution of pottery made at one site but found in others is evidence of trade. A pattern of pottery made in Judea but found at key sites in Galilee would provide more credible support to the theory of massive Judean migration to Meiron and other villages in Galilee.[41] If we find the inscription from Caesarea credible as evidence for a general reconstitution of the priestly courses at particular Galilean villages and cities and the rabbinic tradition in *y. Ta'an.* 4,68d, credible as evidence for Yehoiariv at Meiron, then the implied relocation could have happened anytime between 70 and 250 c.e.

The hypothesized influx of newcomers would have posed severe problems of adjustment and assimilation, for both the indigenous villagers and the immigrants. Those problems would only have been exacerbated for the indigenous village community if a large number of the newcomers had been high-status priests recently from Jerusalem. The villagers of Upper Galilee had staunchly resisted Josephus, who represented the provisional priestly government in Jerusalem. Had a Jerusalem or Judean priestly clan become resident among ordinary Israelite villagers, the purity codes meant to keep the priestly families distinct would only have compounded the usual problems of outsiders coming into the ancestral village.[42] A dramatic expansion and rebuilding would have disrupted, not stabilized, the more traditional life of the native population, particularly if it had been done in a nontraditional way as "a Roman-style town plan." We may well be skeptical of just how much and when the "village life was expanding" and the population "burgeoning."[43]

The conclusions drawn by the excavators regarding the economy of Meiron point to the need for correlation between excavation of ancient sites and comparative studies of traditional agrarian societies. The excavators jump in steadily escalating steps from conjectures about two distinctive artifacts found in one room of a house — "a rounded stone installation" and "a bronze plane or scraper with an iron handle" — to "a large domestic-industrial complex" and even a complete commercial economy with "the vicinity of Meiron as the center of the entire olive oil industry in Roman Palestine."[44] A conjecture that the scraper was used in barrel-making leads to the possibility that the room was a barrel-making shop, which in turn leads to the hypothesis of an olive oil industry, with rabbinic references adduced in support. As noted in chapter 3, however, most traditional village households would presumably have done their own crafts. Even most selling was done from households, judging from rabbinic literature. Thus it seems that the room where the rounded stone and the scraper were found, which also contained an oven, a grinding stone, and other domestic objects, was probably an open courtyard. It is doubtful, moreover, that the bronze scraping tool could have sustained a sufficient cutting edge to be effective in woodworking.[45] The rabbinic references cited, finally, mention only the legendary quality of the oil in Meiron and Teqoʻa or Khirbet Shemaʻ, not its quantity.[46]

That Meiron and other villages of Upper Galilee were trading their oil to Tyre for grain appears unlikely. Numerous coins from Tyre do not indicate trade with Tyre, as explained in chapter 3, and overland transport was costly. In the villages of Upper Galilee, as elsewhere in the Roman empire, self-sufficiency was the fundamental principle.[47] To be sure, the villagers would have produced a "surplus" of oil beyond their own needs — because the ruling authorities demanded taxes in kind. Given the legendary quality of Upper Galilean oil, it is likely that some (probably that taken in taxation by government officials or rents by absentee landlords) was transported to Tyre and elsewhere, despite the cost. *Exchange* of oil for grain, however, would not have been the basis of the Upper Galilean village economy. There, as elsewhere in traditional agrarian societies, each household surely attempted to produce most of what it consumed, just as it consumed much of what it produced. The passing rabbinic reference to an extraordinary shipment of beans sent to Meiron from outside the area (*t. Dem.* 4.13) indicates that ordinarily beans were locally produced.[48] As Josephus's account of the "imperial grain stores" in Upper Galilee indicates, that included grain, which they not only produced for themselves, but for the demands of their rulers. Beyond the produce taken out of the area in taxes, trade would likely have been primarily in luxury goods for the local elite.

Meiron appears to have undergone some significant developments in the Late Roman period (250–365). The two domestic buildings, the "Patrician House" and the "Lintel House," somewhat larger than the others, contained significant fine wares. Fine wares were not unprecedented in the Upper Galilean villages. A first-century B.C.E./C.E. sherd inscribes with *arist...* in Greek (="best"?) was found at Gush Halav.[49] The quantity of fine wares found in the Late Roman period, however, attests an increase in the amount of trade with the outside world in luxury goods for the local elite. The construction of more spacious houses and of an impressive basilica-style synagogue building, moreover, presupposed the mobilization of considerable resources in labor and materials. Thus those large buildings, along with the increase in fine wares, may be good indications of an increasing social-economic differentiation between modestly wealthy families and the ordinary villagers.

Archaeologists themselves differ on how to interpret several items found in the Late Roman houses at Meiron.[50] The cavity identified as a *miqveh*, or pool for ritual bathing, is extraordinarily small, requiring unusual size or agility to enter and exit. Comparison with the numerous *miqva'ot* found from the same period at Sepphoris might suggest a lack of concern for ritual purity at Meiron, which would be puzzling if the priestly division of Yehoiariv had settled there. On the other hand, several installations identified as *miqva'ot* were found at nearby Khirbet Shema'. The excavators interpreted the charred remains of foodstuffs in storage jars found in what appears to be a storeroom of the "Patrician House" as evidence of the conservative piety of the family who had purposely burned the "devoted property" (*heqdes*). Yet to other trained eyes nothing in the assemblage found in this storeroom appeared unusual. What appears to the excavators as an "inscription" (*'esh* = "fire") on one of the storage jars, finally, seems rather to be a simple decoration typical of Late Roman patterns made with a comb-like tool with five teeth before firing the pot. A tendency toward overinterpretation in the flush of excitement over the initial discovery of artifacts can give way to more comparative and contextual interpretation.

For those familiar with rabbinic lore, finally, there remains the question of what to make of the traditions that Meiron was the burial place of Simeon bar Yochai and his son Eliezer, even that Hillel was buried at Meiron and his great rival Shammai buried at nearby (Khirbet) Shema'. In the Middle Ages Meiron became important as a pilgrimage site, with its wondrous cave of Hillel and Shammai. "The importance of Mciron grew through the ages as later generations sought to place their stamp of legitimacy on many sacred places in the Holy Land,"[51] a process that paralleled Christian projections onto the "Holy Land" at sacred sites such as the villages of Nazareth and Capernaum (see chapter 5). Until recently, the tendency has been to follow earlier studies of Galilee and/or the rabbis in accepting such traditions. With the expansion of critical examination of rabbinic literature, however, it is becoming clear that when the rabbis relocated to Galilean "villages" after the Bar Kokhba Revolt, they were concentrated in towns on the southwestern frontier of Galilee, at Usha, Shefarʿam, and Beth Shearim. The latter was hardly a typical village but in earlier times had apparently been on royal land in the Great Plain (Besara, a location of Herodian royal grain stores near the military base of Gaba; Josephus, *Vita* 118–19) that later became a genuine sacred place because of the rabbinic presence and especially the burial there of Judah the Prince. The rabbis then quickly established their principal academies in the cities of Sepphoris and Tiberias. Although some sages apparently were located in villages, it would be difficult to argue that the rabbinic circles remained village-based for very long.

Given "the rather meager collections of literary sources for Meiron in the rabbinic sources," therefore, it would be inappropriate to imagine that the village was "a center of learning."[52] We can only imagine what the relationship was between the rabbis and Meiron and the other villages of Upper Galilee. The casual mention of Meiron as an illustration for an uncertainly tithed crop of beans (*t. Dem.* 4.13) hardly suggests "that the place of Meiron in rabbinic thinking warranted significant halakhic discussion" and it says nothing about "trading practices and halakhic norms" in the village itself.[53] The later tradition (PRK 11,23) about the dispute between Meiron and Gush Halav over which town would be the final resting place of R. Eleazar ben Simeon is a source for rabbinic honor or a revered sage rather than for the villagers' own attitudes.[54] By medieval times, however, perhaps because there was a gap in occupation after 365, Meiron had become an important pilgrimage site where pilgrims visited the tomb of Simeon and Eleazar and especially the tomb of Hillel. Most important of all was the cave of Hillel and Shammai and their thirty-two disciples.

> There all Israel, and the Ishmaelites gather on Second Passover, and Israel prays there and chants psalms. And as they watch, water emerges from inside the cave and all rejoice, because it is a sign that the year is blessed. (Ish-Shalom, *Totsaot Eretz Israel*, dated 1270–91)

The villages of Upper Galilee maintained a traditional Israelite culture throughout the Roman period, judging from the use of Aramaic and Hebrew — and the almost complete lack of Greek — in inscriptions. That was made possible by the combination of topography and political geography of Galilee. Because of the rugged terrain, Upper Galilee had historically been less directly affected and less effectively dominated by the series of rulers based in distant cities and/or in the cities of Galilee that developed during Roman times. Beginning with Antipas's rebuilding of Sepphoris and foundation of Tiberias, Roman political culture and Roman-Hellenistic culture generally became more and more prominent in those cities. In contrast with the villagers of Lower Galilee, many of whom could actually see either Sepphoris or Tiberias, the Upper Galileans living at a more comfortable distance had little contact with urban culture. Indeed, since the Romans never "urbanized" the villages of Upper Galilee into the jurisdiction of either Sepphoris or Tiberias, even tax collection remained under direct Roman imperial administration of the *tetracomia* ("four villages"). Conceivably, the less direct and intensive contact of the Upper Galileans with the cities meant less friction and hostility, at least with city-based officials. Judging from the insurrection of Upper Galilean villagers in 66–67 c.e., however, they were ready, given the chance, to assert their independence of their rulers. It remains to be seen whether the villagers of Upper Galilee were any more independent-minded than those of Lower Galilee.

Chapter 5

VILLAGES OF LOWER GALILEE

What then did you go out to see? Someone dressed in soft robes? Look, those who put on fine clothing and live in luxury are in royal palaces.

—LUKE 7:25

The Galileans, seizing this opportunity, too good to be missed, of venting their hatred on one of the cities which they detested, rushed forward, with the intention of exterminating the population, aliens and all.

—JOSEPHUS, *Life* 375

The motive force behind the original archaeological explorations of the villages of Nazareth and Capernaum was Christian veneration for the holiness of the hometown of Jesus and the principal town of his ministry. Ironically, it is now necessary to dig through the previous archaeology of holy places in order to gain access to the historical social world of the figures and movements that later became the objects of such intense veneration.

Not until Constantine established Christianity did ordinary Galilean villages and towns such as Nazareth and Capernaum become Christian sacred sites in what rapidly became the Holy Land. The holiness of these sites then intensified during centuries of holy wars over the Holy Land as well as through ancient and modern pilgrimage. Standing in the tradition of veneration of holy places, Christian archaeologists have been digging specifically for the sacred loci, artifacts, and aura of Jesus and his followers. Their purpose is to provide empirical verification for traditions adhering to sacred sites rather than to illuminate the concrete historical social context of Jesus and the rabbis. It has been only in recent years that the traditional assumptions and conclusions of "bible-land" or "pilgrimage" archaeology have been questioned.[1]

One major operating assumption in the excavation of Nazareth and Capernaum has been that there was some sort of continuity through "Jewish Christianity" from Jesus and his followers to the fourth-century churches and other "Christian" artifacts and institutions identified by excavators. Found regularly in archaeological reports and in Jewish and Christian histories are references to "Christians" alongside "Jews" and "pagans" in Galilee during the Roman period. Neither literary nor archaeological sources, however, provide evidence for "Christian" communities or remains in Galilee prior to Constantine's establishment of Christianity. The "Christianity" that suddenly appears in Galilee in the mid-fourth century was not indigenous to Galilee, but was something developed outside and then imposed on the landscape. The churches built in Capernaum and Nazareth were not buildings in which communities of people in those villages met, but sacred shrines to which outside Christians came on pilgrimage. After converting to Christianity, Joseph of Tiberias, previously an emissary of the Jewish Patriarch, received permission from Constantine to build churches in Jewish villages that had special significance for Christian pilgrims.[2] The assumption on which much of the archaeological exploration of Nazareth and Capernaum has proceeded thus turns out to be invalid. There were apparently no "Jewish-Christian" communities in these villages which would have transformed a Jewish synagogue building into a Christian church (Nazareth) or transformed "Peter's House" into a house-church (Capernaum).

Nazareth and Other Villages Near Sepphoris

Ancient Nazareth was a relatively small village on a broad ridge between the Beth Netopha basin to the north and the Great Plain to the south. Most of what has been found beneath the churches and shrines of sacred Nazareth, including what were previously interpreted as distinctively "Jewish" or "Christian" installations or artifacts, pertains to the agriculture from which the villagers of Nazareth lived. The rock-cut features of the area around the Grotto of the Annunciation include Middle Bronze Age tombs,

Iron Age and later silos, olive-pressing and wine-pressing installations, cisterns, and holes for storage jars.[3] Clearly the area was
used for agricultural processing. The basin (roughly two meters
square and two meters deep into which descend five steps) found
underneath one of the mosaics in the Byzantine Basilica of the Annunciation, originally thought to be a "Jewish-Christian" initiation
bath, was rather part of a wine-pressing complex. In the recess of
this basin was found a curved knife of a type used for grape har-
vesting and its floor was paved with a mosaic. This basin and a
similar one (with seven steps) found underneath the Church of
St. Joseph, whose floor and steps were also paved with mosaics,
must have been settling or straining vats in wine-pressing installations. In Palestine the latter included a treading area with a sloping
floor and a collecting vat connected either by a pipe or an open
channel. Between them was often a settling vat, usually with steps
and a depression in the corner, as in the two basins at Nazareth.[4]

While Nazareth had clearly been occupied earlier, in the Middle Bronze Age and Iron Age, recent interpreters concluded that
a more substantial village was "refounded" in the second century
B.C.E. (i.e., prior to the Hasmonean takeover in the Galilee), judging from more extensive remains from that time. "This implies
that the village was less than two-hundred years old in the first
century C.E., but that it continued to be attractive to settlers."[5]
There is no reason to imagine that Nazareth was refounded as
part of the Hasmonean expansion, somewhat along the lines of
a colonization model of the Hasmonean takeover of Galilee.[6] In
fact, archaeologists recently pushed back the "refounding" to the
third century B.C.E., well before the reestablishment of Jerusalem
rule in the Galilee.[7] Estimates of the population of the village have
come down recently, from an earlier estimate of 1600–2000 to "a
maximum of 480" at the beginning of the first century C.E. In the
fourth century, Jerome still referred to Nazareth as a *viculus* rather
than an *oppidum*. It had not grown much since the first century.[8]
Clearly, if the first-century village was as small as 400–500 and if
there was an older village on the site, a "refounding" would be
difficult to determine and of questionable significance.

The suggestion that Nazareth had been "refounded" was connected with concern for the cultural ethos in Nazareth at the
time of Jesus in archaeologists' interpretations. It helped bolster

the essentialist assertion that Nazareth "was a thoroughly Jewish settlement," for which archaeologists offered the circumstantial evidence of the tradition about the priestly courses having resettled at various sites in Galilee and elsewhere after Jerusalem was destroyed in 70 C.E.[9] The priestly division of Hapizzez is listed as located at Nazareth in the Late Roman inscription found at Caesarea. As pointed out above, assuming there is historical reliability in this tradition, the date of resettlement may well be well into the second (or even the third) century. The reasoning from such circumstantial evidence is that "to be acceptable to priests [Nazareth] would have to be an unmixed city." Yet another priestly course, that of Yedaiah, supposedly resettled in Sepphoris, which was clearly a "mixed city." This piece of "circumstantial" evidence is thus not only about an uncertain later development, but its application is based in flawed reasoning. A less circumstantial but equally flawed argument for the culture of Nazareth is based on the belief that the multishafted burial chambers (*kokim;* or *loculi,* in Latin) of the kind found at Nazareth had become "the canonical form of the Jewish family grave" from around 200 B.C.E. The *loculi* form of burial, however, was a more general Hellenistic-Roman practice and not a distinctively Jewish custom of the time.

The attempt to establish the culture of Nazareth as "Jewish" and the assertion of a "refounding" of the village are both rooted in an "essentialist" orientation. The shakiness of the evidence in the case of Nazareth is yet one more reminder of how difficult it is to establish ethnicity and religiosity on the basis of archaeological evidence.[10] Archaeologists are now ready to acknowledge that they "cannot really characterize or identify definitively the ethnographic makeup of any [Early] Roman strata very well."[11] To understand the dynamics of ancient Galilean society it is necessary to abandon the essentialist concerns to which the material remains of Nazareth and other villages seem impervious, and to focus instead on issues of historical political-economic relations.

Nazareth was only three or four miles from the city of Sepphoris, but off of a main road that went through the nearby village of Japha. Judging from its somewhat out-of-the-way location and small size, it was a village of no special importance, surely overshadowed by the much larger Japha. Like other villages in Galilee, Upper and Lower, Nazareth was brought under the rule of the

Jerusalem temple-state by the Hasmoneans about a hundred years before Jesus's birth. Assuming that the pre-Hasmonean villagers were descended from former Israelites, they already lived according to Mosaic covenantal traditions. It is unlikely, however, that Jerusalem priestly authorities and scribal retainers had mounted a serious program to "resocialize" Galilean villagers in order to bring local practice into conformity with the official Judean Torah. An incident Josephus relates about the nearby village of Japha, "the largest village in Galilee, very strongly fortified and containing a dense population" (*Vita* 230), may indicate the attitude of such villages to the high-priestly regime in Jerusalem, even seventy years after they had been under the direct rule of the temple-state. We cannot trust the motive that Josephus attributes to the villagers in his highly self-serving account — their loyalty to himself as their "excellent general." It is evident nevertheless that when a (Pharisaic) delegation from the provisional high-priestly government of Jerusalem visited Japha and the surrounding villages (such as Nazareth?) during the great revolt in 66–67 C.E., they received a hostile reception (*Vita* 230–31).

All of the villages of western Lower Galilee were ruled and taxed from Sepphoris. Because of their proximity to Sepphoris, Nazareth and Japha would have been unusually sensitive to administrative pressures from the regime based there, whether that of Herod or Antipas or, later, the city of Diocaesarea. Relations between villagers and their rulers are generally not harmonious. It is curious that most treatments of ancient Nazareth do not mention events in and around Sepphoris in 4 B.C.E. (about the time Jesus was born), that is, the popular insurrection led by Judah son of Hezekiah and brutal Roman suppression of the revolt with massive show of military force. Those events not only manifest the conflict between Herodian rule and the Galilean peasantry that had been building toward an explosion but indicate the trauma that would have left a persistent wound in the village communities around Sepphoris for generations.

After the death of Herod, Judah son of Hezekiah, the famous brigand chief, "organized a large number of desperate men" and attacked the royal fortress. They armed themselves with weapons from the royal armory there and "made off with all the goods that had been seized there" (*Ant.* 17.271–72; *B.J.* 2.56). Josephus makes clear that Judah's insurrection, like the parallel movements in Judea and Perea, was based in the countryside, presumably among the peasants in the villages in the area around Sepphoris (*B.J.* 2.55–57, 65; *Ant.* 17.271, 273–85). Judah's followers may have been "desperate" because of the heavy demands Herod had made on the peasantry to fund his grand building projects and lavish court. The distinctive Israelite form of popular kingship (and "messianic" movement) taken by Judah's Galilean movement, as well as the parallel movements in Judea and Perea, suggests that the popular memory of the stories of Saul and David, Jeroboam and Jehu was very much alive in the oral "little" tradition of the traditional village life.[12] In retaliation, according to Josephus, the Romans sent a huge army and burned Sepphoris and enslaved the inhabitants (*B.J.* 2.68). That recent excavations of Sepphoris have not found evidence of the supposed Roman destruction in the Early Roman stratum suggests that the Roman attack may have been directed against the villages in the immediate area. Either way, the mass enslavement and destruction would have left severe scars on the social body of Galilean village communities for generations to come. As we shall see below, the tensions between Sepphoris and the nearby villages such as Japha and Nazareth continued, escalating again into popular insurrection of villagers against their urban rulers.

Capernaum and Other Villages Near Tiberias

As with Nazareth, so with Capernaum the first step must be clearing the debris of Christian reconstruction of the site. Underneath the octagonal church of the fifth century was found a "house-church" of the fourth century, which was a transformation of domestic buildings of the late Hellenistic period which had undergone some subsequent modifications. The excavators concluded that the "house-church" was constructed as early as the late first century over the site of the original house of St. Peter, assuming that there had been a "Jewish-Christian" presence from the first century onward. The whole assumption of a "Jewish Christianity" in Galilean towns is unfounded, as noted above.[13] Since it has become clear that the *minim* mentioned in rabbinic texts are not identical with (Jewish-) Christians, the *minim* of Capernaum mentioned in *Qohelet Rabba* 1:8 are almost certainly not "Jewish Christians" — eliminating one of the principal bases of the assumption determining the excavators' interpretation of the "House of St. Peter."

The very concept of "house-church" is also misleading insofar as it implies a local community meeting in that house. The fourth-century building at Capernaum, small for a church but large for a room, contained no traces of community life and worship. Much of the space around the large room of the "house-church" was apparently used as sleeping space for visitors or an enclosure for their animals.[14] The graffiti on the walls were mainly in Greek, moreover, indicating that the building was used by visitors rather than a local Aramaic-speaking community. In a telling illustration of the Christian overinterpretation of this structure and accompanying material remains, a sherd with three lines of Hebrew was "read" as a fragment of a "Jewish-Christian cultic pitcher:" "Purify [the pitcher of] wine, [your] blood, O Yahweh." Most likely it was an ordinary jug inscribed with the more domestic message in Aramaic: "[name] the winemaker; wine which he squeezed. May it be for good."[15]

A reexamination of the dating of the supposed "house-church," finally, finds no basis for the excavators' dating to the first century.[16] Key are the fragments of Herodian period lamps found embedded, along with fourth-century coins, in the lime pavement that accompanied the transformation of the domestic structure into the "church." But the principal Herodian period remains are found several layers below, suggesting that the lamp-fragments must have come from a refuse dump where the lime pavement material was mixed before packing. It is worth noting also that the two fishhooks found by the excavators — and claimed by some as evidence for the "House of St. Peter," the fisherman — were located in the fourth-century level, not in the floor of the Hellenistic–Early Roman domestic building. The "house-church" would thus appear to date from the fourth century, not the first. It fits well, moreover, in the program of building pilgrimage churches by Joseph of Tiberias, who sponsored a parallel "House of Mary" in Nazareth and the "House of James and John" in Tiberias. This critical reconsideration of earlier archaeological reports finds no material remains that would contradict the report of Epiphanius that, as of the early fourth century, Capernaum was among those Jewish towns in which Joseph of Tiberias wished to construct churches. Prior to the 330s, life in the Galilean village of Capernaum was not complicated by the presence even of a church for Christian pilgrims, let alone a "Jewish-Christian" community in competition with the "synagogue down the street." Both the church as a lively pilgrimage center and the striking white limestone synagogue building at Kefar Nahum were built after the period during which rabbinic circles became established in Galilee. Neither church building nor synagogue building are particularly pertinent to either Jesus or the rabbis.

As a second step, the restoration of more realistic estimates of the population of Capernaum in particular should facilitate a more realistic historical sense of Galilean life in the villages around the lake. A seemingly reasoned recent calculation of the population of Capernaum as "between 12,000 and 15,000" quickly became the basis for elaborate claims of the extensive "urbanization" of Lower Galilee, particularly along the western bank of the lake.[17] Such remarkable "urbanization," in turn, became the basis for a fully "cosmopolitan" culture in the minds of New Testament scholars. That this estimate of Capernaum at 12,000 to 15,000 was fully one-third the size of that for Jerusalem in the same handbook should have given the readers pause. Archaeologists exploring Galilee had not yet taken into account the "carrying capacity" of the land in the environs of a given site. Population estimates have recently been placed on a sound footing, which would bring the estimate down to about a tenth of those exaggerated figures.[18]

The two excavations at Capernaum and reviews thereof display both different approaches and different results, as well as a good deal of mutual criticism among archaeologists. Both teams of excavators agree that the first-century C.E. village had a population of around a thousand at most.[19] The Franciscan excavators of the western end of the site believe that the "village of Nahum" existing at the time of Jesus originated in the Hellenistic period, although they have also found dwellings and pottery from Middle/Late Bronze and Persian periods.[20] In this poor section of the village the houses were constructed very roughly out of basalt field stones bound with smaller stones and earth. The floors consisted of field stones with earth in the interstices, the roofs were built

of branches, earth, and straw.[21] The houses were grouped in in-
sulae of three or four, with family rooms opening off a central
courtyards that opened onto alleyways.

Recent excavations in the Greek Orthodox (east) area of Capernaum have found underneath a second- or third-century Roman
bathhouse the remains of a similar building from the first century, and under that only remains of an Early Bronze wall, but
nothing in between.[22] Little beyond the floor of another building adjacent to the bathhouse was found from the first century. It
would not be an acceptable method to assume that the building
under the later Roman bathhouse had a similar function. Until
we know more about the building it is not justifiable to conclude
either from the later Roman bathhouse or from Gospel texts (Luke
7:1–10 ‖ Matt. 8:5–13, cf. John 4:46–53) that there was a Roman
military presence rather than Roman client-rulers' military presence at Capernaum. Since the area by the lake was ruled by either
Agrippa I or Agrippa II for all but about a decade following the
deposition of Antipas, any "centurion" in Capernaum would likely
have been an officer of the Tetrarch or client-king.

The plan of the second- or third-century Roman bathhouse
suggests "it was built for Roman bathers rather than Jews." After
the Romans took direct control of eastern Galilee at the death of
Agrippa II and particularly after the Bar Kokhba Revolt, there was
undoubtedly greater Roman (military) presence in the area. Even
in the first century the spacious buildings of dressed stones with
plastered walls in the eastern part of the village contrasted with
the smaller houses of basalt field stones in the poorer western section. The difference in construction and the wealth that must have
been behind it are all the more striking in the other large well-
constructed buildings of the second and third century adjacent to
the bathhouse on the north and the east. Such large buildings may
well have served some public function.[23] A jetty wall was built
along the lake (as a port installation?) in this same period. The
covered water course and the paved street running north-south
also form a striking contrast with the irregular dirt alleyways of the
western part of the village. In the Late Roman and Byzantine periods, the domestic structures of the eastern end of the village seem
to be arranged by design behind the larger "public" buildings built
in a line along the lake.[24]

The larger and finer buildings of the eastern section of the village suggest a striking social stratification in the second and third century. The excavators suggest some correlation with a hypothesized influx of Judeans following the great revolt and the Bar Kokhba Revolt and another possible influx of Jews from the cities of Sepphoris and Tiberias following revolt against Gallus in 354. A connection with the second/third-century bathhouse that appears to have been Roman in style would be more likely. Assuming that the other "development" in the village during the second/third century was probably due to outside influence, it could well have come from Tiberias, not far across the lake to the south, which became more Roman culturally at the same time as it was placed administratively in charge of the whole area in the Romans' systematic program of "urbanization" in Palestine and elsewhere.

The situation of Capernaum along the border of the territory of Herod Antipas and that of Herod Philip in the first part of the first century has led to greater trust in the historical verisimilitude of Mark's narrative arrangement of the "call" of a "tax-collector" (2:1, 13–14), suggesting a tax office was located there. It also makes interpreters more confident that trade was important in the village economy.[25] Because of the border situation it seems likely that "trade" was more important at Capernaum than at other villages, although it would have been largely transit trade. Later in antiquity the presence of wealthy families would have increased the importance of trade, including the likelihood that local produce was sent out of the village community not only in the form of taxes but also in rents or interest on debts expropriated by the local elite to exchange for luxury goods. Presumably, given the village's location along the lake, fishing also contributed to the local economy. It may be significant, however, that the fishhooks found in the "House of St. Peter" were in a fourth-century layer, perhaps brought there by pilgrims. Judging from the agricultural equipment such as stone bowls, grindstones, presses, and handmills found in the poorer western end of the village, agriculture constituted the basis of the economy here as elsewhere in Galilee.

The archaeological explorations and literary references to Capernaum give no reason to imagine any unusual Hellenistic-Roman or Judean influence in the village prior to the second/third century other than a possible "royal" garrison stationed there by

Antipas and his successors, the Agrippas. The possible influx from Judea, as well as the increased Roman presence, would have been second century and later.

A great deal of cultural lore adheres to the village of Arbel(a) and the caves halfway up the precipitous cliffs nearby. Located on top of a hill up a valley (Nahal Arbel) from the lake just west of Magdala, Arbel is the burial site for Adam's son Seth and Jacob's daughter Dinah and several of her brothers in later pilgrimage accounts. The Mishnah tractate *'Abot* associates Nittai, of the second pair of "fathers" or sages, with Arbel. The ninth priestly course, of Jeshua-Nisraf, was associated with the village. Later rabbinic traditions and medieval poetry mention the valley of Arbel as the place where redemption would begin, after a fierce battle. Archaeological probes in Arbel have been concentrated on the synagogue building there (see chapter 7), but we do not need excavations to know what the peasants of Arbel and other villages in the area were up to.

The spectacular cliffs full of caves not far from the village would have been enough to make the place famous. In fact, they became a welcome refuge for peasants from the area who took up resistance to their rulers in times of turmoil. Josephus takes great relish in telling the story of Herod literally "smoking out" the large number of "brigands" who fled to these caves in their desperate attempt to resist Herod's conquest of the area as their Rome-appointed "king" (40 B.C.E.; *B.J* 1.305–13; *Ant.* 14.415–30). Josephus and his upper-class Jewish readers were apparently as fascinated by the heroic resistance of Galilean bandits as the English aristocracy were by the adventures of Robin Hood.

Beginning with the Roman invasion in 63 B.C.E., Roman armies and those of rival Hasmoneans had ravaged the countryside in recurrent wars of conquest and reconquest. Cassius's passing slaughter and enslavement of (tens of) thousands of people at Magdala/Tarichaeae just east of Arbel in 52 B.C.E. was only the most devastating of the Roman punitive measures in Galilee during these decades. Since there could not have been many people in Magdala itself, many peasants from the surrounding villages such as Arbel must have been among those enslaved. Not surprisingly, the disruption caused by the recurrent warfare created widespread displacement of people, burgeoning bands of brigands, and popular resistance. As the military governor of Galilee under Hyrcanus II, Herod killed the popular bandit hero Hezekiah and his men along the western frontier. By the time Herod was appointed by the Romans as their designated strongman to control Palestine, many Galileans would have been active in resistance and particularly agitated at the brutal Herod being their "king."

Herod would surely not have taken time and troops from his overall strategy of conquering his realm to mount a campaign against the "brigands" based in the cliffs at Arbel unless they posed a serious force of resistance to establishing his rule in Galilee. Josephus portrays them not as the usual small band of bandits but as a popular insurrection using guerrilla tactics. Combining "the experience of seasoned warriors with the daring of brigands" (*B.J.* 1.305), they held their own for a while against Herod's own professional troops before the latter prevailed and chased most of them along the lake and across the Jordan. But Herod returned later to finally ferret them out of their caves in the cliffs at Arbel. The latter were so precipitous that Herod's soldiers could not mount an assault from below on the "brigands" holed up in the caves halfway up the cliffs. So Herod "lowered the toughest of his men [over the cliffs] in large baskets/scaffolds until they reached the mouths of the caves where they slaughtered the brigands and their families and threw firebrands [into the caves to smoke out] those who resisted" (*B.J.* 1.311).[26]

Popular resistance to Herod appears to have continued, however, particularly in the villages such as Arbel around the lake. In what Josephus portrays as the last major action in a series of popular insurrections, "the Galileans rebelled against the powerful in their country and drowned those who were partisans of Herod in the Lake" (*Ant.* 14.450; cf. *B.J.* 1.326).

Conflictual Relations between Villages and Cities

Archaeological reports have emphasized the economic and cultural reciprocity, interaction, and continuity between the villages and cities of a supposedly highly urbanized Lower Galilee. Arguments for a high degree of economic and cultural interaction provide the basis for a claim of cultural influence of the cities on the villages. This appears to be one of the intended connotations of the recent emphasis on the "urbanization" of Galilee in the first century and after.[27]

As mentioned in chapter 4, a principal point of the regionalism hypothesis was that the "great urban centers" linked to the Greek-speaking West, with its more "cosmopolitan atmosphere," provided dominant cultural influences that small towns such as those associated with Jesus (Nazareth, Nain, Cana, Capernaum) could not have escaped.[28] The indigenous "culture was already...to some extent Hellenized, and therefore prepared for Roman dominance" so that imposing a "Roman urban overlay" was unproblematic.[29] Such cultural influence and continuity between city and village depend upon a high volume of "trade" and a dependency of villages on the city for markets and services as well as protection. An interpreter who acknowledged the urban-rural tensions in the first century imagines that later on "people from the surrounding area probably also flocked to Sepphoris...to attend the theatre or to hawk their wares."[30]

Such an irenic picture of city-village relations in Lower Galilee can only be drawn by ignoring the literary sources, which indicate latent and occasionally manifest hostility between Galilean villages and their rulers in Sepphoris and Tiberias. Since critical attention to urban-rural relations in Galilee is relatively new, a careful review of the limited evidence available is in order. Issues of the relations between the cities and villages of Lower Galilee, including the influence of the former on the latter, moreover, should be posed far more precisely. To establish that there were certain (cosmopolitan or Roman urban) cultural features present in Sepphoris or Tiberias does not take us very far. Cultural influences cannot be assessed aside from the context of political-economic relations through which they work and the reaction of the people influenced, which would also be determined both by their background and by the predominant forms of social relations.

1. Any influences from Sepphoris or Tiberias on Galilean villagers would have been mediated through the structure of political-economic relations in Galilee, which would have determined the impact of those influences and the people's reactions to them. The general (structural) relationship between Sepphoris or Tiberias and the surrounding villages was, as noted above, one of ruling city and ruled/taxed villages. Sepphoris had been the

principal town from which Galilee was administered, that is, from which the people were taxed, since at least Ptolemaic and Seleucid times; it continued in that function under the Hasmoneans and Herodians. Some recent discussions have imagined Nazareth and other villages as "satellite" or "dependent" villages of Sepphoris. As noted in chapter 3, however, dependency worked the other way, cities obtaining their support from the villages, precisely because villages and towns were subjected to regimes based in cities. One need only note the implications of Josephus's observation that Sepphoris was in a strong position politically/militarily because it was surrounded by numerous villages that would supply its economic needs (*Vita* 346).[31]

On the other hand, villages and towns strove to be self-sufficient economically and generally handled their own internal affairs. As in most comparable societies, the ruling cities attended to the villages primarily when collecting taxes — or suppressing unrest. Given that most villagers would have produced most of what they consumed (including most crafts), plus a percentage for taxes taken by the officers based in the city, it seems unlikely that villagers' trips into the city to market their produce would have been a major factor of urban-rural interaction. Visits for economic reasons to the city would have been infrequent and specialized (e.g., the potters of Kefar Hanania delivering their cooking pots).

The urban literate elite of ancient Roman cities believed that the cities provided certain "services" such as peace, protection, law, entertainment, and religious ceremonies to the surrounding villages. Peace and protection, however, were of concern to the urban elite to protect their own property and privilege. Local conflicts and disputes were handled locally by the semiautonomous village or town governance ("assemblies" and "courts," as noted in chapter 6). Peasants were generally suspicious of "higher courts" and apparently for good reason. The royal and urban courts of Sepphoris and Tiberias would have differed little from courts in the rest of the empire, where justice received depended on one's wealth and status.[32] Cultural interaction of villagers with Sepphoris was probably infrequent. Mary Boatwright finds that outside Rome itself theaters were normally used only five to twenty-five times a year and, more important, were used predominantly for political-cultural affairs.[33] The Sepphoris theater (which may not have been built until after the time of Jesus) had a capacity of only 5,000, that is, only enough for the adult Sepphorites themselves. Thus it seems highly unlikely that peasants from the area around the city "flocked to Sepphoris" on such occasions as theater spectacles.

2. Far from simply positing urban impact and influence on villages, we must also consider the reaction of the people to the impact, again as mediated through the political-economic structures. Although Galilean villagers may not have interacted frequently with the cities, that did not mean that they did not have images of what went on in the rulers' cities. Because peasants generally do not leave literary remains, we have precious little textual evidence for their views of rulers and cities. Yet the synoptic Gospels may provide a window or two onto some of their images: "great banquets" and rulers' birthday celebrations (Luke/Q 14:16–24; Mark 6:17–28); "look, those who put on fine clothing and live in luxury are in royal palaces" (Luke/Q 7:25). Several synoptic Gospel texts containing "urban features" express serious suspicion if not hostility about "urban" institutions such as the courts, councils, governors, and kings (e.g., Matt. 5:25–26 ‖ Luke 12:57–59; Matt. 10:17–19).[34]

The impact of and reaction to new or intensified cultural influences from the cities cannot be separated from the impact of and reaction to new or intensified political-economic forces. There appears to be a paucity of material evidence. The literary evidence of villagers' reaction to Sepphoris or Tiberias indicates hostility. Was the targeting of the royal palace by the rebels around Sepphoris in 4 B.C.E. simply to obtain arms, or also an attack on a political-cultural symbol or Herodian rule? When numbers of "Galileans" joined the riff-raff of Tiberias in the attack on the royal palace in Tiberias in 66 C.E., were cultural hostilities mixed in with political-economic resentment?

3. Insofar as Galileans appear to have been reacting against cultural and political-economic impact stemming from Sepphoris and Tiberias in the first century, they must have been reacting on the basis of and in defense of some culture, as well as concrete interests, of their own.[35] Archaeologists themselves are recognizing that material remains do not necessarily yield evidence for ethnic and cultural identity, as noted above in connection with Nazareth. It

is a sobering realization that, when looking for evidence of Galilean popular culture in the first century, we come up empty — except for the reflections contained in the Christian Gospels and a few indications in early rabbinic literature and certain accounts of Josephus.

Since most Galileans appear to have been descendants of Israelites (as opposed to pagans/Gentiles or Judeans), local community life must have been guided by Israelite customs and traditions. That Galilean villages cultivated Israelite traditions is confirmed by a number of literary sources. Although many passages in the synoptic Gospels express opposition to rulers and ruling institutions in Jerusalem, many sayings of and stories about Jesus in Mark and Q and other Gospel sources presuppose, mention, or "renew" the cultural traditions of Israel. Josephus also provides a few windows onto common Israelite practices of circumcision and sabbath observance in Galilee, and mentions at one particularly dramatic point that the leader of the popular party in Tiberias used a copy of the "laws of Moses" as a rallying symbol (against the ostensible representative of the provisional Jerusalem government, interestingly enough!).[36] These incidents that Josephus recounts have previously been taken as indications of Galilean loyalty to the (Jerusalem) Torah.[37] The Israelite (not just Judean) traditions they attest, however, must have been deeply rooted among the Galilean village communities long before the Hasmoneans took control of Galilee. Although early rabbis complain about lack of respect for their own rulings, they assume that the variant customs operative in Judea and the different regions of Galilee all belong in and are to be related to the heritage of Israel. The Israelite traditions that Galilean village communities shared with the "official" tradition based in Jerusalem, moreover, would have been reinforced during the century of direct rule from Jerusalem. As Josephus reports, from the time of the Hasmonean takeover of Galilee, the inhabitants were expected to live "according to the laws of the Judeans." Thus, although Galilean village culture would not have become conformed to Jerusalem culture (e.g., the Torah), which is somewhat better known from literary sources, it would appear to have been solidly rooted in Israelite traditions. It was apparently on the basis of and in defense of this indigenous culture that Galileans reacted to the political-economic impact and cultural influences stemming from the recently built or expanded cities in Lower Galilee.

4. In the particular case of the impact on Galilean villagers by Sepphoris and Tiberias in early first-century Galilee, we would also have to consider how recently and suddenly the "urbanization" had happened. The rebuilding of the fortified city of Sepphoris as Antipas's "ornament" and the completely new foundation of Tiberias were carried out within the first twenty years of Antipas's reign (Jesus' generation). Such massive and prolonged construction would have meant an unusually heavy economic burden on the Galilean peasantry subject to Antipas. Compounding the economic impact of such "development" on the peasantry would have been the political-cultural impact of a Roman client-ruler and his "Roman urban overlay" located directly in newly built or expanded cities right in Galilee (whereas previously the Hasmoneans and Herod were at a distance in Jerusalem). That would seem to provide reason to believe that popular resentment may have been building early in the first century. The economic pressure on Galilean villagers must then have been the principal cause of the social disintegration that becomes evident in the almost epidemic banditry after mid-first century, with many bands of brigands already active at the outbreak of revolt in 66.

Villagers' Active Opposition to the Cities

The picture that emerges from this analysis of urban-rural relations in Galilee is that the cities were indeed having an impact on the villages of Galilee, but that at least many of those villagers were reacting negatively. In fact, the Galilean villagers' reaction to their rulers in Sepphoris and Tiberias escalated into an insurrection in 66–67, just as it had erupted in the attack on Sepphoris after the death of Herod in 4 B.C.E.

The fields of biblical studies and biblical archaeology seldom deal with issues of overt political-economic conflict. Archaeological reports and studies on Galilee frequently comment on the indirect effect on Galilee of the destruction of the Jerusalem Temple in 70 and the Roman devastation of Judea in the Bar Kokhba Revolt of 132–35. Yet they seldom mention the revolt in Galilee in 66–67, let alone explore its significance.

No standard questions and criteria are available to determine whether certain material remains might be pertinent. Nor do ancient texts, which were written by a cultural elite, often provide much information about the ordinary people, whom they looked down upon. The exception, of course, was when the peasantry disturbed the peace and prosperity of the elite. As the traditional patterns of Galilean village life disintegrated under the pressures brought by the building and expansion of Tiberias and Sepphoris, indicators of social unrest such as banditry became epidemic. In the summer of 66 C.E. a peasant revolt erupted in Galilee as well as in Judea. Its scope was sufficiently wide that the minimal Roman presence in the area was unable to restore political order. The "general" (Josephus) that the provisional high-priestly government in Jerusalem sent to restore whatever order he could in Galilee while they attempted to negotiate terms of submission to Rome short of all-out war wrote both a history of the eventual war and his own memoirs, which provide much useful information on the course of the revolt in Galilee.

Most striking, even allowing for exaggeration by Josephus, was the vehement hostility of "the Galileans" to Sepphoris during the time of the revolt. In his first comment about this conflict, Josephus dismisses their hostility as due simply to the pro-Roman stance of Sepphoris (*Vita* 30, 39). Many modern interpreters follow his lead. Yet the Galileans' hostility to the fortress city cannot be so easily dismissed. It was part of a long-standing Galilean resentment against the city from which they were ruled and taxed (*Vita* 373–75). A survey of Josephus's accounts that mention villages in western lower Galilee, including archaeological information where available, will illustrate just how widespread and intense the Galilean reaction to their ruling cities was.[38]

In the broadest sense the great revolt of 66–67 was against Roman rule. For Judea and part of Galilee, of course, the latter was indirect rule, through the high priesthood or the client-king Agrippa II. Following the death of Agrippa I in 44, the Romans had imposed direct rule in western Lower Galilee. Both western and eastern Lower Galilee, however, were ruled from a city, by Roman officers based in Sepphoris and by officers of Agrippa II in Tiberias, respectively. Thus to insist on their independence, to revolt against their rulers, in western Lower Galilee, meant rejecting the rule of Sepphoris. Given all the resentment that had built up over the generations, the Galilean villagers in the area were eager to attack Sepphoris directly. Toward the beginning of the revolt, when the Romans had apparently been driven out, the Galileans pillaged the city; later they would have wrought a frightful slaughter had not the Sepphorites fled into the fortress and Josephus invented a ruse to divert them, at least according to Josephus (*Vita* 30, 375–80). In the absence of their Roman patrons, the Sepphorites were resourceful enough to hire a huge band of brigands under the head of a certain Jesus as mercenary forces to protect them and, presumably, to take steps to check the impetuosity of the hostile Galilean villagers.

The Galilean villagers' hostility was not focused exclusively on Sepphoris. In the one case Josephus recounts of overt insurrectionary action, young men of Dabaritta (a village on the western slope of Mount Tabor, to the east of Nazareth, along the frontier with the huge royal estates in the Great Plain) ambushed the wife of Ptolemy, the overseer of King Agrippa II.

> She was travelling in great state, protected by an escort of cavalry, from territory subject to the royal administration into the region of Roman dominion when, as she was crossing the Great Plain, they suddenly fell upon the cavalcade, compelled the lady to fly, and plundered all her baggage. (*Vita* 126–27; cf. *B.J.* 2.595–98)

It is clear from Josephus's account of this incident in his *Life*, where he is not presenting himself as the general in control of organized preparation for war, that this was an ad hoc strike against the Herodian regime and its expropriation of village produce, against wealth and privilege, planned and executed by local villagers.

We might surmise that villages in the immediate proximity to Sepphoris would exhibit less independence, either because they had close social-economic ties with the city or because they lived under the shadow of the fortress. The village of Shikhin illustrates that such villages were also capable of taking a stand over against their rulers. The site of the ancient village of Shikhin has recently been identified with some certainty as the two northernmost hills on a ridge just below Sepphoris to the northwest.[39] Surface pottery indicates that the site was occupied from the Iron

Age through Byzantine times but flourished particularly in the
Roman period, when it must have been a fairly large village. Josephus was very familiar with the village, which he called Asochis.
Shikhin was unusual among Galilean villages in two important
ways that made it dependent on the city of Sepphoris. One was
its immediate proximity to the ruling city, living directly under the
shadow of its fortress and in view of its Roman theater. During
the Hasmoneans' struggles to consolidate their control of Galilee,
Ptolemy Lathyrus, the king of Cyprus, attacked Asochis (Shikhin)
on the Sabbath and took it by storm, but failed in his attack against
Sepphoris, presumably defended by a Hasmonean garrison (*Ant.*
13.337–38). Shikhin was also apparently one of two most important sites of pottery-making. While Kefar Hanania produced the
cooking pots used all over Galilee, Shikhin produced what became
the standard storage jars that are found in abundance at Sepphoris
as well as in more distant villages such as Hammat-Tiberias, Capernaum, and Meiron. Neutron-activation analysis now confirms
the many rabbinic references to the village's reputation for such
storage jars.[40] Thus the village was unusually dependent economically on selling pottery to the city as well as particularly vulnerable
to political control by the ruling city because of its immediate
proximity.

On the other hand, Shikhin appears to have exhibited a degree of independence from Sepphoris as well. By no means was
pottery-making the only means of livelihood in the city. Among
the "features of archaeological interest" found simply by surface
survey and soundings are a screw-type olive press carved from
bedrock and a fragment of another olive press. Villagers were
also clearly engaged in agricultural production as well as pottery
production. Most intriguing are Josephus's accounts of Asochis
during the great revolt in Galilee in 66–67, which imply the village's relative independence of the fortified ruling city that loomed
over it. When the delegation from the high-priestly provisional
government in Jerusalem that aimed to displace him made their
rounds of villages and towns (with their military escort!), they met
separately with Sepphoris and Asochis/Shikhin. They also found
that while the Sepphorites were solidly loyal to the Romans, the
people of Asochis, like those at the large village of Japha near
Nazareth just to the south, were almost as resistant to direction

from Jerusalem as they were hostile to Roman rule (*Vita* 230–33).[41] Despite living under the shadow of the fortress at Sepphoris, which had also recruited a sizable force of mercenaries under the bandit-chieftain Jesus, the people of Shikhin were not afraid to pursue a course independent of the city in the turmoil of 66–67.

The first impression we have, once we recognize that Josephus's accounts of the Galilean phase of the Jewish War constitute one long self-glorification of his own exploits as the great Jewish general worthy of engaging in war with the future emperor Vespasian, is that there was not much of a war. The principal Galilean cities and towns simply capitulated, except for Jotapata, where the Romans did have to conduct a prolonged siege, as recent archaeological explorations have shown. If we look more carefully at implications behind Josephus's account, however, it becomes evident that numerous villages were engaged in the conflict. Having asserted their independence from the summer of 66, they continued to resist the Roman reconquest, many of them to the bitter end of slaughter and enslavement. A partial "surface survey" of Josephus's accounts is indicative.

The peasants in Chabulon and neighboring villages bore the brunt of the Roman attempt to intimidate the Galileans and of the first assaults in the Roman campaign of reconquest (*B.J.* 2.503–5; *Vita* 213–14). Situated along the frontier with Ptolemais, Chabulon had houses of the same style as those in the Phoenician cities of Tyre, Sidon, and Berytus. The villagers having fled, the Roman troops pillaged and burned Chabulon and the other villages near the frontier. The villagers, however, apparently struck back guerrilla-style in a surprise attack (*B.J.* 2.506).

Jotapata, like Gischala/Gush Halav in Upper Galilee, had been one of the fortified towns used by the Hasmoneans and Herod to maintain control of Galilee. Given the *pax Romana*, there had been no need to garrison the town since that time, hence it must have become much like other large villages in Galilee. Given its topography — built on a steep hill and virtually inaccessible from the east — and the fact that the Romans besieged it, Jotapata is the one town for which Josephus's claim about fortification has at least some credibility. The town is currently being excavated and reports on those excavations are eagerly anticipated.[42] Even on the basis of a few passing comments in Josephus's lengthy self-serving account of the siege, however, it is evident that the people of Jotapata itself and those of surrounding villages took an active role in resisting the Roman reconquest generally and the siege of Jotapata in particular.

People from other villages in northwestern Lower Galilee are among the heroes Josephus mentions in his account of the siege of Jotapata: Eleazar son of Sameas from the village of Saba, and Netiras and Philip, also Galileans, from the village of Ruma. But these were merely the standouts among the rebels, and there must have been many more from the surrounding villages active in the insurrection (*B.J.* 3.229, 233). Other villages that crop up as important in Josephus's narratives are Cana (*Vita* 86), Simonias (*Vita* 115), Sogane (*Vita* 262–65), and Garis (*Vita* 395, 412).

Galilean villagers, however, were not suicidal. Faced with the overwhelming might of the Roman army in the open country or in indefensible villages (as at the village of Garis, near Sepphoris, *B.J.* 3.129), they usually fled to what seemed more defensible sites. One of the places where "a vast multitude" of villagers took refuge was Mount Tabor, which rises abruptly nearly 2000 feet above the Great Plain to the north — yet another place that Josephus claims to have fortified (*Vita* 188; *B.J.* 2.573, 4.56). Tabor had been used as a base from which to dominate the surrounding area by King Solomon and later by Alexander Janneus (*Ant.* 8.37, 12.396). In the ensuing battle with the Roman cavalry, "masses were slain, . . . [some] fugitives fled to Jerusalem, and those indigenous [to the immediate area] surrendered to [the commander] Placidus" (*B.J.* 4.60–61).

About the most valiant resistance offered to the devastating Roman reconquest was offered by the large village of Japha, close to Nazareth (*B.J.* 3.289–306). Josephus claims that the village was fortified, although we must again doubt that he was responsible for the fortifications (*B.J.* 2.573). Like other villages in the orbit of Sepphoris, Japha turned a cold shoulder to the delegation from the provisional high-priestly government in Jerusalem in 66 (although we cannot trust Josephus's statement that their motive was loyalty to himself as "their excellent general"). Again, while we cannot trust the details, including the exaggerated numbers, we must take seriously the basics of his account of Japha's resistance to the Roman reconquest (*B.J.* 3.289–306; he even gives the date, 13 July

67). That is, persisting in their insurrection, the villagers offered stiff resistance to the Roman troops, the women as well as the able-bodied men doing whatever they could to fight back. In reaction to such resistance the angered Roman commanders became all the more vicious in retaliation. As Josephus reports, virtually the whole population (thousands, but not 15,000) was massacred. "For no males were spared except infants; these, along with the women, the Romans sold as slaves." Similar to the effect of the Roman onslaught and enslavement among the villages near Sepphoris in 4 B.C.E., so again in Japha and neighboring villages such as Nazareth in 67, the devastation and slaughter and enslavement of the people would likely have made a serious impact on the surviving people of the area for generations.

In eastern Lower Galilee, the villages around the lake similarly attacked the royal palace, symbol of their subjection, and the officers of Agrippa II in the royal city of Tiberias. Even before the outbreak of the hostilities, being suspicious of the devious ways in which the fearful royal officers in Tiberias were maneuvering in anticipation of popular unrest, Galilean villagers had taken punitive action against one of those officers (*Vita* 177). The ruling elite in Tiberias was particularly vulnerable once the minimal royal garrison was driven out because the vast majority of people in Tiberias itself organized under the city magistrate Jesus son of Sapphias, and made common cause with the Galilean villagers in the surrounding area. Their first target was the lavish royal palace built by Antipas. They plundered its gold and other luxurious furnishings and set it on fire (*Vita* 66). Behind Josephus's accounts of his alliance with "the Galileans" we can detect serious hostility to the ruling elite in Tiberias, which Josephus claims only he was responsible for restraining (*Vita* 99). In general the Galilean villagers around the ruling city of Tiberias did not simply withdraw into the temporary respite of independence from the Roman client-rule of Agrippa II, but maintained an active network of surveillance on the attempts of the royal officers in Tiberias to communicate with Agrippa and the Romans (to betray their revolution!) and periodically attacked and intimidated the ruling elite in the city (*Vita* 381–92).

The Galileans were also rightly suspicious of the intentions of "their general," as Josephus himself admits in his boast about his own perfidy. One such account reveals that the villagers of western Lower Galilee were in active communication with those of the area near the lake. When Josephus seized the booty that the young men of Dabaritta had taken from the royal baggage train in the Great Plain, "the young men went to the villages around Tiberias, declaring that I intended to betray their country to the Romans" (*Vita* 129; *B.J.* 2.598).

It may say something about the importance of the village of Arbel that it is the only one mentioned by name in Josephus's accounts of the revolt in the area of Tiberias. The heritage of insurrection had obviously not died out in Arbel and nearby villages since the struggles against Herod over a hundred years before. While we are completely skeptical of Josephus's reports that he fortified so many sites, his lists indicate that he knew of villages where the peasants had made preparations for the Roman reconquest that was sure to come. Among them were "the villages of the cave of Arbela" (*Vita* 188; cf. *B.J.* 2.573). That Arbel held some prominence among rebel villages, as well as a strategic location, is indicated by Josephus's convening a meeting of "the Galileans" there at one point (*Vita* 311).[43]

As in the area around Sepphoris, so in the area around Tiberias, the peasants could not hold their own against the Roman armies. Masses of villagers from the area made a last stand at Tarichaeae/Magdala, the other administrative town along the lake to the northwest of Tiberias, and the site of the mass enslavement of Galilean villagers nearly 120 years before. This time the emperor-to-be enjoyed a game of cat and mouse with the Galileans before implementing the massive slaughter of the aged and infirm and enslavement of the young and healthy, to the number of 36,000, says Josephus (*B.J.* 3.532–42).

From close scrutiny of Josephus's accounts of affairs in Galilee during the great revolt, it appears that the villagers of Lower Galilee were not much less resistant to the Rome-imposed order than the villagers of Upper Galilee. After Josephus, our sources are silent about any popular resistance in Galilee. Yet the widespread resistance that erupted in the so-called Gallus revolt in mid-fourth century indicates that the spirit of independence did not disappear in Lower Galilee.

Chapter 6

BEFORE SYNAGOGUES
WERE BUILDINGS

*As these remains were the first of the kind that we had yet seen,
and were of a style or architecture utterly unknown to us; we were
at a loss for some time what to make of them. They were evidently
neither Greek nor Roman. The inscription, if authentic, obviously
makes both structures as of Jewish origin, and as such, they could
only have been Synagogues.*
— EDWARD ROBINSON (the "father" of biblical archaeology)

*The research of the past two–three generations has been blessed with
structures that have been called temples or worship-sites on the basis
of most doubtful proofs.*
— S. YEIVIN (1973)

Lack of attention to concrete social realities and social structures
blocks historical understanding the most, ironically, with regard
to the synagogues, the most social of ancient institutions. Much
of the previous discussion of ancient synagogues has been skewed
by the assumption of a synthetic construct of the synagogue that
includes the building with its orientation and furnishings, as well
as the congregation itself and its activities. It is not only the archaeologists who excavate them who almost invariably assume that
synagogues were religious buildings. And it is not only textual
scholars who almost invariably assume that Torah scrolls were *read*
to the congregation.

Recent excavations and examinations of other evidence, however, have raised several difficulties regarding such a synthetic
assumption about ancient synagogues. Three facts pertinent to

synagogues, at least synagogues in Palestine/Galilee, have become increasingly evident. (a) There were virtually no "synagogue" buildings until the third century c.e. and after in Palestine/Galilee. (b) In a traditional agrarian society such as ancient Galilee, where the vast majority of people lived in villages and towns, the religious and social-economic aspects of community life were virtually inseparable, in contrast with modern Western assumptions. (c) The basic meaning of the ancient Greek term *synagōgē* (from which "synagogue" derives) and the parallel Hebrew term *knesset* is "assembly" or "congregation." The conclusion to be drawn from those three facts might seem obvious: the synagogues in first- and second-century Galilee, the context of both Jesus and the early rabbis, must have been local community assemblies or congregations.

Scholars of "early Judaism" and "early Christianity" have been reluctant to draw this conclusion and face the implications: for example, that local communities had forms of social cohesion and celebration that did not necessarily involve a building, or that to presume the affairs of those local congregations were primarily "religious" is reductionist and abstracting. Although only a small number of the buildings identified as "synagogues" date from the very end of the period with which we are concerned and most date from later, it is important to have a general sense of the emergence of public buildings in Late Roman Galilee. Some attention to "synagogue" buildings from even later can help highlight the features of the Late Roman buildings by comparison. Recognition of what emerged in the third century and developed through Byzantine times should also serve to indicate what was not present earlier and help to redirect the focus of our investigation for the late second-temple period. A review of the numerous references to *synagogai* in the Gospels similarly leads to a refocusing on the concrete social forms taken by community life. Focusing on the concrete social forms in first-century Galilee should then, in turn, enable us better to appreciate the later construction of public buildings for activities of the synagogues.

Architectural Typology and Dating of Synagogue Buildings[1]

The early twentieth-century investigations of Kohl and Watzinger on "the ancient Synagogues in Galilee" established the dogma that the earliest known synagogue buildings in ancient Palestine dated from around 200 c.e. It was assumed that synagogue buildings existed earlier, but were destroyed in the two Jewish revolts of 66–70 and 132–135. An eager audience thus greeted archaeologists' claims in the 1960s and 1970s to have identified several "synagogues" from late second-temple times, at Masada, Herodium, Gamala, and Magdala. More cautious voices have subsequently concluded that the evidence was not convincing.[2] There now seems to be a critical consensus emerging that "no synagogue [buildings] have been found in Palestine for the almost two hundred years following the destruction of the Temple."[3] They begin appearing only the second half of the third century c.e. Then from the fourth to seventh centuries there is evidence of scores of synagogue buildings, with more than fifty in the Galilee, a dozen in Judea, and several more around the periphery of Judea.

Previous dating of synagogue buildings was done according to an architectural typology that was thought to fall into a tidy historical sequence. The basilica or "Galilean" type, thought to be "early," featured rectangular rows of columns running mainly north-south and a (short-side) facade facing south (usually interpreted as meaning toward Jerusalem) having three entrances. In the "transitional" type, the principal subset of which was a "broadhouse," the orientation is toward one of long walls rather than toward the end or short wall. The "apsidal" of "Byzantine" type, finally, which came mainly "later," had an apse (which pointed in the direction of Jerusalem) separated from the auditorium as the center of worship, with entrances in one or more of the other walls. In contrast with the attention focused on the external facade in the "Galilean" type, emphasis in the "Byzantine" type is internal, including elaborate mosaics often depicting biblical scenes and/or a zodiac with a sun-chariot at center.

Recent excavations have thrown the previous typology into question, particularly with regard to correlation between the building types and dating. Virtually none of the earlier dating of synagogue buildings was done by carefully controlled stratigraphy or epigraphy, which is now standard archaeological procedure. Quite apart from the question of sequence, "even the concept of a standard basilica can no longer be maintained."[4] Earliest use of the "broadhouse" architecture pre-dates most if not all basilical buildings.[5] The "Galilean" or "basilica" type, moreover, can hardly be a stage in a general sequence since it correlated more with geography than time-span. That is, the "basilica" type occurs in the relatively confined area arcing from the Golan Heights through Galilee and perhaps over to Carmel, with no clear examples elsewhere. The "transitional" type in all its variety is predominant outside of Galilee and Golan from the second/third to the fifth/sixth centuries. The "apsidal" type then not only becomes the standard design in Byzantine times and after, but occurs further south than the "basilica" type, overlapping only at Hammat-Tiberias. There is thus no fixed universal typological-chronological pattern, but there does appear to be a very rough regional-historical pattern.

With so much attention and excitement focused on the discovery of the buildings themselves, a number of questions remain to be addressed. Few have been explored in more extensive relation to their surroundings, taking into account the importance of contextual factors and social functions within their villages or towns.[6] If, as seems to be the case, public buildings began to be constructed in any numbers only during the third century, what factors may have played a role in their emergence, for example in several villages in close proximity in Upper Galilee? Moreover, considering the great expense and cooperative effort that such a major construction project would require in a small town or village and the reconstruction made necessary by earthquake damage, what was the source of those resources and what were the political circumstances that made such major construction projects possible in the third and fourth centuries?[7] The story in the Gospel of Luke about the centurion having "built" the synagogue for the people of Capernaum suggests one possibility: patronage by some wealthy benefactor. Ancient Near Eastern temples, of course, had always been sponsored by kings, such as Herod, and it was the wealthy who underwrote monumental public buildings in the cities of the Roman empire. Had certain wealthy "big men" emerged in the villages and towns of Galilee and paid for construction of public buildings as a way of giving something back to their communities? Although not all that large and ostentatious, the "Patrician house" and the "Lintel house" found in the Late Roman stratum of Meiron in Upper Galilee (i.e., contemporary with the construction of the public building there) are suggestive in this regard.[8]

Particular Synagogue Buildings

To illustrate "synagogue" building in Galilee we take four geographically and temporally related sets, of four third-century
buildings in close proximity in Upper Galilee, but varying types,
three third- or fourth-century buildings from Lower Galilee rang-
ing from the Sea of Galilee to near Nazareth, two later and larger
buildings at the north end of the Sea of Galilee, and a sampling
from later buildings in Tiberias and Beth Shean.[9]

Upper Galilean Villages

Of the two buildings at Gush Halav,[10] the lower one (in the Wadi
to the east of the contemporary village) was a basilica erected in
the second half of the third century, then rebuilt and expanded
after an earthquake in 306, lasting into the sixth century. In contrast with other early basilicas that have three entrances on the
south facade, the Gush Halav building had only one in the center,
with a down-facing eagle carved into the underside of the lintel.
Two north-south rows of columns divided the internal space of
roughly 14 x 11 meters into three aisles. To the west is a corridor,
perhaps storage area, to the east are some rooms, and perhaps a
gallery extended to the north. Off-center to the west of the door
in the south facade was a *bema* or a platform from which, presumably, the Torah was recited or read.[11] Despite the limited permit
that confined the excavation to the lower synagogue building itself,
the excavators were able to ascertain its relation to its immediate
surroundings. The facade of finely trimmed ashlar blocks was the
only exterior wall, the others, made of rough-hewn field-stones,
bordering adjacent buildings, perhaps domestic structures. It is
not situated on any height or other conspicuous place drawing
attention to it. Of potential significance historically, "the interior
benches were built over a preexisting wall with a slightly different orientation."[12] Similarly, "large quantities of tesserae" in the
east corridor of the building were "concentrated well below floor
level." These may indicate "the existence of a fine building — perhaps even some sort of public building — standing in this area
of the *tell* sometime between the Hellenistic and Middle Roman
periods."[13]

At Meiron the unusually long (13.5 x 28 meters) basilica was set on a rock-cut terrace, with its west wall carved into the rock near the summit of the hill. Besides the usual three entrances in the south-facing facade, a shallow portico with six columns graced the facade (as at Bar'am). No *bema* or Torah ark was evident. Built in the late third century, the synagogue along with the village was apparently abandoned after the earthquake in 363 c.e.

At Khirbet Shema'[14] was a third-century broadhouse building. In the east-west orientation of its columns it differs from the only two other clear broadhouse buildings in Palestine that approximate its plan, both located in southern Judea, at Susiyah and Eshtemo'a. This broadhouse type of structure appears also in the diaspora, at Dura Europas along the Euphrates River and at Naro. A menorah was carved into the lintel over the northern door at Khirbet Shema', and an eagle in one of the doorjambs of the western entrance. After its destruction in an earthquake in 306 it was reconstructed as a broadhouse, which lasted until another severe earthquake in 419. At this stage a *bema* was built in the long southern wall over part of the bench there, indicating perhaps a change of orientation.

At Nabratein a third-century basilica with two rows of three columns each had one entrance from the columned porch on the south and, unusual for this early a building, a fixed Torah shrine (with figures of lions above). Preceding the basilica, however, was a second-century broadhouse. Although it had no Torah ark, two *bemas* flanked the entrance on the south wall. The Byzantine basilica that replaced the third-century basilica had no *bema* and apparently only a wooden Torah ark instead of a fixed shrine.

Lower Galilean Villages

In Arbel, a settlement perched on the top of a hill above a valley just to the east of Magdala, was a fourth-century basilica (20 x 18 meters) built mainly of light-colored limestone, in contrast with the black basalt of the village houses. The two long rows of columns run north-south, with the orientation toward the south, but the entrance is toward the north end of the east wall.[15] Also unique are the benches along the east and west walls, which feature a 1.4-m wide platform below the outer-upper bench, with more benches below the platform almost filling the space ordinarily comprising the side aisles. There was also a hewn rock "chest" to the east end of the north wall. The unique single main entrance, made of a single stone, required stepping downward on the stepped benches to the main floor. When the structure was rebuilt in Byzantine times, a round niche (for the Torah shrine) with a *bema* in front of it was added in the center of the south wall, and a courtyard added to the east of the building. This building at Arbel is the northernmost among those with niches, which are completely lacking in Upper Galilean buildings.

At Khirbet Ha-'Amudim ("Ruin of the Pillars"),[16] amidst the ruins of an ancient village situated on the plateau at the eastern end of the Beth Netopha valley, stood some monumental columns of another "Galilean" building, apparently erected at the turn of the fourth century, then abandoned a century later. Two north-south rows of columns divided the internal area of 22 x 14 meters into a nave and two aisles with benches along the sides. The (standard) three entrances on the south-facing facade were decorated with stone carvings, including a monumental lion carved lintel. This building provides the earliest example of a mosaic covering the floor, one part of which featured an Aramaic inscription. Stones forming a square toward the center just inside the southern (facade) wall may not have been the base of a Torah shrine, given their similarity to other partitions in the southeast section of the structure. A stone found earlier at the site contained the dedicatory inscription: "Yoezer the hazzan and Simeon his brother made this gate of the Lord of Heaven." Again excavation focused on the "synagogue" building, producing no information on its relation to the rest of the ancient village.

Further west at Yaphia (Japha) near Nazareth was either a broadhouse or a basilica facing east. This building, perhaps from the fourth century, had a floor mosaic with a circle set within a square frame, divided into twelve medallions, which contained either symbols of the tribes or zodiac signs. A panel on the southwest corner of the mosaic had an eagle standing above a head of Helios.

North End of the Sea of Galilee

At Capernaum, just to the west of where the Jordan River enters the north end of the Sea of Galilee, was a large (24.3 x 17.25 meters) basilica with the usual three entrances. It also had both a porch along the south facade and a court (24 x 13 meters) to the east, and the complex was surrounded by streets on at least three sides. In contrast with the modest basalt houses nearby and the basalt of other public buildings such as at Chorazin, this building was of white limestone brought from some distance. Despite considerable resistance by some interpreters, the building can be dated from material in the fill under the floor to the fifth century c.e. On the other hand, underneath the fifth-century building may have been a public building of the first century c.e. (although except possibly for Nabratein, no example exists of an earlier "synagogue" building replaced by a Byzantine structure). There was apparently no permanent place for a Torah ark along the south wall. Among the unusually elaborate ornamentations were a Roman imperial eagle carved into the lintel of the central entrance, other eagles, several lions at points on the facade, the face of a Medusa and animals carved into the bench along the western wall, and a menorah, shofar, and incense shovel carved on a Corinthian capital.

At Chorazin, a large fourth-century basilica (70 x 50 ft) built of basalt has been reconstructed among many other buildings in what must have been a fairly large village. A flight of stairs ascended from a square to a platform in front of the south-facing facade, with the usual three entrances. Two tiers of benches lined the internal walls. Some of the elements found scattered in the area may have belonged to a possible Torah ark and an aedicula that may have served as a platform for reading. Most intriguing is the "Moses' seat" discovered among the ruins to the south of the building in 1926. Among the decorations were human figures, a lion attacking a centaur, another lion devouring an animal, and a Medusa's head. That no traces of any earlier building were found under the synagogue is consistent with the conclusion that the site of this third/fourth-century village is different from that of the first-century village of Chorazin.

Culture of the Galilean Synagogue Buildings

If we examine the architectural forms and building styles and ornamentation of these Galilean public buildings of late antiquity in comparison with the culture of the wider area, there seems at first to be little that distinguishes them from corresponding buildings elsewhere, in Syria and beyond. In architectural form and style, Galilean buildings were patterned after some form of Roman civic building. The broadhouse buildings, for example, resemble the basic Syro-Palestinian broadhouse temple. The facades of many of the "Galilean"-type buildings are virtually indistinguishable from contemporary "pagan" structures, with identical plans and decorations: a main entrance flanked by two side entrances, decorated windows, columns, and a semicircular arch above the main entrance, and a gable crowning the facade. The Babylonian Talmud has a story of a man who walked along the street and bowed down before a building, thinking it was a synagogue, and only afterward realized that it was a pagan temple (*b. Šabb.* 72b). The later Galilean basilicas parallel Christian basilicas.[17] Construction techniques in eastern and south Syria, such as the mixing of ashlar masonry on one wall with field stone on another, have influenced those used on the Galilean buildings. The Upper Galilee buildings, on which the execution of forms does not always match the highest standards, may have been somewhat removed from the mainstream of imperial Roman art forms.[18] Nevertheless, generally the ornamental elements such as the "Syrian Gable," the so-called oriental style in relief sculpture, as well as the diverse repertoire of Greco-Roman symbols all point to a common culture in the area that the Galilean "synagogue" buildings share.

This is dramatically illustrated in several motifs that are prevalent in the decor and ornamentation of the Galilean buildings. Lions, winged victories, wreaths that had cultic significance in pagan art, figures treading grapes in a wine-press, and mythical figures such as centaurs and Medusas all appear in the decor carved into the lintels, doorjambs, and elsewhere on these Galilean buildings.[19] Of special significance may be the nearly ubiquitous eagle, which had long been a symbol of kingship and imperial sovereignty. As Herod lay on his deathbed the students of two distinguished sages of Jerusalem chopped down the golden eagle that he had erected over the gate of the Temple. "Yet by the fourth century C.E. the eagle had become one of the most ubiquitous symbols gracing the synagogue [building]s of Galilee!"[20] Similar figures of eagles are found on "pagan" temples not far away in Syria (e.g., Kadesh) apparently as symbols of Zeus-Jupiter-Baʿal Shamin —

and almighty Rome. Most fascinating to many, perhaps, has been the prominent appearance of zodiacs with the sun-god Helios and the four seasons in the mosaic floors of Byzantine buildings, the earliest of which is at Hammat-Tiberias (which is also the only one in Galilee, unless the mosaic at the building in Yaphia has signs of the zodiac rather than symbols of the twelve tribes). The fifth-century "synagogue" building at Capernaum, the most elaborately decorated in Galilee, comes the closest in decor to imperial Roman art.[21]

An Increasingly Explicit Jewish Orientation

By comparison with the culture they shared with the wider area, the third-century buildings were almost entirely devoid of distinctively Jewish/Judean motifs. The menorah carved into the lintel at Khirbet Shema' was a notable exception to the general pattern. "Until the early fourth century C.E. very few Jewish symbols appear in a synagogue [building] context."[22] Even the elaborate decor on the basilica at Capernaum exhibited only one minor representation of a set of clearly recognizable Judean symbols, a menorah, shofar, and incense shovel, on one Corinthian capital. Only in the Byzantine period did distinctively Jewish cultic motifs such as menorah, shofar, lulab, ethrog, and the incense shovel begin appearing with any regularity.[23] It is extremely difficult to approach the question of a distinctive significance in these buildings and their decor without reverting to some sort of essentialist dichotomy between "Jewish" and "pagan" culture. At least there has been some critical discussion of a few of the most pertinent issues, such as the orientation of the buildings, Torah shrines and Torah reading, and "the seat of Moses."

Most of the "Galilean" basilicas were clearly oriented to their southern walls, which had elaborated facades. That has usually been interpreted as an orientation to the holy city of Jerusalem (for the biblical practice of praying toward Jerusalem, see 1 Kgs. 8:44, 48=2 Chron. 6:34, 38; Dan. 6:11; and the later rabbinic injunction in *y. Ber.* 4,8bc). On the other hand, the doorways in the southern wall in most "Galilean" basilicas stand contrary to the rabbinic requirement that the entrances of synagogues face east (*t. Meg* 3.22), and if any group in third- through fifth-century Galilee was cultivating the temple and priestly traditions from Jerusalem, it was the rabbis who produced the Mishnah and Tosefta. Also, several Galilean buildings, such as those at Yaphia, Arbel (and perhaps Khirbet Shemaʿ?) as well as Sumaqa on Carmel, were oriented toward the east, like pagan temples.[24] In Galilee as elsewhere in Palestine, there was thus a significant minority of buildings not oriented toward Jerusalem.[25]

The hypothesis of an orientation toward Jerusalem also usually assumes some sort of Torah shrine on the south wall, either portable or permanent. As the excavator of several buildings notes, however, "none has been found *in situ*."[26]

"In later synagogues of the Byzantine period, the Torah shrine was accorded a permanent installation."[27] Apparently by extrapolation backward into earlier centuries, it is hypothesized that portable Torah shrines must have been brought into the main sanctuary when needed. Perhaps it should also be questioned whether the primary or only function of the *bema* or platform found, usually but not always along the south wall, was for the *reading* of the Torah. It may have served other purposes as well. That variations in the arrangements within the buildings have been found[28] suggests that no standard pattern of usage should be assumed for the third- and fourth-century buildings. The construction of later buildings with apses in which a more elaborate shrine for the Torah was built into the overall structure, by contrast, makes clear that a principal function of the building had to do with the Torah. In a possibly related matter, portrayals of biblical scenes do not appear in Galilean buildings, and in "synagogue" buildings outside of Galilee those portrayals do not appear until the Byzantine period and after (e.g., the binding of Isaac in the floor mosaic at Beth Alpha).

One occasionally finds the suggestion in archaeological reports that either the "synagogue" buildings themselves or the courts or rooms adjacent to them served as a "house of study" (*bet ha-midrash*). This seems highly unlikely, however, on the basis of rabbinic texts that assume that the "houses of study" were separate from the "houses of assembly." Those same rabbinic references also make clear that the rabbis had little to do with the ordinary "houses of assembly," while they focused their own activities, study, and discourse, in their own "houses of study." That there were actual houses in Galilee, particularly in Tiberias and Sepphoris, whether residences or not, in which such study took place seems a likely conclusion on the basis of an inscription found in the Golan: "This is the house of study of Rabbi Eliezer Ha-Kappar."[29]

The discovery of stone chairs identified as "Moses' seat" (cf. Matt. 23:2) at the synagogue buildings in Chorazin and Hammat-Tiberias has helped fuel discussions of supposed competition and conflict between "the synagogue" ("Judaism") and "the church" ("Christianity") in the late first century. These chairs provide an example of how inappropriate it may be to draw direct connections between given artifacts and certain texts, and how wider critical consideration in connection with pertinent textual and comparative materials is necessary to establish the significance of particular artifacts.[30]

At the synagogue building in Dura Europas the raised seat connected to the highest bench seems to have been a seat of honor for the elder or *archisynagogos*. The stone "chairs" found in the synagogue buildings at Chorazin and Hammat-Tiberias apparently stood isolated from all other seats and next to the Torah ark/shrine. The latter (which subsequently disappeared and is known only from a drawing) lacks armrests or side rails and the seat slopes forward, making it inappropriate for someone actually to sit in, but it has three distinctive holes in a row toward the front of the "seat." The Chorazin chair stood upon a dais approached by some stairs. It has handrails with a gap between them and the seat, which has a 2-centimeter-wide depression toward the front.

Various interpretations have been given, but each one is problematic. These chairs cannot be the symbolic seats of "Jewish legal authority" because the head of a court would not have sat alone in judgment but among other members of the court.[31] They cannot have been the seat of the rabbi "who taught Torah to the congregation" in the synagogue, not only because the teacher's "sitting at the head" pertains only to the "house of study" but also because the rabbis did not have such functions in the synagogues even in Byzantine times. These chairs seems highly unlikely to have been the seats of the *archisynagogos* or other major functionary since "the elders [always in the plural] sit facing the people and with their backs to the holy" (*t. Meg.* 4.21).

The few literary references to "chairs" are suggestive. Insofar as it was forbidden to sit on the king's throne (*m. Sanh.* 2:5) or even in one's father's seat (*p. Qidd.* 1:7 61a; *b. Qidd.* 31b), it would have been unthinkable that anyone actually sit on Moses' seat, if there were such a thing set aside. The phrase "seat of Moses" may have been a short form of "seat for the Torah of Moses," considering how frequent expressions connecting the Torah and Moses are in biblical and rabbinic literature.[32] The "seat of Moses" appears only once in rabbinic literature, in the fifth-century *Pesiqta de Rab Kahana* 7b, citing a Palestinian sage of the fourth century, R. Aha, who said the throne of Solomon (1 Kgs. 10:19) "resembled the seat of Moses," suggesting that a "seat of Moses" was known, if rarely discussed and rarely present as a piece of furniture. The Babylonian sage Rabba, also of the fourth century, refers to a chair (Aramaic *korsia*) in a synagogue building on which he saw a Torah scroll placed (*b. Meg* 26b).

Considering the degree to which Galilean synagogue buildings share common cultural motifs and decor with neighboring Syrian buildings, the chairs in pagan temples may be suggestive as well. Near contemporary to the chairs found in the Chorazin and Hammath synagogue buildings is the basalt chair at Suweida in southern Syria, with handrails in the form of two lions, parallel to the lion and eagle handrails on the Chorazin chair. The Suweida chair represents the "empty throne" of a deity, probably Astarte, and likely held her image or symbols of her authority and power. Long a standard motif in ancient Near Eastern societies, "empty thrones" were transferred from deity to ruler in the Hellenistic East after the death of Alexander. At least one "empty throne" was taken over by imperial Roman emperor worship, the emperor's insignia on the "chair" or "throne" represented the deity or ruler (in absentia).[33] Early Christianity simply applied the image of the enthroned emperor and his "empty throne" to Christ. The "empty throne" appears repeatedly in fifth/sixth-century reliefs, mosaics, and sarcophagi. All the more suggestive, the Gospel was enthroned at the head of great church councils and also apparently placed on a throne-shaped edifice in fourth/sixth-century North Syrian churches. There is also a contemporary "empty throne" of Mani, "raised upon a dais of five steps, carrying his Gospel and icon."[34]

These parallels suggest that these stone chairs next to the Torah shrine or ark must have been an "empty throne" on which the Torah was placed during an assembly before and/or after it was read/recited. The chairs are about the right size, and the holes in the Hammath chair and the depression or channel between the seat and the handrails in the Chorazin chair must have held the Torah scroll in place. Given the close association of the Torah with Moses, moreover, it is conceivable that such a chair was known as the "chair of Moses."

Functions of the Public Buildings

A comparison of the third/fourth-century buildings in Galilee with the synagogue buildings of Byzantine times and later indicates that the former were simpler structures with little of the internal differentiation and specialization that developed in the later basilicas in Galilee and apsidal buildings to the south. With one possible exception, moreover, there is no archaeological evidence to indicate that activities in these early buildings were centered on the Torah or that prayer was a primary activity. Only on evidence of Torah shrines in later buildings, and the assumptions of the interpreters, is it posited that portable Torah shrines must have been brought in and that the *bema* was basically for the reading and interpretation of Torah. It has even been suggested that the "synagogues of Galilee" may represent "a conservative tradition which adopts Torah-centered worship only at a relatively late date."[35]

Assuming that we should not simply assume what the functions of these public buildings in Galilee were, what activities occurred there, and given the continuity between these Galilean buildings and similar buildings in Syria and beyond, then the functions of the latter may provide some clues to the possible functions of the former. For example, benches along the sides of buildings or large rooms, far from being unique to these "synagogues," are found in *odea*, forecourts of Nabatean temples, Greek and Roman dining rooms, council halls, and temples of Mithras. They appear in Greek and Roman as well as Mesopotamian and Syrian temples. Benches also appear in smaller public buildings and even private houses, such as the small community meetinghall found in northern Syria dating from the early first century C.E. Similarly, rows of columns are found in buildings that enclose sufficient space to accommodate some form of assembly, such as a reception hall in a palace, a council hall, and the porches of a church.[36] That most of the public buildings in Galilee were located in villages and towns, one would presume that the sorts of meetings or meals that occurred there were not royal receptions and councils of state, but rather local gatherings and communal activities.

In fact, the rabbinic literature contemporary with these buildings provides some indication of the principal activities conducted in them. Of course we must take into account the special perspective of the sages, as a social and educational elite who chose not to associate on a regular basis with villagers and their gatherings. It may have been only later, in Amoraic times (late antiquity), that prayer came to be the primary activity (as in *y. Ber.* 4.4 [8b]; 5.1 [8d]). An earlier tannaitic source mentions reading/recitation, study, and teaching/homilies, but not prayer (*t. Meg* 2.18), and other traditions mention prayer last, after reading and study. In fact, as suggested by several scholars recently, the "house of assembly" seems to have served more broadly as what was in effect a community center with several functions in addition to reading, study, and prayer. Public gatherings, discussion and administration of community affairs by communal leaders, collection of charity, sessions of local courts, announcements of lost property, and perhaps even community meals (e.g., *y. Ber.* 2.5 [5d]; *y. Ta'an.* 4.5 [68b]; *y. Sanh.* 15.2 [26b]; *t. Šabb.* 16.22; *t. Ter.* 1.10; *y. Dem.* 3.1 [23b]; *Lev. Rab.* 6:2; *m. Mak.* 3:120).[37]

Synagogues as Local Community Assemblies

The recognition that even when "houses of assembly" began to be constructed in the third and fourth centuries they functioned broadly as community centers and not simply as houses of prayer or worship leads to the conclusion that the synagogues were local community assemblies — as both the Greek term *synagōgē* and the Hebrew term *knesset* indicate. We can then explore the purposes for which they gathered and the functions they had in the villages and towns of Galilee.

Once the first-century landscape has been cleared of the synagogue buildings so desperately sought by modern scholars we can more readily catch sight of the community assemblies that had al-

most certainly been there for centuries. The basic meaning of the
key terms should have been the clue. That the Hebrew term *knesset* in early rabbinic literature means "assembly" or "congregation"
has not been in doubt, but that literature has often been neglected
in discussions of "synagogues." What has most blocked discernment of the local assemblies has been the synthetic and synchronic
construct of "synagogue" through which the Greek term *synagōgē*
has been read.[38] That the term referred primarily to an assembly
or congregation in the first century has been clarified by several
recent studies that have attended more precisely to the literary and
historical contexts of its usage.[39]

The Greek word *synagōgē* indicates an assembly or gathering, without any special religious connotations. The Septuagint,
the Jewish Bible in Greek, uses the term to translate *edah*, and
sometimes *qahal* (which is more frequently rendered by *ekklēsia*),
referring to the local or tribal assembly or the congregation of
all Israel. In inscriptions and Jewish literature in Greek from diaspora communities of the first century C.E. and before, *synagōgē*
almost always indicates a congregation or assembly of people,
while *proseuche* and other terms refer to the place or building in
which the assembly meets.[40] Only in the second half of the first
century is *synagōgē* used for the place or building in which the
congregation met. An inscription from Cyrenaica dated 56 C.E. indicates how the term was being extended from the assembly to its
building: "It was resolved by the *synagōgē* of the Jews in Berenice
that those who donated to the repairs of the *synagōgē* would be inscribed on the stele of Parian marble." Most accessible are three
instances where Josephus used *synagōgē* to refer to buildings where
Jews met in Dora, Caesarea, and Antioch (all in cities outside of
Judea; *Ant.* 19.300–305; *B.J.* 2.287–92, 7.44–47).

In all of these references, moreover, whether to the assembly
proper or to the building in which it met, the *synagōgē* is clearly
more than a worshipping community or a place of worship. As indicated in Josephus's account of the Jewish communities at Sardis
and elsewhere, the social-political dimensions were inseparable
from the religious. Such communities "from earliest times . . . had
an association of their own [*synodos idia*] in accordance with their
native laws and their own place, in which they decide their affairs
and controversies with one another" (*Ant* 14.235).

Insofar as other documents indicate that they were gathering funds and/or sending funds to Jerusalem, they clearly had a significant economic dimension as well.[41] In all three cases where Josephus refers to the building in which the congregation assembled as well, the *synagōgē* is a center for a community concerned about its political rights and existence, not simply religious exercises, with the "twelve leading men" (*dynatoi*) in Caesarea (*B.J.* 2.287, 292), their long-recognized political rights and their own "magistrate" (*archon*) in Antioch (*B.J.* 7.44, 47; cf. *c. Ap.* 2.39), and the references to their having been allowed heretofore to conduct their community life according to "the [ancestral/traditional] laws" (*B.J.* 2.289; *Ant.* 19.301, 304). Thus in Jewish usage outside of Judea and Galilee in early Roman/late second-temple times, not only does *synagōgē* refer primarily to an assembly, with extension to the place of assembly only in the second half of the first century, but that assembly of the Jewish community was concerned with political-economic as well as religious affairs.

The most appropriate sources for the situation in Palestine and particularly Galilee itself are surely the Christian Gospels. The traditional impression and standard construct of the "synagogues" in which Jesus supposedly preached and healed has surely been heavily influenced by two Lukan stories: that of the synagogue in Capernaum which the centurion had supposedly built for the people (Luke 7:1–5) and that of Jesus supposedly reading the scroll of Isaiah in the synagogue at Nazareth on the sabbath (Luke 4:16–20). Those stories, however, are Lukan projections from his own later experience in diaspora "synagogues" back into the ministry of Jesus. In all other Gospel stories and sayings (and probably in Luke 4 as well) *synagogai* refer to assemblies (or the court constituted in or by an assembly). The parallels with councils or rulers and authorities in Mark 13:9 and Luke 12:11 make it clear that "synagogues" means not buildings but assemblies with political jurisdiction and authority to keep the peace and to discipline agitators. The parallels with "squares" (*agorai*) and "dinners" (*deipnoi*) in Mark 12:38–39 and Luke 11:43 indicate that *synagogai* mean not buildings but public scenes and occasions in those passages. In all other Markan references, whether particular (1:21, 23, 29; 3:1; 6:2) or general (1:39) as well as their Lukan or Matthean parallels, the synagogues are village assemblies in which Jesus teaches and heals.

It seems clear, therefore, that "synagogues" in Galilee, as well as in diaspora communities in the first century C.E., were the assemblies of the local communities. And if they had more comprehensive concern for political-economic as well as religious affairs in the diaspora communities, then that was even more likely in Galilee, where the basic social form was semiautonomous village community.[42] As long as their tax revenues were forthcoming in timely fashion, the Roman imperial authorities and client-rulers left villages and town communities to run their own affairs. In those communities, comprised of a larger or smaller number of patriarchal households in relative continuity over the generations, communal relations and responsibilities were guided by traditional ways and customs, presumably informed by the age-old Mosaic covenantal principles. As recent investigations have recognized, early rabbinic texts simply assume that the people of a village or town are self-governing.

In the local communities of ancient Galilee, however, social forms were fairly simple, with little of the "structural differentiation" among religious, political, and economic affairs that developed in later industrial societies. Those who read rabbinic sources through the assumption that the synagogues were only religious institutions have difficulty discerning whether certain texts refer to "the synagogue itself" or to other community affairs. That confusion disappears immediately when we recognize that "local government is constantly identified in our sources with synagogue government."[43] The conclusion to which we are driven is that what is referred to by *synagōgē* in the Gospels and by *knesset* in early rabbinic literature was the village or town assembly, which was the basic social form of communal cohesion and self-government in local communities. Adaptations of this basic social form then appear in communities of Jews from particular locations now resident in a city to which they had recently moved and who associated with each other, for example, "the assembly of the Tyrians" in Sepphoris.

Limited sources make it impossible to attain a very precise picture of the various activities, patterns, and leadership of such local assemblies. Because the fundamental social forms in a traditional agrarian society such as Galilee were so conservative, that is, retained a high degree of stability from generation to generation and from area to area, it may be possible to extrapolate from later rabbinic sources and inscriptions found in the Hauran area to the east of Galilee to the situation in first-century Galilean villages.

Several early rabbinic passages refer to Monday and Thursday as the "days of assembly" in the villages (e.g., *m. Meg* 1:1). Those days were also therefore the days on which courts convened, since a village court (*bet din*) was constituted from the local assembly (*m. Ketub.* 1:1; *t. Ta'an.* 2:4). This is also why the Torah was to be "read" (recited) on those same days, the "days of assembly," for that was when the people of a village or town congregated for just such purposes (*m. Meg* 3:6, 4:1) — and also helps explain the connection between "reading the Torah" and "municipal institutions" that otherwise puzzles modern scholars. And the "days of assembly" were also the times to declare public fast days, on which public prayer was conducted (in the assembly) in the "town courtyard" (*m. Ta'an.* 2:9). The people may have taken such occasions to engage in selling and bartering as well.[44]

The more abundant information available on the leadership of these local assemblies also illuminates some of their other activities and responsibilities, including more mundane matters of local community life. Some variation is only to be expected considering the diversity of our sources, the range of time over which they are spread, and regional differences. Nevertheless it is still possible to discern some common patterns in community leadership and their responsibilities. The *rosh ha-knesset* or *archisynagogos*, of which there was often more than one (Mark 5:22, 35–38; Acts 13:15), would appear to have been a local head-man or presiding officer — and not a "ruler of the synagogue" in the usual mistranslation of New Testament texts. Rabbinic texts often refer to both *parnasim* and *gabbaim*, whose principal responsibilities appear to have been collection of goods and their distribution to the poor (e.g., *m. Pe'a* 8:7; *m. Dem.* 3:1).[45] These local "treasurers," who usually operated in twos and threes, were clearly different from the "tax collectors" (*moksin*) sent out from (the seat of Roman government) in the cities. Judean documents from Bar Kokhba times have *parnasim* leasing out land (possibly for the village) and certifying ownership of an ox to prevent its confiscation.[46] In addition to tending to social welfare and public works, these "magistrates" are also represented by early rabbinic sources as carrying out the orders of the local "house of judgment." Presumably they are the representatives, leading officers, and/or executive officers of the local assembly and/or court.[47]

Other early rabbinic texts have the *hazzan* of the assembly carrying out the orders of the court, for example, administering the beating ordered by the "house of judgment" (*m. Mak.* 3:12). The *hazzan* also apparently facilitated or led religious ceremonies. The duties of the *hyperetes* who takes charge of the scroll and signals for speakers or responses in Luke's story of Jesus in the assembly at Nazareth seems comparable (Luke 4:16–20). There is no need to imagine two different local officers with the same name, one secular and the other religious, for there was no separation between civil government and religion. Nor should we imagine that the *hazzan* was religious while the *parnasim* and *gabbaim* were civil officers, for the latter were simply facilitating the traditional divinely mandated (biblical) provisions for economic justice and social welfare. Presumably the *archontes* (magistrates) and *presbuteroi* (elders) in other texts refer to local leaders with similarly general functions and responsibilities.[48] Josephus would appear to be alluding to traditional patterns of local leadership when he claims to have structured the government of Galilee during the great revolt of 66–67 with "seven men in each town to adjudicate upon petty disputes" (*B.J.* 2:570–71).

Portrayal of local leadership and responsibilities in rabbinic texts is paralleled by inscriptions found in Syrian villages in late antiquity. These inscriptions represent multiple officers, whose names vary from place to place, but who all carry out similar responsibilities. Operating in groups of from two to seven, they tend to the finances of the village (or the local god), supervise public works such as constructing a gate or public building, or repair of the waterworks, or regulation of the local market. Significantly, even two generations ago, scholars of antiquity recognized that "the religious cult of an ancient community played so important a part in the life of that community that there can have existed no sharp line of division between an official of the cult and an officer charged with ordinary municipal matters."[49] These parallels from villages and towns in the Hauran, just to the east of Galilee, confirm the picture of the leadership of village assemblies in Galilee obtained from rabbinic passages.[50] The relatively autonomous villages maintained their traditional community life and customs within a local democratic pattern of an assembly with its officers responsible for supervising communal finances, public works such as gates and water supply, and religious celebrations. The similarities between Galilee and the Hauran and between earlier Jewish literature such as Judith and Susanna and later rabbinic texts indicate that there was a continuity of patterns across regions and centuries. Such evidence supports the conclusion that the synagogue in first-century Galilee was the local village assembly and that its functions were local self-government and community celebrations and cohesion.

It may be obvious by now that the Pharisees and rabbis do not belong to this reconstruction of the Galilean synagogues as the assemblies of local communities. The old synthetic Christian theological construct of ancient Judaism that pictured the Pharisees and their supposed successors the rabbis as the leaders of the synagogues persists in Christian constructions of both the synagogue and Galilee.[51] Recent critical studies by Jewish scholars, however, make it abundantly clear that far from having been the leaders of the synagogues, the rabbis had little involvement with them until well after the Late Roman period.[52]

According to the usual historical reconstructions, the rabbis did not move to Galilee until after the Bar Kokhba Revolt. Although they located first in the towns of Usha and Beth Shearim on the western frontier of Galilee, most of them became established in Sepphoris and Tiberias by the third century. In Galilee as in Yavneh, they were heavily absorbed in their own academies, socially and religiously as well as intellectually. There is no evidence that the second-century rabbis were even interested in being the "leaders of Jewry."[53] Although in their first few generations in Galilee they lived in certain towns or villages, they apparently were not dispersed into many villages, where they could have been members of a local synagogue (*bene ha-knesset*). Nor were they concerned about village affairs. Remarkably few of their decisions dealt with civil cases.[54] Indeed, the sages apparently held the *'am ha-'aretz*, the peasantry, in contempt, a disdain that was likely mutual. "Morning sleep and midday wine and children's talk and sitting in the assemblies of the peasants drive a man out of the world" (*m. 'Abot* 3:11). The early rabbis made no effort to reach out to the villagers. "They had their own organizations [*havurot*], modes of piety, and way of life."[55]

From the mid-third century on, the rabbis appear more frequently in connection with the synagogues. Yet their actual involvement in synagogue activities remains sporadic and limited in scope.[56] Most cases of their connection with a synagogue are outside of Galilee altogether or in the cities of Sepphoris and Tiberias. In one case, at a synagogue in Tiberias, far from being involved in the congregation, the rabbi complained about the economic demands of the patriarch which stood in competition with those of the rabbis for the people's donations (*y. Sanh.* 2,6,20d). Rabbinic literature itself offers several cases of their conflict with local assemblies, for example, over practices of translation of scripture. Features of the synagogue buildings, from their entrances to their decor, run counter to rabbinic rulings. Several sources, including the Theodosian Code, mention synagogue functionaries in late antiquity, but the rabbis are not among them.[57] One interesting aspect of the slowly evolving relationship between the later rabbis and the synagogues is that as the latter developed more elaborate liturgical activities and orientation, the rabbis took more of an interest.[58]

In sum, the rabbis were not involved in the synagogues of the Galilean villages because they were not members of those local communities. They did not seek or develop influence over the local assemblies and their buildings because they were not agents of the state or possessed of other political-economic power or political-religious authority by which they could control local civic and religious affairs.

If the rabbis were neither leaders of nor influential in the local synagogues of Galilee, then it would be difficult to argue that their supposed predecessors, the Pharisees, were. One can hardly rely on the statement by Luke, writing from some distance, that "Pharisees and law-teachers...had come from every village of Galilee and Judea and from Jerusalem" (Luke 5:17). Most critical reconstructions of the Pharisees have them based and active primarily in Jerusalem. The statements that they look for deference in public and seats of honor at feasts and assemblies (Mark 12:38–39; Luke 11:43) suggest periodic visits to villages and towns, as might be expected from those whose social role has recently been constructed as "retainers" of the temple-state in Jerusalem.[59]

The discourse against the scribes and Pharisees in Matthew 23 has been the principal basis for arguments that the Pharisees were leaders of "synagogues" parallel with Matthew's "church."[60] In both his framing of this discourse and his general treatment of the Pharisees, however, Matthew has them solidly based in Jerusalem and closely associated with the high priests and rulers (Matt. 23:37–39, 15:1, 21:45, 27:62). Moreover, if "Moses' seat" (in Matt. 23:2) was simply symbolic of authoritative interpretation of Torah, its focus is centralized and official, not diffuse and locally based. If at the time of Matthew it already referred to a chair on which the scroll of the Torah was placed, then the saying in Matthew would appear to indict the scribes and Pharisees for placing themselves in the place of the Torah (cf. their displacement of the basic "commandment of God" with their own "traditions of the elders" in Mark 7:2–13).

Other than the passages just mentioned, the synoptic Gospel traditions do not connect with Pharisees with synagogues. Mark 1:21–22 suggests only that the people were familiar with the scribes' social function, not that the scribes taught in the local assemblies. Scribes and Pharisees do not appear in other stories or sayings mentioning synagogues, such as Mark 1:23–29, 39; 6:1–6; 13:9–10 (and parallels). Among the ten "controversy" or "pronouncement" stories in Mark 1–10 in which the scribes and/or Pharisees oppose Jesus, only in one do they appear at a local assembly. In short, the synoptic Gospels portray Jesus as teaching and healing in the synagogues, with the Pharisees as representatives of Jerusalem.

Chapter 7

LANGUAGES AND CULTURAL TRADITIONS

The only phenomenon with which writing has always been concomitant is the creation of cities and empires, that is the integration of large numbers of individuals into a political system, and their grading into castes or classes.

— CLAUDE LÉVI-STRAUSS

A provincial community would in general have had no practical need for more than a limited number of people capable of conversing in one of the dominant languages.

— WILLIAM V. HARRIS

Constructions of culture in Galilee have depended heavily on estimates or assumptions about the language used by Galileans. Treatments of culture in Galilee, moreover, have often been couched in terms of an essentialism that understands language as a direct expression of a distinctive cultural essence. The latter also often is assumed to constitute the cultural identity of the people who use the language: Aramaic or Hebrew was an expression of Judaism and Jewishness, and, by contrast, Greek was an expression of Hellenism and being Hellenistic, cosmopolitan, philosophical. Thus evidence of Aramaic and/or Hebrew justifies the conclusion that the people continued in their traditional Jewish culture and identity, while evidence of Greek indicates that the people had acquired Hellenistic culture more generally, for example, that they were cosmopolitan and acquainted with popular philosophy. Recent recognition that the presence in a given area of Greek language is a "useless barometer of Greek culture" may help jolt biblical scholars and archaeologists out of their essentialist assumptions.[1]

Surveys of language use in Galilee have been problematic in other ways as well. The main question asked has been what languages were used and by what relative proportion or percentage of the populace. Insufficient attention has been given to class and regional variation. Although Galilee is often differentiated from Judea with regard to Hebrew and Aramaic in late second-temple times, it is usually simply lumped together with Judea in most surveys of languages. Their divergent historical development suggests that there may have been significant differences between Judea and Galilee in language usage, just as there would have been language differences between cities and villages within Galilee. And until recently little attention has been devoted to the use of multiple languages by the same people and the relationship among those languages.

Moreover, because the principal sources available are literature and inscriptions, treatment of languages has, in effect, been mainly of written use of language by the literate. Little attention has been given to spoken languages, much less to how the evidence of literature or inscriptions may be related to the question of spoken language. Even though non- or quasiliterate evidence has recently become available, little attention has been paid to what burial inscriptions or ostraca or graffiti may or may not indicate about spoken language. Even when some attention is given to differences between the educated elite and ordinary people, the move directly from inscriptions to language is still a projection of written language onto the everyday use of language. Previous treatment of languages in Galilee and Judea have thus in effect been of literacy in those languages. We are increasingly aware, however, that communications in Galilee as elsewhere in the Roman empire were largely oral, even among the literate. Writing had little importance except for certain functions of the elite. Study of language usage in Galilee must thus be refocused on spoken language, and the first step must be a consideration of the extent and function of literacy in order to highlight the predominant orality by contrast.

Literacy and Orality

It is understandable that scholars who devote their lives to the interpretation of ancient texts project their own assumptions of literacy, along with their bent toward the viewpoint of the literate elite, onto the areas and periods they study. The classic *Hellenistic Civilization* by W. W. Tarn, read closely by every generation since its original publication (in 1927), distinguishes not between the vast mass of illiterate and the tiny minority of literate, but between the highly educated and a much larger public who "had education enough to read greedily but not to read seriously."[2] What they devoured so greedily, Tarn declares, was "popular literature." If we intend "popular" to refer to the ordinary people of Greco-Roman antiquity, however, there was no such phenomenon as popular *literature*, since only a tiny fraction of the population was literate.

Anyone who has seen a copy of an ancient manuscript, written with no breaks between the words let alone the sentences, knows it would have been extremely difficult to read from one. Recent studies of ancient literacy conclude that only a very small number can be called literate, with a somewhat broader percentage (10–15%) able only to write slowly or not at all and to read short simple texts.[3] Of the estimated 100,000 people of Pompeii, the 2,000 or 3,000 who were literate included

> all members of the curial class, some but not all of the artisans and tradesmen, a markedly lower proportion of the women in the families of these latter groups, very few of the really poor, but a substantial number of slaves in the more prosperous households. In the countryside around the town, the proportion of literates will have been lower: there very few of the small farmers or of the farm slaves are likely to have been able to read and write.[4]

Previous claims that the prominence of public inscriptions in the cities of the ancient Mediterranean indicates a high degree of literacy among the populace have been challenged as the cognitive orientation of modern interpreters.[5] Public inscriptions, for example, of emperors' edicts and letters had a symbolic as well as practical function as what Suetonius calls "the imperial power's finest and oldest record" (*Vespasian*, 8). Such political-cultural "messages" on monumental stones and buildings were important media of Romanization, but not a measure of the people's literacy. Coins, the only mass-produced "texts" in antiquity, were another medium of political-cultural propaganda, not an index of literacy.[6] Similarly, graffiti turned out to be unreliable indicators of popular literacy. The numerous graffiti at a city such as Pompeii inform us rather about the erotic fantasies of some Pompeians.[7] Again, that slaves in wealthy households were literate and teachers of literacy indicates not widespread literacy but the opposite.[8] The principal producers of writing in antiquity were the administrations of the Hellenistic and Roman empires. The central regime directed and controlled its provincial officers and army via letters and decrees. The history of literacy, in fact, centers upon the cohesion and power of the political elite.[9]

In contrast to modern literate societies, the peoples of the Roman empire did not need literacy to carry on their relatively advanced-level civilization. Communications of all sorts were oral, mostly face to face and in public gatherings. Well-developed "oral technologies" enabled them "to retain large quantities of information about not only the heroic deeds of the past but also 'technical knowledge'" such as navigation, agriculture, and the calendar.[10] On religious matters, in relation to the unknown, people would consult nonwritten "texts" such as oracles and the flight patterns of birds — or perhaps their entrails. Individuals and groups even knew sacred writing, such as inscriptions on amulets or holy texts, but their function did not depend on literacy but on their awe-inspiring mediatory or sacred symbolic value.

Perhaps especially because both Judaism and Christianity have centered around scriptures, the assumption has been common that ancient Judea and Galilee were highly literate.[11] Yet there is little evidence that the Galileans were different from other people of the Roman empire. The key references cited from rabbinic literature to attest widespread literacy in Galilee have simply been misunderstood according to the modern assumption of literacy.[12] Mishnah texts refer to the people not *reading* but *reciting* from memory, and with varying abilities, certain prayers and psalms (*m. Ber.* 4:3; *m. Bik.* 3:7; *m. Sukk.* 3:10). Rabbinic rulings and comments have also been wrongly taken to pertain to the general population. Rabbinic texts, however, probably do not reflect social practices beyond "the highly literate group within which the rabbinic texts were formed."[13] For example, the ruling about not reading by lamplight, juxtaposed with a ruling about a scribe (*m. Šabb.* 1:3) pertains to rabbinic circles themselves, not the Galilean peasantry generally. Far from suggesting wide literacy, rabbinic texts assume that parents taught their children orally the basic Israelite traditions. Although themselves literate, the rabbis could recite from memory not only "scriptural" traditions, but also the teachings of their mentors. In their schools, moreover, instruction would have been primarily oral.

As in the rest of the Roman empire, literacy in Judea and Galilee was concentrated among the political-cultural elite. The scribes and presumably the Pharisees, as a party of retainers, were the professional literate stratum of the temple-state in Jerusalem. Officers in the Herodian administration would also have been literate, although presumably in Greek instead of (or in addition to) Hebrew and Aramaic. In Galilee itself literacy would have been concentrated in the urban-based administration of Antipas during the time of Jesus and in rabbinic circles as well as the other elites of the cities later. It seems highly unlikely that many villagers were literate.

Written Languages in Galilee and Judea

The question of languages in Palestine in general and Galilee in particular becomes considerably more complicated when we attend to the kinds of issues considered by modern sociolinguistic study of multiple-language situations.[14] Two concepts in particular may be particularly appropriate to Palestine and Galilee in the context of the Roman empire. (1) *Bilingualism* or *multilingualism* involves the same people speaking (although not necessarily writing) more than one language, which may mean people picking up each others' home languages (such as from a merchant, ruler/subject, or other people along a frontier) or peoples with different home languages communicating across communities in a *lingua franca* that may be one of the home languages. Depending on the political and cultural power relations, one language may replace another as the home language used among friends and family.

(2) *Diglossia* involves the same people or community using two

different languages whose relative function is determined by social conventions and/or political power relations. Usually the "lower" one is the language of everyday life used by nearly everyone, while the "upper" language is used in formal speech and/or on formal occasions, such as religious activities, and perhaps in writing (usually by a literate elite in traditional societies of limited literacy). In situations of diglossia not everyone may know the "upper" language, which is usually learned through formal education, although the number of those who understand it will tend to be larger than those who speak and write it.

Considerations such as these may be helpful in reconceptualizing the question of languages in Galilee, in order both to draw some tentative conclusions about the probable relative use of Aramaic, Hebrew, and Greek, and to evaluate the evidence. With regard to the latter, for example, the "home languages" (in a situation of diglossia) or the less-prestigious language(s) (in a multilingual situation), although holding the tenacious loyalty of their users, may not be written (to any great extent), hence would not turn up in epigraphical remains (at least not in proportion to their actual usage). Similarly, taking names as a key to importance and frequency of language in a multilingual situation may be problematic, since native users of a home language may adopt a name or a second name in the politically dominant or more prestigious language.

With such complexities of the linguistic situation in mind, we can proceed to a genealogy of written languages in Palestine.[15] The vast majority of Hebrew biblical literature (now referred to as Biblical Hebrew) was composed by a literate elite in Jerusalem, or by exiles from Jerusalem, in what could be referred to as a Judean or Jerusalem Hebrew. Considering that Jerusalem was not an Israelite city prior to the monarchy, it is all the more likely that its standardized court language differed from the Hebrew spoken among the far-flung villages of Israel. Those differences would likely have increased with time, as the official language became fixed — and later sacred. The exile of the ruling class and literate elite to Babylon would only have exacerbated the differences. Popular language changes more rapidly during times of social-political upheaval, and the literate elite that composed Hebrew biblical literature during or after the exile were meanwhile influenced by the imperial Aramaic with which the Persian regime replaced Babylonian as the administrative *lingua franca*.[16]

The language of the postexilic biblical literature, often referred to as Late Biblical Hebrew, exhibits some significant changes over the earlier Biblical Hebrew. Presumably some commonality remained between this Late Biblical Hebrew and the spoken language in and around Jerusalem. The complaint (in Neh. 13:24) that some (prominent) Judeans who had made marriage alliances with (prominent families in) Ashdod "could not speak Judean" (presumably Judean Hebrew) implies that it was deemed normal — or at least was now official policy — to do so. The comment in the story of Ezra's reading the Torah to the people that it had to be *translated* in order to be understood (Neh. 8:1–8), on the other hand, suggests considerable difference between Late Biblical Hebrew and the ordinary language of the people (was it already some form of Aramaic?). Scribal and priestly circles, however, continued or revived Late Biblical Hebrew in the late third and mid-second centuries, as illustrated by the Hebrew portions of Ben Sira and the Dead Sea Scrolls written in Hebrew.

Mishnaic Hebrew has significant differences from Biblical Hebrew. Early literary witnesses to this language are some of the letters of Bar Kokhba found at Wadi Muraba'at, written between 132 and 135 c.e.,[17] and the Copper Scroll found at Qumran. Mishnaic Hebrew was thus apparently used for correspondence as well as more formal literature. The Mishnah itself, of course, compiled by the rabbis under the leadership of Judah the Prince around 200 c.e., is largely in this language as well. That the Mishnah consists of traditional teachings and rulings that had previously been cultivated in oral form indicates that Mishnaic Hebrew had also been the language at least of formal teaching in the rabbinic academies, a usage short of formal literature yet not necessarily a spoken language of everyday life.

Written Aramaic evolved from the Imperial Aramaic that became the prestigious official language of the Persian empire from Babylonia westward into the more localized later varieties of Middle Aramaic such as Syriac, Jewish Babylonian Aramaic (of the Talmud), and Mandaean. In comparison with the Biblical Aramaic of passages in Ezra and the first parts of Daniel, that of the *Genesis Apocryphon* and other Aramaic documents of the Dead Sea

Scrolls is closer to the western varieties of Middle Aramaic. These documents from Qumran thus suggest there was a wider Judean literature in Aramaic. Josephus, of course, wrote his *Jewish War* originally in Aramaic, but that was for fellow Jews "beyond the Euphrates and the inhabitants of Adiabene" (*B.J.* 1.3–6).

By the time of Josephus, of course, Greek had been the politically and culturally dominant language of the eastern Mediterranean for over three centuries — and, not surprisingly, he quickly translated his *Jewish War* into Greek. What had been imposed by the Hellenistic imperial successors of Alexander the Great was simply taken over by the Romans in the East. Jews in the Hellenistic diaspora had not only long since translated the Hebrew Bible into Greek, but were composing a richly varied literature not only in the Greek language but in Greek genres as well.[18] By the second century B.C.E. Jewish Greek literature was also being written in Palestine, particularly histories such as that by Eupolemus and the epitome of Jason of Cyrene known as 2 Maccabees.[19] Influence of Greek language in Jerusalem was part of the Hellenizing influence to which the Maccabean Revolt reacted, and within two generations after the Hasmoneans took over the high priesthood, "King" Alexander Janneus was issuing bilingual coins inscribed in Greek as well as Hebrew. As the Hasmoneans took control of Hellenistic cities, as well as areas such as Galilee, it is likely that the language of their administration was increasingly Greek. The many Hellenistic cities surrounding the traditional land of Israel had long since used Greek as their official language.

That Herod and his sons went over to purely Greek inscriptions on their coins is representative of the general move by these Roman client-rulers to a more complete Hellenization of their administration. With the political culture of Jerusalem, and later of Sepphoris and Tiberias, setting the tone, the Judean upper class, including the high-priestly families in Jerusalem, moved more and more to Greek in the decor of their mansions and their public and burial inscriptions.[20] At the level of the ruling elite, Jerusalem thus became well acquainted with Greek. Josephus needed help to put his histories into the appropriate Greek literary style, but he wrote his histories in or translated them into Greek himself. His polemic against his rival, Justus of Tiberias, under the patronage of the Herodian king Agrippa II, illustrates that Josephus had competitors in Jewish historiography in Greek based elsewhere in Palestine.

After so many generations as the language of political power and social prestige, Greek also became well established as the language of legal records and business dealings. As illustrated in the correspondence of Bar Kokhba found at Wadi Muraba'at, even in the struggle for independence of Roman rule, communications were conducted in Greek as well as Aramaic (in the first bundle of letters were six in Aramaic, two in Greek, one in Hebrew; the second set of documents consisted of four deeds in Hebrew, two in Aramaic, and fifteen papyri in Greek).[21] These letters are by no means in elegant Greek, but Simeon Bar Kokhba or his scribe and the readers corresponded in Greek. In fact, in the letter most specifically about special religious matters, an appeal for branches and citrons for "the citron celebration of the Jews," the author So[uma]ios (Simeon himself?) explains "this has been written in Greek because a desire has not been found to write in Hebrew," suggesting that writing in Hebrew would have been more difficult for him.[22]

We thus have solid evidence of Jewish literature as well as inscriptions and correspondence in three languages, Hebrew, Aramaic, and Greek in Palestine, particularly in Jerusalem, during late second-temple times and for the following century or two. Latin and other languages are much less in evidence.

Spoken Languages in Galilee and Judea

When we shift the focus to the language spoken among the people, where no direct evidence is available, the issues are far more complex, and the ways of evaluating indirect evidence are unclear and disputed. Even the rare statements in historical sources regarding what language is spoken in a given area are problematic. It is unclear, for example, whether *'ebraisti* in Greek refers to Hebrew or Aramaic. In a situation of diglossia or a *lingua franca* coexisting with home languages, the observer may have assumed that the language s/he heard was the language ordinarily spoken. Another obvious problem is that (some) people may have the ability to speak a certain language but ordinarily speak another.[23]

For Palestine in the Roman period, the question most broadly considered is the relative use of (some forms of) Aramaic, Hebrew, and Greek. While the currency and prominence of each must be considered in relationship with the others, the hypotheses about and evidence for each must be examined in succession.

Most scholars of language history in the Hellenistic and Roman periods believe that, prior and parallel to the emergence of Judean literature in Aramaic, there were local versions of Aramaic spoken among the people in and around Palestine. The consensus is that some Palestinian form(s) of Aramaic was the most commonly spoken language in Palestine, outside of the (Hellenistic) cities, that is. Even defenders of Mishnaic Hebrew as the more important spoken language in Judea itself believe that Aramaic was a close second among the people there.[24] In Galilee, Aramaic would have been the traditional spoken language of the people during Hellenistic times, continuing so after the Hasmoneans brought the area under Jerusalem control. With the successive Ptolemaic and Seleucid administrations in Sepphoris (as indicated in the Zenon papyri) Greek replaced Aramaic as the language of administration, but the traditional spoken language undoubtedly continued in everyday village life.

Official documents or business records may not be good evidence for spoken Aramaic since they will have been produced by professional scribes and/or for official purposes. Ostraca and inscriptions on ossuaries (boxes in which bones were reburied), however, may be more indicative, since Aramaic does not appear to have had the status of an archaic holy language, as did Hebrew. Ostraca from an Idumean town indicate that Aramaic was holding its own as a language of small local transactions.[25] The more discursive inscriptions warning would-be looters may be particularly good indications of Aramaic as common everyday language. Two examples from near Jerusalem: "This burial slot has been made for the bones of our fathers; it is two cubits long, and do not open it!" and "Whatever a man may find for his benefit in this ossuary is an offering to God from him who is within it."[26] The letters of Bar Kokhba found at Wadi Muraba'at, in which Aramaic is the most frequently used language, indicate that it continued as a language of correspondence and official business in Judea, at least. That continuing function of the language at the official and/or business level surely helped it maintain its own as a popularly spoken lan-

guage over the several generations during which Greek had been
the language of Herodian or Roman administration in Judea and
the rest of Palestine.[27] On the other hand, the documents from the
Cave of Letters were predominantly in Greek.[28]

One survey of the numerous Aramaic inscriptions from Galilee
concluded with the broad generalization that the area along Lake
Tiberias and the southern half of Lower Galilee were "bilingual"
(apparently Aramaic-Hebrew and Greek), while Upper Galilee,
which has only a few Greek inscriptions, was dominated by
Hebrew-Aramaic.[29] In order to be more useful in addressing
the question of spoken language, however, surveys of inscriptions could also raise questions of dating, the relative character
of the sites (e.g., city or village; public building or private house),
purpose (monumental, burial, dedicatory), class, and (relative) "literacy." Close attention could also be paid to historical geography.
If "the southern half of Lower Galilee" refers largely to sites in the
Jezreel Valley near Scythopolis, then combined with sites in and
around Tiberias the sample would be mainly one of Hellenistic
urban culture along the southeastern edges or frontier of Lower
Galilee.

Short of a more precise analysis, a survey that concludes that
"as a region, of all sites with epigraphic remains, about 40% report
Greek, 40% report Hebrew, and more than 50% report Aramaic"
may seriously underestimate the importance of Aramaic as a spoken language in Galilean villages, whether in late second-temple
times or late antiquity.[30] While the evidence is not particularly impressive given the elementary previous analysis, what little there
is supports the consensus that Aramaic was the most widely spoken language in Galilee and probably also in Judea during late
second-temple times and in Galilee through late antiquity.[31]

The extent to which Mishnaic Hebrew was spoken, including
its relation with spoken Aramaic, remains unclear and in dispute
even for late second-temple Judea itself. One can readily imagine
a renewed commitment to (Mishnaic) Hebrew emerging from the
Maccabean struggle against the Seleucid regime. Yet the hypothesis "that mishnaic Hebrew was a fully living spoken language in
Judaea at the time of the Maccabean revolt" and that it continued
until the third century C.E. is basically inferential.[32]

As with Aramaic, so with Hebrew as well, there is precious little evidence on which we can determine the extent and ways in which it was a spoken language. It is necessary to examine such evidence all the more carefully in terms of the particular context in which it was found and functioned, and its class and regional location and implications.

As evidence for Hebrew as an ordinary language in Palestine, previous treatments have pointed to both public inscriptions in Hebrew and inscriptions on ossuaries, boxes in which the bones of the (previously buried) deceased were reburied. Since ossuary inscriptions in Hebrew found on the Mount of Olives and elsewhere in and around Jerusalem (e.g., "Mary our mother"; "Salome the proselyte"; "John the craftsman") were supposedly "intended for the family," they are taken to indicate that "Hebrew was a language of daily communication."[33] The reburial of bones, however, was surely the most solemn and holy of contexts, for which a sacred — and perhaps archaic — language would be used.[34] The location of these inscriptions in and around Jerusalem, moreover, is hardly good evidence for village life in Judea or Galilee, given the historical class and regional differences. Public and/or monumental inscriptions would appear to be even less reliable as an indicator of ordinary language usage. Whether it be the inscription on the Tomb of James just east of the Temple Mount or "Belonging to the Place of Trumpeting..." inscribed on a stone found at the southwest corner of the temple enclosure, such inscriptions are unlikely to have reflected the language habits of ordinary people. One need consider only the Latin inscriptions on public and university buildings in the United States to imagine the awe-inspiring function of formal, official, and/or archaic language of monumental inscriptions, whether for the social-cultural elite that frequent such monuments or for the ordinary people who make occasional "pilgrimages" to such sacred sites.

Fragments of biblical writings in Hebrew from Masada, although precisely datable because of the Roman conquest of the fortress, like the storage jars for "offerings" found there, again suggest traditional sacred usage rather than everyday language. Nor do the (minority of) letters of Bar Kokhba and other documents written in Hebrew found at Wadi Muraba'at provide good evidence for Hebrew as a commonly spoken language in Palestine.[35] The biblical fragments in Hebrew, plus a phylactery, a prayer from a burial, two bills of divorce, four deeds, five real-estate transactions, twelve contracts about rental of fields, are all either examples of sacred and/or scribal language. If anything, that the vast majority of the documents from Wadi Muraba'at and Nahal Hever are in either Greek or Aramaic would point to those languages as the more likely to have been spoken. In fact, the explanation in one letter written in Greek that "a desire has not been found to write in Hebrew" is suggestive: Greek was easier for the scribe and/or dictator of the letter, Hebrew less familiar (even if desirable for ideological reasons). The presence of documents in Hebrew among the Bar Kokhba correspondence, moreover, should be greeted with caution, since a sudden upsurge of interest in Hebrew may have been stimulated by the struggle for independence.[36]

That the Mishnah includes many teachings of earlier scribes and Pharisees suggests that Mishnaic Hebrew was used orally at least in formal instruction by the (schools of) the scribal and Pharisaic predecessors of the rabbis in late second-temple Judea. The Pharisaic "traditions of the elders" (mentioned in Josephus, *Ant.* 13.296–98; Mark 7:1–13) may thus have been cultivated orally in Mishnaic Hebrew. Yet one cannot conclude from such oral teaching and transmission of traditions that even the Pharisees themselves were using Mishnaic Hebrew in everyday life, let alone that it was a common spoken language of other Judeans.

Once we become aware of the significant historical regional differences within Palestine, it is evident that all of the potential evidence just examined pertains mainly to Jerusalem and possibly to the Judean environs of the city but not necessarily to wider areas of Palestine. For Galilee itself the Mishnah itself may provide more promising indications. Indeed, a recent hypothesis has Mishnaic Hebrew as the traditional colloquial dialect of Galilee, in continuity with the "Israelian Hebrew" of certain northern traditions included in biblical literature that is otherwise largely in Judean or Jerusalem Hebrew.[37]

Since it seems clear that the rabbinic circles who produced Mishnaic materials came from Judea to Galilee following the Bar Kokhba revolt (132–35 C.E.), the contents of the Mishnah cannot be used as indicators of language in Galilee until rabbinic circles were well established there, around 200 — having been influenced by Galilean colloquial Mishnaic Hebrew (required by Rendsburg's hypothesis) or having consolidated their own Mishnaic Hebrew amid the predominant Aramaic and Greek. More important for the question of the languages spoken among the Galilean people, however, we run into questions of the social strata for whom statements in the Mishnah may have been relevant. The scribal or Pharisaic predecessors of the rabbis may have used Hebrew, although they would presumably have used Aramaic in Galilee to communicate with people there. When the rabbis moved to Galilee following the Bar Kokhba Revolt, they probably continued their use of Mishnaic Hebrew, at least in teaching and transmission of traditions. For rabbinic circles, then, Hebrew would have been the upper language in a situation of diglossia. Rabbinic references to languages provide a few windows onto that situation. The statement about bills of divorce being in Greek or Hebrew (*m. Git.* 9:8), for example, indicates the preferences and practices among the circles of sages, but not necessarily those of the ordinary people. It pertains to a formal, legal document, moreover, not to ordinary speech habits.[38]

A passage often cited as evidence that Hebrew was still spoken (*Sifre Deut.* 26:4) suggests that it was at that point still being preserved but only in a situation that sociolinguists would call "language loyalty." "When the toddler begins to speak, his father shall talk to him in the Holy Tongue and teach him the Law." The child is assumed to have begun to talk in another language (presumably Aramaic). Also assumed is that only the father is carrying on the "Holy Tongue." Yet the teaching appears to be more than simply reciting the Law in the sacred language, but a wider range of "language preservation." There is no reason to believe, however, that this Mishnaic Hebrew was being maintained in circles much wider than those for whom rabbinic teaching was directed, and that the matter is mentioned at all suggests that even among those circles insufficient attention was being devoted to the preservation of the Holy Tongue. Judah the Patriarch is quoted as having said: "Why [use] Aramaic [*sursi*] in the Land of Israel? Either *leshon haqqodesh* ["the language of holiness," i.e., Hebrew] or Greek" (*b. B. Qam.* 82b–83a). That is, to Judah's mind it would have made more sense for Jews either to speak the traditional holy language of Hebrew or the language of the politically dominant culture in the eastern Roman empire, Greek. Since most Israelites in Galilee at the time were (presumably) using Aramaic, apparently the emergent rabbinic class and allied sections of the population were also speaking Aramaic. Mishnaic Hebrew is thought to have died out as a spoken language in the third century, although a recent study contends that it must have continued several generations more in rabbinic oral instruction.

Most important to assess critically are the extent and the ways Greek was used as a spoken language, due to the effect it was supposedly having on the traditional culture of Galilee and Judea. The increasing supply of Greek inscriptions found in the Jerusalem area and elsewhere have been taken as more or less direct indications of spoken language among the people generally. As with the Aramaic and Hebrew inscriptions, however, adequate assessment for implications about spoken language will require more comprehensive critical analysis in terms of function, location, literacy, and class and regional differences. Prior to such analysis, only a few cautious probes and highly tentative conclusions are possible.

Public inscriptions are not good evidence for spoken language among the ordinary people. The warning in Greek and Latin inscribed in the Jerusalem Temple that "no gentile shall enter inward of the partition and barrier surrounding the sanctuary"[39] was obviously directed to outsiders who knew (one of) those languages. Even the inscription by the Seleucid emperors Antiochus III (223–187 B.C.E.) and Seleucus IV (187–175 B.C.E.) from Hephzibah in Scythopolis ordering that copies be set up "in the surrounding villages" does not mean that the peasants could speak, much less read, Greek.

It is indeed striking that two-thirds of the ossuary inscriptions found largely in and around Jerusalem from late second-temple times are in Greek. Greek had long since been the language of political power and social-cultural prestige in the eastern Mediterranean. As noted above, the Hasmoneans and particularly Herod made it the language of administration, with the corresponding impact on life in and around the royal court and even among the high-priestly and other powerful families who were Herodian clients. Moreover, as encouraged first by the Hasmoneans and then much more aggressively by Herod, Jerusalem with its Temple, rebuilt in grand scale and style by Herod, had become the center of international Jewry. Many pilgrims came for shorter or longer sojourns from diaspora communities in Hellenistic cities around the eastern Mediterranean. Thus the large percentage of ossuary inscriptions probably do indicate that most of the wealthy and powerful and their clients knew and used a good bit of Greek, while retaining Aramaic as their original "home language." Since Greek was the language of prestige, it would likely be used for special occasions and purposes such as reburial.

More difficult to determine would be the relative use of Greek and Aramaic in everyday life among upper-class families in Jerusalem.[40] In their temple and other ritual roles the high priests, like the ordinary priests, presumably would have continued using Hebrew. Until we know the relative demographic range of the ossuaries, however, we cannot move directly to conclusions about ordinary people in Jerusalem, much less in the villages of Judea.[41] On the other hand, with so many Greek-speaking Jews from the diaspora and nearby Hellenistic cities (and Gentiles) in Jerusalem, there would have been no lack of spoken Greek in the city. It is not surprising to find a number of "Hellenists (Greek-speakers)" playing an important role in a renewal movement, and opposed by yet other groups of Greek-speaking Jews in Jerusalem, "the assembly of the Freedmen, Cyrenians, Alexandrians, and others from Cilicia and Asia" (Acts 6:9).

Previous treatments of languages in Palestine have tended to allow for greater penetration of Greek into Galilee than into Judea proper — perhaps because of the longer period during which Galilee had been under Ptolemaic or Seleucid imperial administration and the lack of anything corresponding to the Maccabean Revolt in Judea. More problematic recently have been the broad surveys of inscriptions that do not consider critically the kinds of sites from which they come in the wider context of the historical geography of Galilee. In particular, the large number of burial inscriptions in Greek (196) from Beth Shearim are included without distinction with isolated Greek inscriptions from other sites. Moreover, comparisons are made with the overall number of Aramaic or Hebrew inscriptions (which appear in very limited numbers in particular Galilean sites).[42]

Beth Shearim was hardly a typical village, however, and it is unclear when it would have been appropriate to include it as part of Galilee. Judging from Josephus's works, the "village" of Besara, near the southwestern frontier of Galilee, must have been an administrative base for the rulers who enjoyed the revenues generated from the royal estates in the Great Plain. During the middle of the first century C.E. (some of) "the grain belonging to Queen Berenice was collected from the neighboring villages and stored in Besara" (*Vita* 118–19). After the Bar Kokhba Revolt, Beth Shearim became one of the towns where a circle of rabbis including Judah the Prince set up an academy for a time, before becoming established in the city of Sepphoris. In the early third century Judah the Prince, who had established such power and influence in Galilee that Origen compared him to a "king" (*Ep. ad Afric.* 20, 14), as well as wide influence among diaspora communities and who had spearheaded the compilation of the Mishnah, was buried in Beth Shearim. Soon thereafter and into the fourth century, Beth Shearim became a privileged burial site where the bones of thousands of (presumably well-off) Jews from the diaspora were taken for reinterment.[43] The hundreds of Greek ossuary inscriptions from the necropolis of Beth Shearim (which comprise 80% of the inscriptions there) are thus not representative of life and language in Galilean villages.[44]

To contribute much to the question of spoken language in Galilee, analysis of Greek inscriptions would have to be more precise and sensitive to historical social context and to bi- or multilingual and diglossia situations, as noted above with regard to Aramaic inscriptions. Particularly important would be separate consideration of the situation in Sepphoris and Tiberias, where the Herodian and later the Roman administrations would have used Greek, with a corresponding impact on everyday speech. By early second century, of course, these cities were more fully Hellenistic and Romanized. There we would expect a considerable percentage of the residents, and not simply the upper strata, including the educated elite such as the rabbis, to have spoken Greek, with many having been bilingual. Presumably the height of Greek as the language of political power and social prestige, and its influence on village life, would have been during the second century C.E., after all of Lower Galilee was "urbanized" under one or the other city's control. In the villages of Upper Galilee, as archaeologists have pointed out, only a few Greek inscriptions have surfaced, in contrast with many in Aramaic and/or Hebrew. That strongly suggests that little Greek was spoken in that more mountainous area further from the cities. Yet once we remove inappropriate evidence such as the numerous Greek ossuary inscriptions at Beth Shearim from the pool of evidence pertaining to the villages of Lower Galilee, and particularly if we consider separately the sites close to Tiberias, there is much less of an indication that Greek was an everyday language in the rest of Lower Galilee. Pidgin Greek may have been common, but a bilingual situation seems unlikely given evidence now available.[45]

Cultural Traditions

Some of the same problems entailed in previous treatments of languages in Galilee also attend standard assumptions about Galilean culture. Assumptions that only high culture commands loyalty become tied up with certain modern religious and/or political interests in the standard dichotomy of Jewish versus Hellenistic, Hebrew biblical language and culture over against Greek language and culture.

> In the context of the first century C.E., both Greek and Biblical Hebrew stood for a rich cultural content, each in its own way. Mishnaic Hebrew stood for the values and folklore of Judaean Jewry. But neither literary nor spoken Aramaic carried in the world of first-century Palestine any cultural message. This was before the time of cultural resistance of the East to Roman-Hellenistic civilization and the emergence of national literary languages out of middle Aramaic. Aramaic was a means of communication, no more. It commanded no loyalty.[46]

As noted above (end of chapter 5), however, popular resistance to the rule of Rome and its clients preceded the appearance of resistance at the literary level, in Galilee at least. That popular resistance, moreover, appears to have been rooted in Israelite and other Galilean cultural traditions. And, given the consensus that Aramaic was the principal spoken language in Galilee, then those traditions were carried in Aramaic as well as in Hebrew.

Early rabbinic literature provides repeated reminders of the regional differences between Galileans and Judeans. It may not be surprising, given that Galilee was brought under the rule of the temple-state only at the very end of the second century B.C.E., that Galileans were accused of "ignorance" with regard to heave-offerings and "things devoted to the priests" (*m. Ned.* 2:4). With regard to a number of matters, such as marriage, measures, land-tenancy, and observance of the sabbath and festivals, customs and practices in Galilee differed from those in Judea (e.g., *m. Ketub.* 13:10; *m. Ter.* 10:8; *m. Ketub.* 5:9; *m. Ḥul.* 11:2; *m. B. Bat.* 3:2; *m. Pesaḥ.* 4:5; *m. Ḥul.* 5:3). In addition to the regional differences between Galilee and Judea, there were regional differences within Galilee, such as agricultural customs dependent on differences in climate between the hill country and the basin around the lake (e.g., *m. B. Qam.* 10:9; *m. Seb.* 9:2). In their rulings on a number of issues, the early rabbis state repeatedly that they are simply deferring to "local custom," particularly with regard to agriculture (e.g., *m. B. Mes.* 4:11; 7:1; 9:1). Indeed, local custom could even override the Law and the rabbis' own rulings (*m. B. Mes.* 7:8).

Age-old indigenous local religious practices and attachments also persisted in Galilee. Unlike Judea, which had been dominated by the Temple and high priesthood in Jerusalem for centuries, Galilee was ruled by a series of imperial regimes and never developed a central sacred place. A number of literary references indicate a strong local or even regional attachment to Mount Tabor. In ancient times the tribes of Zebulun and Issachar gathered there to "offer the right sacrifices" (Deut. 33:19), and it was remembered as the place where Deborah and Barak had called those tribes in preparation for battle against the Canaanite kings (Judg. 4:6). Other references suggest that it may have been a traditional holy place where Canaanite kings and, later, Israelite kings established a royal fertility cult (Ps. 89:12; Hos. 5:1).[47] As noted (end of chapter 5), Galilean peasants fled to Mount Tabor as a refuge from the Roman reconquest of the area in 67 C.E. That it was still a sacred site, not simply an inaccessible hill, is suggested by a rabbinic reference to Tabor as the place where flares went up signaling the beginning of the new year (*t. Ros Has.* 2.2). The symbols found on a number of Upper Galilean synagogue buildings suggest a cultural survival of a traditional indigenous attachment to "holy sky god." The eagle appearing over the doors of the temple of Zeus-Jupiter in Kedesh, just across the frontier into Tyrian territory, suggests a Hellenistic overlay of the traditional Syrian Baal Shamin and offers a fascinating comparison.[48]

Besides such local cultural tradition, Israelite cultural traditions remained strong in Galilee. Once we are aware of the class and regional differences between the Galileans and the governing and scribal circles in Jerusalem, including the difference between the written form and the oral form of cultural traditions that constituted one aspect of those differences, however, the Israelite traditions can no longer be discussed simply in terms of "scripture" or "the Law." The distinction anthropologists often make between the "great tradition" and the "little traditions" may be of some help in formulating the issues. A "society" may develop cultural traditions at two levels: the traditions of origin and customary practice continue as a popular tradition cultivated orally in the villages, while specialists codify those same traditions in a standardized and centralized form as an official tradition, which is cultivated orally but perhaps also reduced to written form. Something like this distinction between official tradition and popular tradition may help explain the situation in Galilee as seen both in sources from the first century c.e. and in early rabbinic literature.[49]

Although some of the inhabitants of Galilean villages may have been of non-Israelite background, most of the Galileans must have been descendants of the northern Israelite tribes.[50] While living under a series of foreign imperial rulers, Israelite traditions such as the exodus/passover, Mosaic covenant (including sabbath observance), circumcision, and stories of Elijah would have been cultivated in the village communities of Galilee. Thus when the Hasmoneans incorporated Galilee under the jurisdiction of the Jerusalem temple-state, the Galileans were already living according to traditions and customs stemming from the same Israelite heritage as the "laws of the Judeans" (Josephus's phrase) that constituted the official code developed in Jerusalem.

The Israelite heritage as the popular tradition cultivated in the villages of Galilee surfaces at three points that can be discerned in our written sources. First is the movement led by Judas son of Hezekiah in the area around Sepphoris at the death of Herod. That this movement was informed by the popular tradition of "messianic movements" of which Saul, (the young) David, and Jeroboam were historical paradigms is evident from the other movements in Judea that took the same social form, headed by a popularly acclaimed (anointed) king.[51] Second is the prominence of Israelite traditions in the synoptic Gospels, particularly in the Synoptic Sayings Source Q and in Mark. Jesus appears as a prophet like Moses and Elijah (Mark 4–9), he declares and enacts the renewal of Israel (Luke/Q 13:28–29, 22:28–30), he reinvigorates Mosaic covenantal instruction (Luke/Q 6:20–49), and pronounces prophecies against the Temple and high priesthood, like the earlier Israelite prophets (Luke/Q 13:34–35; Mark 12:1–9, 13:1).

The third appearance of Israelite traditions comes in Josephus's narratives of certain incidents involving Galileans. When the emperor Gaius (Caligula) ordered the Legate of Syria to mount a huge military expedition through Galilee into Judea to install his statue in the Temple, large numbers of Galileans joined in (what was in effect) a peasant strike, refusing to sow their crops, on which the empire depended for its tribute (*B.J.* 2.184–203; *Ant.* 18.261–88; cf. Philo, *Leg.* 188–249). The motives of the Galileans may need to be sorted out from the highly apologetic accounts of Josephus (and of Philo), so we may not infer that they were necessarily acting in defense of the Temple. Yet they were certainly acting in defense of the Mosaic decalogue. In the course of his attempt to control the chaotic outbursts of the great revolt in Galilee in 66–67 c.e., Josephus dealt with a move to circumcise two royal officials of Agrippa II as a condition of their remaining in Galilee. The popular party were insisting that the strangers should conform to "the customs" of the Galileans, that is, circumcision, a key symbol of belonging to the covenant people of Israel (*Vita* 112–13, 149). In such incidents, we can see Galileans taking a stand on the basis of their Israelite covenantal traditions at times of crisis and acute threat to their traditional way of life.

Far more explicitly than the Galilean villagers' cultivation of popular Israelite traditions is the rabbinic program of consolidating official Judean traditions following the two devastating wars in which the land and people had been ravaged by Roman military might. That such a large percentage of material in the Mishnah pertains to the Temple and priesthood indicates that the rabbis stood in continuity with the official scribal tradition in Jerusalem. Now they were engaged in a program of saving and perpetuating what had been the official tradition based in the Temple, only now without the actual Temple and the institutional base it had provided. By establishing mutually supportive circles of sages focused in academies, in which the traditions could become the basis for communal life of ever-widening circles of the descendants of Israel, they provided the social and ideological basis for perpetuation of the traditional way of life and resistance to assimilation into the culture sponsored by the empire.

JESUS AND THE RABBIS IN HISTORICAL SOCIAL CONTEXT

Jesus and the rabbis, of course, are not the only reasons for interest in Roman-period Galilee. Indeed, they could easily be viewed as an illustration or subset of broader issues. From the perspective of Roman imperial policy, Galilee was situated at a sensitive point along the eastern frontier vis-à-vis the Parthians. The maintenance of a sizable contingent of troops as well as of effective administration (i.e., public order) in such territories was a key to Roman policy in the east. The punitive Roman treatment of Galilee and Judea in 67–70 and the Roman devastation of Judea again in 132–135, and the resulting migration of sages and priests to Galilee, fit into the broader program of empire. Or Galilee would offer an excellent study of the impact of Roman imperial rule and the "civilizing" (pacifying) influence of "urbanization" that the Romans imposed on "backward" peoples in more remote areas among whom cities had not yet developed. Both Jesus and his movement and rabbinic circles might appear as illustrations of the ways in which subject peoples reacted and adjusted to the pressures of imperial rule and "urbanization."

The analysis above purposely focused on Galilee itself so that investigations of social relations, institutions, and historical dynamics would not be overly skewed by special interest in Jesus or the rabbis. Those investigations, more carefully, critically, and completely considering the results of archaeology and rabbinic studies than I had previously, have significantly affected my own understanding of Galilee.[1] For example, in contrast to the previous categories in which we attempted to comprehend the social-cultural changes Galilee was undergoing in Roman times, that is, the dichotomy between "Hellenistic" and "Jewish," two matters of particular importance have emerged. The theater in Sepphoris, the Roman client-ruler's palace in Tiberias, and the reconstitution of Sepphoris as Diocaesarea exemplify just how important Roman political culture became in first- and second-century Galilee. Closely related, moreover, is the importance of focusing on political-economic-cultural relations (e.g., between Roman imperial rule and the cities or between the administrative cities and the villages) rather than on cultural essences. If we then factor in the historical dimension, it becomes all the more striking how sudden and dramatic the impact of Antipas's rule must have been in Galilee and how dominant Hellenistic-Roman influences must have been in the cities where rabbinic circles established centers for the maintenance of Jewish cultural identity and the practice of Jewish traditions.

The investigations above have also convinced me that the regional approach pioneered by archaeologists is valid and important in discerning regional differences, and must be further developed and refined. Rabbinic literature and Josephus as well as archaeology indicate that there were cultural differences (related to topographical) among the regions of Galilee as well as within Palestine. Analysis of regional differences can be coordinated with analysis of political-economic relations and historical changes.

A final example of the ways these investigations have affected my understanding of Galilee is the importance of oral communication in social interaction and cultural expression and the continuing use of the indigenous Aramaic and Hebrew alongside or as an alternative to the more prestigious and officially dominant Greek. Greek language and culture clearly were influential, increasingly so during Roman times, but did not displace the indigenous languages, certainly not in the villages.

Since Galilee was the location in which the Jesus movement began and in which the rabbinic circles became established, however, and given the long-established academic division of labor, much of the historical importance of Galilee focuses on its being the context of these movements that resulted in world-historical religions. With that focus, therefore, we can sum up provisionally some of the general implications that emerge from the analyses in the chapters above.

Jesus and the rabbis emerged at very different points in the history of Galilee. Because so little source material is available for Galilee in general, and for the early Roman period in particular, the tendency is to draw a synchronic as well as synthetic picture of Galilee as a context in which to place a Jesus or the early rabbis. While the resulting picture of Galilee may be a fair representation of the cumulative effect of developments under Roman rule by the third century, it may blunt the sharp edges of the dramatic changes that were imposed on Galilee in late second-temple times.

Jesus and his movement emerged at the end of a series of developments that had a profound impact on life in Galilee. In successive generations, Galilee was incorporated into the temple-state by the Hasmonean high priesthood, invaded repeatedly by Roman armies, subjected by Herod, and finally ruled by Antipas, who (re)built two cities for his regime directly in Galilee. The impact of Antipas's massive city-building and Roman client-rule located in Galilee itself must have been sudden and dramatic. Jesus and his initial followers, who formed a movement rooted in villages, were from a generation struggling to adjust to and/or resist the dramatic changes that had so suddenly come upon their communities.

The rabbis, apparently descendants of earlier scribes and sages, moved to Galilee from Judea in the wake of a second major Roman devastation of a widespread popular revolt against Roman rule. The newcomers to Galilee had to adjust to displacement as well as to the tragic devastation of the society they had helped lead and guide according to the "tradition of the elders." They eventually concentrated in the Galilean cities that had become more completely Roman/Hellenized in the course of the second century. While located in the cities, however, they attempted to preserve the traditional Palestinian Jewish way of life in resistance to the homogenizing Roman-Hellenistic culture.

Jesus and His Movement

Investigations of the historical Jesus are only beginning to take the concrete historical social context into account. Earlier studies compared Jesus and his first followers only to an abstracted "sectarian Judaism," particularly the supposedly normative Pharisees and, since the discovery of the Dead Sea Scrolls in 1947, the Essenes or Qumran community.[2] Such literate groups comprised only a tiny fraction of Judean society and, as we now realize, were hardly representative of the ordinary people. Not until very recently did we attend to other *popular* movements with which Jesus and his movement could be compared.[3] Careful consideration of Jesus and his movement in the particular context of a Galilee more precisely discerned remains to be done.[4] At this point, all we can do is note how some of the principal portrayals of Jesus appear problematic when we attempt to place them in Galilee as discerned through the consideration of literary and material remains in the chapters above.

1. What were almost passing comments by an archaeologist about cosmopolitan influences in Lower Galilee and provisional interpretations of archaeological finds as evidence of urbanization there became the basis for constructions of Jesus as a Cynic-like countercultural sage in the midst of a cosmopolitan Hellenistic culture in Lower Galilee.[5] Review of the archaeological and literary evidence in chapter 2, however, suggests that there may have been little more than a thin veneer of cosmopolitan culture even in the cities of Lower Galilee in the early first century c.e.. Even more problematic in the case for a Cynic-like Jesus is the failure of its advocates to consider extra-Gospel evidence for how Galilean villagers may have responded to "influences" upon them from the newly rebuilt Sepphoris and the newly founded Tiberias. Critical consideration of Josephus's accounts of events in 4 b.c.e. and 66–67 c.e. in chapter 5 indicates a widespread and long-standing reaction against the urban-based rulers and their culture.

It is difficult, moreover, to understand how Cynic influence in particular would fit the specific circumstances of Galileans forced to adjust, both economically and culturally, to the recently intensified urban presence in their midst. We have the general sense that Cynic philosophers were indeed "unconventional" or "countercultural," challenging and even flouting the conventional culture and morality. That would better fit a situation of a long-standing conventional culture. Both Judean culture and Roman-Hellenistic culture, however, would have been relatively new in Galilee and (from the extremely fragmentary evidence we have reviewed above) present primarily in the capital cities. Over against which culture would a Galilean Cynic have been unconventional? The traditional mores and popular tradition of the villages, the relatively new official Judean traditions which Pharisees or other representatives of the official Judea centered in Jerusalem were likely pushing, or the Roman urban overlay so recently imposed in Sepphoris and perhaps Tiberias? In the Galilean context, the last two simply were not conventional established culture. The traditional Galilean way of life, on the other hand, was already being threatened by the disintegration of the basic social forms of family and village; attacks by caustic Cynic sages were hardly needed. Jesus and his movement would appear to have been "cynical" in a more "class-conscious" prophetic mode, about kings in their palaces and finery or fancy banquets among the elite (cf. Luke/Q 7:24–25, 14:16–24; Mark 6:17–29).

Nor is there reason to believe that Jesus and other low-level artisans and peasants were assimilating imperial and/or urban cosmopolitan cultural influences any more than were the rabbis later, who were even more exposed to those influences in Diocaesarea and Tiberias. In compiling the Mishnah, Judah the Patriarch provides a vivid illustration of preserving the traditional culture while playing imperial politics to the hilt on its own terms. For a leader of a popular movement, of course, actively renewing the traditional culture would likely have meant more oppositional politics, by contrast with Judah's cultivating friends in high imperial positions.

2. For Jesus and his first followers to have launched a radical itinerant lifestyle of "wandering charismatics" requires a Galilee with a number of people who are poised to become rootless in response to a compelling call or challenge, that is, individuals who are already rootless.[6] That there was the requisite number of such people makes sense if one assumes an overburdened populace *and* a somewhat overpopulated Galilee (Josephus's exaggerated image of villages burgeoning with 15,000 people each). The reports on archaeological sites reviewed indicated that not only the population of already settled sites but also the number of sites were expanding during the early Roman period. That is, Galilee was not already "full" of people; there was room for people cut loose

from their land and villages to relocate. Yes, there were movable people, but they had other good options more in accord with traditional values than those posited by the hypothesis of an itinerant individualist lifestyle.

An alternative way of construing the situation would appear to fit the evidence for the political-economic situation of first-century Galilee better. Certain areas of Galilee must have suffered extreme social trauma during the Roman conquests and prolonged civil wars between rival Roman and Hasmonean factions during the first-century B.C.E. and again at the Roman repression of the insurrection following the death of Herod in 4 B.C.E. Then the massive urban building program of Antipas, following upon Herod's heavy taxation and compounded by the tribute owed to Rome (and, supposedly, tithes and offerings to Jerusalem), must have made a dramatic and sudden economic impact on households and villages.[7] The economic impact of Antipas's building programs following upon Herod's heavy taxation would likely have left many producer-households seriously in debt. Expansion of settlements would fit the same situation, with either Herod or Antipas or both managing the expansion of settlements in order to expand their economic base (cf. Herod's practice in Batanaea and Trachonitis, and Antipas's means of populating Tiberias; *Ant.* 17.23–26, 18.36–37).

Jesus' call for the mutual cancellation of debts (Luke/Q 11:2–4; cf. Matt. 18:23–34) and for people to respond to each other's acute distress and basic needs (Luke/Q 6:27–36, 12:22–31) would fit handily into such a situation whether or not one construes it simply as teaching or as part of a more concrete program of local community renewal. What is distinctive about the Gospel tradition's representation of Jesus' teaching is not an itinerant radical individualism, but the renewal or revitalization of local community (and marriage/family; e.g., Mark 10:1–45; Luke/Q 6:20–49, 22:28–30). The Gospel traditions of Jesus simply do not fit a situation of the disappearance of the traditional community life (in the basic social form, the village) in which a radical individual lifestyle was a viable alternative. They rather fit a situation in which the traditional covenantal way of life based on reciprocity in village communities was threatened, such that Galilean villagers responded to Jesus' attempt at a renewal of the Mosaic covenantal cooperation and reciprocity.

We thus cannot return to the overly simple essentialist categories of "Jesus and Judaism," much less the opposition "Jesus versus Judaism."[8] Those who still want to retain the term "Judaism" have been forced to resort to serious qualifiers, such as "formative" (since what later became identified as "Judaism" had not emerged yet in late second-temple times) or to use the plural, "Judaisms" (because the particular communities or ideas reflected in our sources were so richly diverse). For some time we have been aware of the differences among Pharisees, Sadducees, and Essenes. More recently we have realized that ordinary Judeans did not necessarily share the views of the Pharisees and often came into conflict with the priestly aristocracy. Closer attention to the literary and material sources for Galilee now forces us to take regional differences into account as well.

The regional differences between Galilee and Jerusalem (and Judea) were rooted in many centuries of separate historical development prior to the Hasmonean takeover. Galilee was then under Jerusalem rule, presumably with exposure to the Torah or "laws of the Judeans" and some sort of relations with the Temple, for only a hundred years before the death of Herod and the birth of Jesus. There is no literary or material evidence and little historical likelihood — given the political crises raging in Jerusalem, Palestine, and the Roman empire during the first two-thirds of the first century B.C.E. — that over such a short period of time traditional Israelite culture and local customs in Galilee had become conformed to what may have been standard in Jerusalem or Judea. It is highly doubtful that the high priesthood or its scribal "retainers" (including the Pharisees) would have been able to mount a program by which the Galileans could have been effectively "resocialized" into habitual loyalty to the Temple and the Torah (or the "laws of the Judeans").

The inhabitants of Galilee in late second-temple times appear to have been of Israelite heritage, for the main part, although the indications are admittedly indirect. Jesus and the initial members of his movement, from such villages as Nazareth, Cana, Capernaum, and Chorazin, appear to have been rooted squarely in Israelite traditions. There is no basis, therefore, in evidence for the identity of the Galileans or in the early strata of the Gospel tradition, for the claim that Jesus and/or the Jesus movement in the first three or four decades was somehow invoking judgment against "[all] Israel" or "Judaism."[9] Jesus and/or the early Jesus movement, at least those branches of the movement behind Mark and Q, were engaged in the renewal of Israel. This is evident once we relinquish the standard theologically determined paradigm of the "universalist" religion Christianity breaking with the "particularistic" religion Judaism and arrive at a more appropriate interpretation of passages such as Luke/Q 13:28–29, 13:34–35, and 22:28–30. Indeed, the last passage is a prophecy of the renewal of Israel, symbolized in the Twelve on thrones "doing justice for" the twelve tribes.[10] Far from condemning "all Israel," Jesus, in both Mark and Q, is engaged in the renewal of Israel.

Such a vision and program was fully consistent with a sharp opposition to the high-priestly rulers and the Jerusalem Temple in which they were based, as well as to Antipas in his palace in Tiberias. Not only is that opposition the dominant conflict in both the Gospel of Mark and the Q discourses, as well as in the Gospel traditions behind them (Mark 6:17–29; 11:15–18; 12:1–8; 13:1; Luke/Q 7:24–25; 13:28–29, 34–35), but it is also rooted in the fundamental structure of political-economic-religious relations in Palestine.[11] The regional differences between Galilee and Jerusalem compounded the class differences between the village communities and the ruling groups, both high-priestly families and Herodian kings.

For there to have been social conflict, of course, there has to have been some social relationship. We can thus analyze the conflict between Galileans and Jerusalem more appropriately in relational terms than in essentialist categories. The opposition between Jesus and the Pharisees is another aspect of the conflictual relations between Jerusalem rulers and the Galilean villagers. As noted in chapter 7, the distinction anthropologists make between the "great" or official tradition and the "little" or popular tradition may help us understand this conflict.[12] Those traditions generally run parallel and influence each other, while also usually standing in some tension. An illustration of how precisely such a distinction fits the Gospel sources for traditions about Jesus is the "pronouncement story" in Mark 7:1–23 (previously used as an illustration of "Jesus vs. the Law/Judaism"), in which the Pharisees and scribes based in Jerusalem are represented as pressing their "traditions of the elders" upon the Galilean villagers, over against which Jesus appeals to the "commandment of God."

It is virtually impossible, given the lack of sources, to know what may have happened to the Jesus movement(s) in Galilee after the great revolt. If, as seems to be the case in both pre-Markan traditions and the Q discourses, the movement understood itself as a renewal of "Israel," apparently in the revitalization of village communities, then we should not be looking for congregations of a new religion separate from the already existing village forms — a "church" down the street from the "synagogue." Presumably in a given village, the Jesus movement would have been identical with or involved a certain number of the members of a local synagogue or assembly of Israel. In discourses such as Luke/Q 6:20–49 and Mark 10:1–45, the "agenda" or aim of the movement appears to be the revitalization of covenantal social-economic relations at the level of the local community (village). The tradition behind the Teaching of the Twelve Apostles would appear to provide windows onto a similar sort of movement based in village communities. It seems likely that the tradition of Jesus' teaching behind such literature as Mark, Q, and the Didache would have been cultivated in Galilean communities. Yet we do not know how long — whether, for example, the movement survived the Roman suppression of the great revolt of 66–67 and/or simply affected certain village communities, which then continued as covenantal village communities, presumably temporarily revitalized by the movement.

Much of the textual as well as archaeological study of Galilee and Judea is based on the assumption that some form of "(Jewish-) Christianity" continued in both cities such as Sepphoris as well as villages such as Nazareth and Capernaum. Given the paucity of evidence, the idea that there were two (or three if we add "paganism") rival "religions" operating in Galilee and Judea from the late first to the early fourth century may be yet another product of the standard paradigm of the emergence of "Christianity" from "Judaism." Archaeologists exploring Sepphoris, for example, conclude that "Judaism," "Christianity," and "Roman paganism" were all flourishing side by side in Sepphoris, while acknowledging candidly that to date "archaeology has only illuminated the Jewish and Roman [pagan] presence there."[13] Contrary to previous deductions from synthetic theological constructs of "Jewish Christianity," literary sources do *not* document "Jewish-Christians" in Sepphoris or Tiberias or Nazareth or Capernaum, along with Jews and Romans.[14] As mentioned in chapter 5, "Christianity" in Galilee was apparently the product of interest in "the Holy Land" for outsiders' pilgrimage to sacred sites, following the establishment of Christianity under Constantine. Acting with the blessing of Constantine, the wealthy Jewish convert Joseph of Tiberias constructed pilgrimage churches in Sepphoris and Tiberias as well as in the sacred sites of Nazareth and Capernaum (*Pan.* 30.12.1–9).[15] Until archaeological findings indicate otherwise, it would seem appropriate to assume that there were no "churches down the street" identifying themselves as "Christians" as distinguished from "Jewish synagogues" during the third century when rabbinic circles were establishing their prominence in Sepphoris and Tiberias.

The Rabbinic Circles in Galilee

Estimates of the rabbis' role and importance in Galilee in particular and/or in Jewish society of late antiquity generally have ranged from political as well as religious dominance to peripheral unimportance.[16] A common and influential portrayal of the rabbis pictures them as artisans based in Galilean villages.[17] Recent critical treatments of rabbinic literature focusing more restrictively on such traditions as case laws and legal rulings present a credible nuanced picture of the social location and role of the rabbis in the historical context of second- and third-century Galilee.[18] Whatever intermediate steps they may have undergone in the transition to Galilee in mid-second century, the standard picture of the rabbis as artisan-scholars requires revision.

The view that the rabbis supported their own study by work as artisans is not sustained by the literary evidence of the rabbis themselves.[19] At least some of the rabbis held large estates on the coastal plain during the Yavneh period. A number of texts indicate that, by the third century, after many of them had relocated to Galilee, many of the sages managed to establish themselves as wealthy landowners in Galilee or enjoyed the patronage of wealthy landowners.[20] The rabbis thus had a secure economic basis for the role they assumed as an elite academic-religious class in the third and fourth centuries.[21]

In the first generations after their migration to the north, rabbis established schools in Usha and Beth Shearim on the western frontier of Galilee. By the early third century, under the influence of Judah the Patriarch, many of the rabbis had moved to Sepphoris, and later in the century many (others) to Tiberias. As noted in chapter 7, Beth Shearim was hardly a typical Galilean town, having been a storage site for the produce of royal estates in the Great Plain and later becoming a favored site of reinterment for diaspora Jews. The short period during which early academies were located at Usha and Beth Shearim therefore hardly provides a basis for viewing the rabbinic movement as primarily rural, anchored in villages rather than cities for a time, only to be transformed into a primarily urban movement in the third century.[22] By the middle of the third century, in any case, the rabbis in Galilee were heavily concentrated in Sepphoris and Tiberias. After several influential rabbis moved to Tiberias in the mid-third century, the leading rabbis in the academy were priests from Babylon.[23] Tiberias, meanwhile, became an important center for the reinterment of diaspora Jews. Those two factors suggest that the prominent rabbinic circles of Tiberias may have been oriented as much to Jewish affairs around the Roman empire and beyond as to Galilean society. Although the rabbis gave more attention during the course of the third century to agricultural matters, they were by no means oriented primarily to typical village affairs. The residence of the sages in the cities was probably a key aspect of the social distance between the rabbis and the Galilean people.

After their relocation to Galilee, moreover, the subjects of their rulings indicate that the rabbis had very little interaction with or influence on social-economic life in Galilee.[24] Their rulings covered a narrow range of issues, such as the calendar, purity, and marriage/divorce. Apparently the Galilean peasants simply disregarded their rulings regarding agricultural matters such as tithes, heave-offerings, firstlings, mixed cropping, sabbatical year, and small cattle. The rabbis themselves in turn remained aloof from the peasants whose impurity they suspected and whose practices they distrusted: "Morning sleep and midday wine and children's talk and sitting in the assemblies of the peasants put a man out of the world" (*m. 'Abot* 3:11). They had virtually no interest in civil and criminal cases, which were handled by local village or city courts. And they had little contact with — let alone any decisive role in — the local village assemblies; indeed, they did not take a leading role in the synagogues until the sixth or seventh centuries.[25] The rabbis were focused on the *bet-midrash*, not the *bet-knesset*, that is, on their own teaching and learning in the academy, not local village affairs in the assembly. During the course of the third century, however, they became less focused on issues of purity and devoted more attention to civil and agricultural matters.

The rabbis were not agents of the Roman state any more than they were communal leaders of Galilean or Palestinian Jewish society. There is no evidence that they were even interested in being leaders of Jewry during the second century.[26] Even had they been interested, their political influence would have been closely confined because Roman-imposed urban structures held political jurisdiction. The rabbis began to gain some influence in Galilean social life only during the third and fourth centuries, and then only through its association with the Patriarchate first established by Judah the Prince. They gradually established more influence of their own, first by association with Judah the Prince and his successors in the Patriarchate, and then by assumption of some of the Patriarchate's functions, such as influence over training and appointment of judges. While many of them criticized the patriarch, others supported him and some even entered his service. Interestingly enough, those who cooperated with the patriarch appear in subsequent rabbinic traditions as the leading sages of their generation, while his critics appear as less important. The latter, moreover, either lived in Tiberias when the patriarch was based in Sepphoris/Diocaesarea or lived outside both major urban centers of rabbinic activity.[27] Emergent rabbinic influence and authority in Galilee would thus appear to be dependent on the de facto power of the patriarchs. The rabbis' role in Galilee, however, remained primarily "academic," their political authority marginal, and their influence in Galilean society at large still minimal.[28]

Following the leadership of Judah the Prince and the Patriarchate that became the legacy of his consolidation of social-economic power in the network of imperial relations, the rabbis gradually emerged as a new but unofficial social infrastructure in the cities of Galilee.[29] Assessments of the role of the rabbis in Late Roman Galilee and the relevance of archaeological findings can take into account the two directions in which they faced: From their social-economic base as landowners resident in Sepphoris and Tiberias, they were attempting to cultivate ancestral Jewish traditions over against the dominant Roman imperial political culture while also asserting their version of those Jewish traditions to the people of Galilee.

The most remarkable fruit of early rabbinic activity in Galilee was the Mishnah, given shape under the leadership of Judah the Prince around 200 C.E.[30] The systematic topical arrangement of rabbinic traditions and opinions arranged into tractates has been thoroughly analyzed and variously interpreted by rabbinic scholars, with debate continuing about the agenda and purpose of the rabbis in gathering this mass of material. The relative weight given to topics and the structure of the Mishnah derive from a tradition oriented to the Jerusalem Temple and priesthood. Speaking through the style and persona of the Judean scribes, the rabbinic authors of the Mishnah advocate a religious-economic program that perpetuates priestly interests, ideally at least. The center of interest economically is the village made up of household units of agricultural production. Village life and household production, however, are coordinated with the Temple as the focus of holiness.[31]

It should be abundantly evident by now that much rethinking and fresh analysis remains to be done before we can adequately understand Jesus and the rabbis in historical context, once we have dismantled misleading old paradigms and come to grips with newly discerned aspects of the Galilean landscape. The outlines of both Jesus and the rabbis in historical Galilean context are nevertheless already becoming clear.

Galilee in the first century — as discerned from a combination of artifactual and textual sources — consisted of a traditional Israelite covenantal society beginning to disintegrate under the pressures of Roman rule and newly (re)built royal cities. There is neither evidence nor, apparently, any historical likelihood that Galilean villagers were eagerly assimilating cosmopolitan culture; indeed the newly (re)built cities were not all that cosmopolitan. Far from an individualistic Cynic sage, therefore, Jesus must be understood as the prophetic leader of a movement of Israelite renewal based in the villages, the fundamental units of social life. In Galilee itself, moreover, that movement apparently never became a separate "religion" known as Christianity. Whether or not any local communities of the Jesus movement survived the great revolt, "Christianity" was first established in Galilee as a series of pilgrimage sites under the sponsorship of Constantine.

Ironically, whereas the indigenous Galilean movement catalyzed by Jesus did not become well established in Galilee after the great revolt, the rabbinic circles who migrated to Galilee only after the Bar Kokhba revolt did establish a continuing presence in Galilee from which rabbinic Judaism emerged. After a generation or two in towns on the western frontier of Lower Galilee, the rabbis established their most prominent academies in the cities of Sepphoris and Tiberias. By their own admission they had little influence among the Galilean people and had little interest in the village assemblies (synagogues) until centuries later. Although they never held official positions of authority recognized by the Romans, they did become an academic-religious elite with increasing influence in the diaspora as well as in Galilee itself.

NOTES

Introduction

1. Statements about cosmopolitan influence on Lower Galilee were in Eric M. Meyers, "Galilean Regionalism as a Factor in Historical Reconstruction," *BASOR* 221 (1976): 95; and "The Cultural Setting of Galilee: The Case of Regionalism and Early Judaism," *ANRW* 2.19.1 (1979): 687–98; implications drawn for more Hellenistic and cosmopolitan ethos for Jesus by Burton L. Mack, *A Myth of Innocence: Mark and Christian Origins* (Philadelphia: Fortress, 1988), 53–78; John Dominic Crossan, *The Historical Jesus: The Life of a Mediterranean Jewish Peasant* (San Francisco: HarperCollins, 1991), 18–19.

2. In contrast to the previous historical reconstruction by Sean Freyne, *Galilee from Alexander the Great to Hadrian, 323 B.C.E. to 135 C.E.: A Study in Second Temple Judaism* (Wilmington, Del.: Michael Glazier, 1980), esp. 195; repeated in *Galilee, Jesus, and the Gospels* (Minneapolis: Fortress, 1988), 145.

3. Eric M. Meyers, "Roman Sepphoris in Light of New Archaeological Evidence and Recent Research," in *The Galilee in Late Antiquity*, ed. Lee I. Levine (New York: Jewish Theological Seminary of America, 1992), 326; Eric M. Meyers, Ehud Netzer, and Carol L. Meyers, *Sepphoris* (Winona Lake, Ind.: Eisenbrauns, 1992), 12.

4. See Meyers, "Roman Sepphoris," 327.

5. One of the principal contributions of E. P. Sanders, *Jesus and Judaism* (Philadelphia: Fortress, 1985), esp. introduction and chaps. 6 and 9.

6. Although they did not state it that way, this is the thrust of Marcus Borg, "A Temperate Case for a Non-Eschatological Jesus," *Foundations and Facets Forum* 2, no. 3 (1986): 81–102; Crossan, *Historical Jesus*, chap. 12; and the implications of much of the work of the "Q Seminar" of the Society of Biblical Literature, as drawn out by Mack, *Myth of Innocence*, and others.

7. Gerd Theissen, *The Sociology of Early Palestinian Christianity* (Philadelphia: Fortress Press, 1978); Richard A. Horsley, *Jesus and the Spiral of Violence: Popular Jewish Resistance in Roman Palestine* (San Francisco: Harper & Row, 1987), and *Sociology and the Jesus Movement* (New York: Crossroad, 1989); Crossan, *Historical Jesus*.

8. The program of Jacob Neusner and his students is well known and embodied in many works too numerous to mention; for a general picture of

the Mishnah itself that results from this intensive study, see Jacob Neusner, *Judaism: The Evidence of the Mishnah* (Chicago: University of Chicago Press, 1981).

9. Martin Goodman, *State and Society in Roman Galilee, A.D. 132–212* (Totowa, N.J.: Rowman and Allanheld); Shaye J. D. Cohen, "The Place of the Rabbi in Jewish Society of the Second Century," in *Galilee in Late Antiquity*, ed. Levine, 157–73; and Lee I. Levine, *The Rabbinic Class of Palestine in Late Antiquity* (New York: Jewish Theological Seminary of America, 1989).

10. See, e.g., the section on pottery in Eric M. Meyers, James F. Strange, and Carol L. Meyers, *Excavations at Ancient Meiron* (Cambridge, Mass.: ASOR, 1981).

11. Evident, for example, in the use of only one of Josephus's accounts of John of Gischala in discussion of coins and trade by Eric M. Meyers, "Introduction," in Richard S. Hanson, *Tyrian Influence in the Upper Galilee: Meiron Excavation Project 2* (Cambridge, Mass.: ASOR, 1980).

12. Adolf Büchler, *The Political and Social Leaders of the Jewish Community of Sepphoris in the Second and Third Centuries* (London: Jews' College, 1909); S. Klein, *Beiträge zur Geographie und Geschichte Galiläas* (Leipzig: Haupt, 1909).

13. See the review by Gunther Stemberger, "Galilee — Land of Salvation?" in W. D. Davies, *The Gospel and the Land* (Berkeley: University of California Press, 1974), 409–38.

14. The subtitle of the first major study focused specifically on Galilee, Freyne, *Galilee from Alexander the Great to Hadrian*, may be a measure of the hold that the standard paradigm has in literary and historical studies.

15. Earlier archaeological exploration of Galilean sites such as Nazareth and Capernaum are summarized, e.g., in Bellarmino Bagatti, *Excavations in Nazareth*, vol. 1, *From the Beginning til the XII Century* (Jerusalem: Franciscan Printing House, 1969); Jack Finegan, *The Archaeology of the New Testament: The Life of Jesus and the Beginning of the Early Church* (Princeton, N.J.: Princeton University Press, 1969); but see now the critical appraisal by Joan E. Taylor, *Christians and the Holy Places: The Myth of Jewish Christian Origins* (Oxford: Clarendon Press, 1993). Investigation of isolated synagogue buildings is discussed in chapter 6 below, with numerous citations. The excavations at Meiron and nearby villages are well reported in journal articles and books: e.g., Meyers, Strange, and Meyers, *Excavations at Ancient Meiron*. Other references in notes to chapter 4 below.

16. Eric M. Meyers and James F. Strange, *Archaeology, the Rabbis, and Early Christianity* (Nashville: Abingdon, 1981).

17. See the critique by S. R. F. Price, *Rituals and Power: The Roman Imperial Cult in Asia Minor* (Cambridge: Cambridge University Press, 1984), 15–19, 239–48.

18. Thus when isolated aspects of Galilee are treated as adjuncts or incidentals of (a) religion, the result is to make the social reality of Galilee dissolve into a modern construct such as "Judaism" or "Christianity."

19. Archaeologist Anthony Snodgrass, in "Archaeology," *Sources for Ancient History*, ed. Michael Crawford (Cambridge: Cambridge University Press, 1983), 139 (and 168–69), notes how *classical archaeology* also *decontextualizes* its finds.

20. Recent construal of the Pharisees as scribal retainers is laid out most completely by Anthony J. Saldarini, *Pharisees, Scribes, and Sadducees: A Sociological Approach* (Wilmington, Del.: Michael Glazier, 1988).

21. Snodgrass, "Archaeology," 164, points out that archaeologists outside the classical field have become increasingly uneasy, e.g., about the validity and application of the whole concept of "cultures," that is geographical assemblages based on similarity of artifact-types.

22. E.g., Meyers, "Roman Sepphoris," 322–25; Werner Kelber, *The Kingdom in Mark: A New Time and Place* (Philadelphia: Fortress, 1974).

23. Most of our sources for the Hellenistic-Roman period suggest that ethnic "Jews" inside Palestine as well as in the diaspora had assimilated Hellenistic culture in some degree; see, e.g., Martin Hengel, *The Hellenization of Judea in the First Century after Christ* (Philadelphia: Trinity Press International, 1989). Anthropological archaeologists find that, generally speaking, "ethnicity is difficult to recognize from the archaeological record." See Colin Renfrew and Paul Bahn, *Archaeology: Theories, Methods, and Practice* (New York: Thames and Hudson, 1991), 169.

24. E. J. Hobsbawm, "From Social History to the History of Society," *Daedalus* 100 (1971): 41.

25. John H. Kautsky, *The Politics of Aristocratic Empires* (Chapel Hill: University of North Carolina Press, 1982), 13.

26. Anthony F. C. Wallace, *Culture and Personality* (New York: Random House, 1970 [1961]), 110.

27. See, e.g., Eric Wolf, *Europe and the People without History* (New York: Harper and Row, 1982).

28. E.g., Kelber, *Kingdom in Mark*.

29. I have attempted to sort out the different groups, their distinctive characteristics and actions, and the sequence of their activities in a series of articles. See esp. "The Sicarii: Ancient Jewish Terrorists," *JR* 59 (1979): 435–58; "Ancient Jewish Banditry and the Revolt against Rome, A.D. 66–70," *CBQ* 43 (1981): 409–32; "Menahem in Jerusalem: A Brief Messianic Episode among the Sicarii — Not 'Zealot Messianism'" *NovT* 27 (1985): 334–48; "The Zealots: Their Origin, Relationships and Importance in the Jewish Revolt," *NovT* 28 (1986): 159–92.

30. R. A. Horsley, *Galilee: History, Politics, People* (Valley Forge, Pa.: Trinity Press International, 1995); Horsley with John Hanson, *Bandits, Prophets, and Messiahs: Popular Movements at the Time of Jesus* (Minneapolis: Winston Press, 1985; pbk: San Francisco: Harper and Row, 1987).

31. On structural power relations in general, see especially Kautsky, *Politics of Aristocratic Empires;* and Wolf, *Europe and the People without History.* Within

the wider range of archaeological literature pertinent to study of Galilee are Robert McC. Adams, *Heartland of Cities* (Chicago: University of Chicago Press, 1981); and Charles Redman, *The Rise of Civilization: From Early Farmers to Urban Society in the Ancient Near East* (San Francisco: Freeman, 1978). The ways in which archaeology could contribute to the analysis of inequality or social class within particular sites or among sites are exemplified in numerous studies of skeletal remains, burials, and the production, use, and display of ceramics. E.g.: M. N. Cohen and G. J. Armelagos, eds., *Paleopathology at the Origins of Agriculture* (Orlando, Fla.: Academic Press, 1984); R. G. Wilkinson and R. J. Norelli, "A Biocultural Analysis of Social Organization," *American Antiquity* 46 (1981): 743–59; M. P. Pearson, "Mortuary Practices, Society, and Ideology: An Ethnoarchaeological Study," in *Symbolic and Structural Archaeology*, ed. Ian Hodder (Cambridge: Cambridge University Press, 1982), 99–114; Michael Shanks and Christopher Tilley, "Ideology, Symbolic Power, and Ritual Communication: A Reinterpretation of Neolithic Mortuary Practices," in *Symbolic and Structural Archaeology*, ed. Hodder, 129–54; C. Kramer, "Ceramic Ethnoarchaeology," *Ann. Rev. Anthro.* 14 (1985): 77–102; S. E. van der Leeuw and A. C. Pritchard, eds., *The Many Dimensions of Pottery* (Amsterdam: von Griffen Institute, 1984); and Dean E. Arnold, *Ceramic Theory and Cultural Process* (Cambridge: Cambridge University Press, 1985).

32. Social inequality and conflict have drawn more attention in the wider field of archaeology in recent years. See, e.g., A. Gilman, "The Development of Social Stratification in Bronze Age Europe," *Current Anthropology* 22 (1981): 1–23; J. Haas, *The Evolution of the Prehistoric State* (New York: Columbia University Press, 1982); T. C. Patterson and C. W. Gailey, eds., *Power Relations and State Formation* (Washington, D.C.: American Anthropological Association, 1987); Robert Paynter, *Models of Spatial Inequality* (New York: Academic Press, 1982); M. Spriggs, ed., *Marxist Perspectives in Archaeology* (Cambridge: Cambridge University Press, 1984).

33. In the wider field of archaeology, awareness of how the modern European-based world capitalist economic system determines economic life far from the centers of power (partly stimulated by such historical studies as Immanuel M. Wallerstein, *The Modern World-System I: Capitalist Agriculture and the Origins of the European World Economy in the Sixteenth Century* [New York: Academic Press, 1974]) has stimulated recent studies of core-periphery power-relations in earlier ages, such as the ancient Near East and the Roman empire, studies directly pertinent to ancient Galilee. See esp. M. Rowlands, M. Larsen, and K. Kristiansen, eds., *Centre and Periphery in the Ancient World* (Cambridge: Cambridge University Press, 1987). Although some of these studies focus on trade, they are aware that the ancient Near East and some sections of the Roman empire were basically tributary political-economic systems.

34. Hobsbawm, "From Social History to the History of Society," 40–41:

We may find, paradoxically that the value of our study [of a movement or revolution] itself is in inverse proportion to our concentration
on the brief moment of conflict.... The analytical advantage of the
colonial situation... is that here an entire society or group of societies
is sharply defined by contrast with an outside force, and its various
internal shifts and changes, as well as its reactions to the uncontrol-
lable and rapid impact of this force, can be observed and analyzed as a
whole.

35. The basic works pertinent to the ancient Mediterranean and Near East
are Karl Marx, *Grundrisse* (Harmondsworth: Penguin, 1973), the key sections
of which are immediately accessible with introduction in Karl Marx, *Pre-
Capitalist Economic Formations*, ed. E. J. Hobsbawm (London: Lawrence and
Wishart, 1964); Max Weber, *The Agrarian Sociology of Ancient Civilizations* (At-
lantic Highlands, N.J.: Humanities Press, 1976); and Karl Polanyi et al., *Trade
and Market in the Early Empires: Economics in History and Theory* (Glencoe, Ill.:
Free Press, 1957).

36. Gerhard E. Lenski, *Power and Privilege: A Theory of Social Stratification*
(New York: McGraw-Hill, 1966); Kautsky, *Politics of Aristocratic Empires.*

37. To apply generalizations based on anthropological studies of part-
societies such as particular villages in the modern Mediterranean directly to
ancient Christian literature, as do some of the essays in Jerome H. Neyrey,
The Social World of Luke-Acts: Models for Interpretation (Peabody, Mass.: Hen-
drickson, 1991), is highly questionable without taking into account particular
historical social context of the ancient text and the historical distance between
the first and the twentieth centuries.

38. As in James F. Strange, "Some Implications of Archaeology for New
Testament Studies," in *What Has Archaeology to Do with Faith?* ed. James H.
Charlesworth and Walter Weaver (Valley Forge, Pa.: Trinity Press International, 1992), 24–31. It hardly makes sense, however, to develop two
different models, one derived from archaeological materials and the other
from literature, and then compare them. The usual procedure of archaeologists when investigating historical societies, including Strange himself, is to
utilize the literary remains even in devising a research strategy. The need is for
both textual scholars and archaeologists to draw (critically) on both kinds of
evidence as well as to become more critical and intentional about the models
that they are using in their constructions and interpretations.

39. See esp. Elisabeth Schüssler Fiorenza, *Jesus: Miriam's Child, Sophia's
Prophet* (New York: Continuum, 1994).

40. Bruce G. Trigger, "Alternative Archaeologies: Nationalist, Colonialist,
Imperialist," *Man*, n.s. 19 (1984): 355–70. See also Neil Asher Silberman,
"Promised Lands and Chosen Peoples: The Politics and Poetics of Archae-
ological Narrative," and other essays in *Nationalism, Politics, and the Practice*

of Archaeology, ed. Philip L. Kohl and Clare Fawcett (Cambridge: Cambridge University Press, 1995).

41. As in western Europe (and not only Nazi Germany!) and Mexico, for example; see Don D. Fowler, "Archaeology in the Service of the State," *American Antiquity* 52 (1987): 229–48. For current practices in the Eastern Mediterranean and the Middle East such as Turkey, Egypt, and Israel, see Neil A. Silberman, *Between Past and Present: Archaeology, Ideology, and Nationalism in the Modern Middle East* (New York: Holt, 1989).

42. A classic example: when cultures seemingly more elaborate than those known in historical times were discovered in the Ohio and Mississippi Valleys, they were assigned to a lost race of "Moundbuilders" who were different from Native Americans. See R. Silverberg, *Moundbuilders of Ancient America* (Greenwich, N.Y.: New York Graphic Society, 1968).

43. British archaeology may be the classic example; see D. K. Grayson, *The Establishment of Human Antiquity* (Cambridge: Cambridge University Press, 1983). More generally, in a process that included the early development of "biblical archaeology," western Europe claimed that they, rather than modern peoples that live in the Near East, were the true spiritual heirs of ancient Near Eastern civilizations. On the development of biblical archaeology, see Neil A. Silberman, *Digging for God and Country: Exploration in the Holy Land, 1799–1917* (New York: Knopf, 1982).

44. See the grounding of such an approach between positivism and constructivism in recent philosophy by Marianne Sawicki, "Caste and Contact in the Galilee of Jesus: Research Beyond Positivism and Constructivism," in *Archaeology of Galilee and the Jesus of History*, ed. Richard A. Horsley and J. Andrew Overman (Valley Forge, Pa.: Trinity Press International, forthcoming).

Chapter 1. Galilee, Crossroad of Empires

Epigraph: Fernand Braudel, *The Mediterranean and the Mediterranean World in the Age of Philip II* (New York: Harper & Row, 1972), 1:34.

1. Our term "Galilee" stems from *galilaia* in the Septuagint (the Greek Jewish Bible) and other ancient literature in Greek such as the Christian Gospels and the Jewish historian Josephus. The few references in the Hebrew Bible are not consistent. "Circle of the peoples" in Isa. 9:1 seems to include both "the land of Zebulun and the land of Naphtali," that is, roughly, western Lower Galilee and Upper Galilee. Discussion and references by Rafael Frankel in *ABD* 2.263–74.

2. On the *hapiru*, see Moshe Greenberg, *The Hab/piru*, AOS 39 (New Haven: American Oriental Society, 1953); Marvin Chaney, "Ancient Palestinian Peasant Movements and the Formation of Premonarchic Israel," in *Palestine in Transition: The Emergence of Ancient Israel*, ed. D. N. Freedman and D. F. Graf (Sheffield: Almond, 1983), 39–94, esp. 72–83; Richard A. Horsley, "'*Apiru* and Cossacks: A Comparative Analysis of Social Form and Historical

Role," in *New Perspectives on Ancient Judaism: Religion, Literature, and Society in Ancient Israel, Formative Christianity and Judaism*, vol. 2., *Ancient Israel and Christianity*, Presented to Howard Clark Kee, ed. J. Neusner, P. Borgen, E. Frerichs, R. Horsley (Lanham, Md.: University Press of America, 1987), 2:3–26.

3. Yigael Yadin, *Hazor: The Schweich Lectures of the British Academy 1970* (London: Oxford University Press, 1972), 108–9, 129–32.

4. For summary of the archaeological reconstruction of the context of early Israel, see Neil Asher Silberman, "Who Were the Israelites?" *Archaeology* (1992/2): 22–30; Israel Finkelstein, *The Archaeology of the Israelite Settlement* (Jerusalem: Israel Exploration Society, 1988).

5. Finkelstein, *Archaeology of the Israelite Settlement* (including references to significant work by Adam Zertal published in Hebrew); Lawrence Stager, "The Song of Deborah: Why Some Tribes Answered the Call and Others Did Not," *BAR* 15 (1989): 53.

6. Cf. the survey of settlements by Zvi Gal, "The Late Bronze Age in Galilee: A Reassessment" *BASOR* 272 (1988): 79–84. His conclusion that Galileans must not have played much of a role in the conflict between early Israelites and the Canaanites seems to depend on an assumption that *hapiru* and Israelites are mutually exclusive.

7. Zvi Gal, "The Settlement of Issachar," *Tel Aviv* 9 (1982): 79–87, is more confident when an occupational gap occurs, as at Taanach in the eleventh century B.C.E., that it must have been the Israelites who destroyed the city.

8. On the hypothesis that Israel found its origin in a prolonged sequence of revolts against or withdrawals from the Canaanite rulers rather than by a "conquest" of or a process of gradual immigration into the land, see George E. Mendenhall, "The Hebrew Conquest of Palestine," *BA* 25 (1962): 66–87, and *The Tenth Generation: The Origins of the Biblical Tradition* (Baltimore: Johns Hopkins University Press, 1973); Norman K. Gottwald, *The Tribes of Yahweh* (Maryknoll, N.Y.: Orbis, 1979); Chaney, "Ancient Palestinian Peasant Movements," 39–90. For alternative reconstructions, see, e.g., Baruch Halpern, *The Emergence of Israel in Canaan* (Chico, Calif.: Scholars Press, 1983); Robert B. Coote, *Early Israel: A New Horizon* (Minneapolis: Fortress, 1990).

9. Stager, "Song of Deborah," 54.

10. Cf. Zvi Gal, *Lower Galilee during the Iron Age* ASOR DissS 8 (Winona Lake, Ind.: Eisenbrauns, 1992), 106.

11. On the development and use of Elijah-Elisha traditions, see now the essays in Robert B. Coote, ed., *Elijah and Elisha in Socioliterary Perspective* (Atlanta: Scholars Press, 1992).

12. Shulamit Geva, "Archaeological Evidence for the Trade Between Israel and Tyre?" *BASOR* 248 (1982): 69–72.

13. Bustenay Oded, *Mass Deportations in the Neo-Assyrian Empire* (Wiesbaden: Reichert, 1979), 54–57, 91–109. As Oded points out, his title by no means indicates *total* deportations, but "only a portion" of a given area.

14. Convincing analysis by Stuart A. Irvine, "The Southern Border of Syria Reconstructed," *CBQ* 56 (1994): 21–41.

15. Yohanan Aharoni, *The Land of the Bible: A Historical Geography*, rev. ed. (Philadelphia: Westminster, 1979), 374–76; *ANET*, 283; H. Tadmor, "The Southern Border of Aram," *IEJ* 12 (1962): 114–22; Martin Noth, *The History of Israel* (Edinburgh: T. and T. Clark, 1958), 261. See further H. Tadmor, "Some Aspects of the History of Samaria during the Biblical Period," *Jerusalem Cathedra* 3 (1983): 1–11; and John H. Hayes and Jeffrey Kuan, "The Final Years of Samaria (730–20)," *Biblica* 72 (1991): 153–81.

16. Gal, *Lower Galilee during the Iron Age*, esp. 109–10; cf. Gal, "The Lower Galilee in the Iron Age II: Analysis of Survey Material and Its Historical Implication," *Tel Aviv* 15–16 (1988–89): 56–64; and N. Zori, *The Land of Issachar* (Jerusalem: Israel Exploration Society, 1977). These surface surveys find a suddenly resettled Lower Galilee in the Persian period following a suddenly unsettled Assyrian period. Would that lead to the conclusion that the Persians launched a massive repopulation campaign in Galilee, the counterpart to the total depopulation supposedly carried out by the Assyrians? Such studies suggest the need for coordination of archaeological surface surveys and other historical research. Recent broad-ranging surveys of settlement patterns elsewhere in antiquity combined with more complex analysis may be suggestive for research on Galilee and elsewhere. Cf. Susan E. Alcock, *Graecia Capta: The Landscapes of Roman Greece* (Cambridge: Cambridge University Press, 1993).

17. Most recent critical discussion of the limited and problematic sources and complex issues, with synthetic reconstruction by Lester L. Grabbe, *Judaism from Cyrus to Hadrian*, vol. 1 (Minneapolis: Fortress, 1992), chap. 2. On the chronology of the restoration, see Frank M. Cross, "A Reconstruction of the Judean Restoration," *JBL* 94 (1975): 3–18.

18. On this complicated problem, see esp. Cross, "A Reconstruction of the Judean Restoration," 231–46; James D. Purvis, "The Samaritans and Judaism," in *Early Judaism and Its Modern Interpreters*, ed. Robert A. Kraft and George W. E. Nickelsburg (Atlanta: Scholars Press, 1986), 81–98.

19. Given the power struggles between various priestly factions in Jerusalem and the emphasis on boundaries between themselves and their own "people of the land" as well as the Samaritan elite, it is highly doubtful that Jerusalem priestly groups mounted any effort to influence, let alone include Galileans. Grabbe, *Judaism from Cyrus to Hadrian*, 1:131–38; E. Stern, "The Persian Empire and the Political and Social History of Palestine in the Persian Period," in *The Cambridge History of Judaism*, vol. 1, ed. W. D. Davies and L. Finkenstein (Cambridge: Cambridge University Press, 1987), 70–87, esp. 82–86.

20. Sean Freyne, *Galilee from Alexander the Great to Hadrian, 323 B.C.E. to 135 C.E.: A Study in Second Temple Judaism* (Wilmington, Del.: Grazier, 1980), 27–35.

21. See the discussion in Richard A. Horsley, *Galilee: History, Politics, People* (Valley Forge, Pa.: Trinity Press International, 1995), 39–52.

22. In the classic study of ancient Mediterranean materials Arthur Darby Nock, *Conversion: The Old and the New in Religion from Alexander the Great to Augustine of Hippo* (Oxford: Clarendon, 1933), defines conversion as "the re-orientation of the soul of an individual...from an earlier form of piety to another" (7). Shaye J. D. Cohen, "Respect for Judaism by Gentiles Accord-ing to Josephus," *HTR* 80 (1987): 409–30, points out that Josephus has no term for "conversion," which is at best "an ill-defined concept." Cf. Cohen's attempt to broaden and adapt the concept in "Crossing the Boundary and Becoming a Jew," *HTR* 82 (1989): 26.

23. See Menahem Stern, *Greek and Latin Authors on Jews and Judaism*, 3 vols. (Jerusalem: Israel Academy of Arts and Sciences, 1974–84), sec. 11a; Steve Mason, *Flavius Josephus and the Pharisees* (Leiden: Brill, 1991), 97–106; and both Pierre Briant, "The Seleucid Kingdom, the Achaemenid Empire, and the History of the Near East in the First Millennium B.C.," and Shaye J. D. Cohen, "Religion, Ethnicity, and Hellenism in the Emergence of Jewish Identity in Maccabean Palestine," in *Religion and Religious Practice in the Seleucid Kingdom*, ed. Per Bilde et al. (Aarhus: Aarhus University Press, 1990), 58–59, 218–19. See also the discussion in Horsley, *Galilee*, 47–49.

24. Bezalel Bar-Kochva, "The Beginning of Jewish Settlement in Gali-lee," in "Manpower, Economics, and Internal Strife in the Hasmonean State," in *Armées et Fiscalité dans le Monde Antique* (Paris: Éditions du Centre Na-tional de la Recherche Scientifique, 1977), 191–94, sharply rejects the view that "assumes that Galilee was already densely populated by Jews before the Hasmonean State" as not based on critical assessment of the sources.

25. On Sepphoris as an administrative fortress town, see further chap. 2 below.

26. Analysis of archaeological and textual evidence for Hasmonean for-tresses and garrisons in Israel Shatzman, *The Armies of the Hasmoneans and Herod* (Tübingen: Mohr, 1991), esp. 44, 83–87, 94–97.

27. Cf. Richard S. Hanson, *Tyrian Influence in the Upper Galilee: Meiron Excavation Project 2* (Cambridge, Mass.: ASOR, 1980), for the way in which the almost equally large number of Tyrian coins in middle-late Roman times are interpreted as evidence of a thriving trade between the "businessmen" of Upper Galilee and the metropolis of Tyre.

28. Cf. Eric M. Meyers, James F. Strange, Carol L. Meyers, and Richard S. Hanson, "Preliminary Report on the 1977 and 1978 Seasons at Gush Halav," *BASOR* 233 (1979): 36. See further Richard A. Horsley, "Archaeology and the Villages of Upper Galilee: A Dialogue with Archaeologists," *BASOR* 297 (1995): 7–11.

29. In a sustained argument that Galilee was not a hotbed of the "Zealot" movement (now known to be nonexistent prior to the great revolt of 66–70), Sean Freyne, *Galilee from Alexander the Great to Hadrian*, contends that

opposition to Herod came primarily from the "Hasmonean nobility" (who seem to be the same as the "Galilean aristocracy"?). For a criticism of and alternative to that contention, see Horsley, *Galilee*, 54–56.

30. Review of literature in James F. Strange, "Archaeology and the Religion of Judaism in Palestine," *ANRW* 2.19.1 (1979): 651–55.

31. See Richard A. Horsley, "Popular Messianic Movements around the Time of Jesus," *CBQ* 46 (1984): 471–95; with John Hanson, *Bandits, Prophets, and Messiahs* (San Francisco: Harper and Row, 1985, 1987), chap. 3.

32. Eric M. Meyers, "Roman Sepphoris in the Light of New Archaeological Evidence and Research," in *The Galilee in Late Antiquity*, ed. Lee I. Levine (New York: Jewish Theological Seminary of America, 1992), 323.

33. S. Safrai, "The Temple," in *The Jewish People in the First Century*, CRINT 1.2, ed. S. Safrai and M. Stern (Assen: Van Gorcum, 1976), 898–902; and the critical review of the issue in Horsley, *Galilee*, 144–46.

34. Sean Freyne, *Galilee from Alexander the Great to Hadrian*, chaps. 7 and 8.

35. For this reason Antipas is often characterized as "a pious Jew," e.g., recently by Gerd Theissen, *Gospels in Context* (Minneapolis: Fortress, 1991), 29, 81–97, who is still working with the standard but unwarranted synthetic concept of "the Jews" and tends to move directly from sources such as Josephus and the Gospels to historical events without sufficient critical analysis.

36. On the revolt in Galilee, see the full discussion and documentation in Horsley, *Galilee*, 72–88.

37. Fuller reports of the excavations will be published in the near future by their director, Mordechai Aviam.

38. See esp. Benjamin Isaac, "Judaea after A.D. 70," *JJS* 35 (1984): 44–50.

39. Further references and discussion in Martin Goodman, *State and Society in Roman Galilee, A.D. 132–212* (Totowa, N.J.: Rowman and Allanheld), 147–48.

40. The principal archaeological argument has been that the population growth of certain villages in the late second century must have been due to Judean immigration, which is supposedly evident in "the building of synagogues." Unfortunately only a few of the synagogue buildings discovered can be dated as early as the second or third centuries. See further the discussion and references in Horsley, *Galilee*, 97–98, and esp. 307–8, nn. 22 and 23.

41. On the origins of the Patriarchate and its relations with the rabbis, see Lee I. Levine, "The Jewish Patriarch (Nasi) in Third-Century Palestine," *ANRW* 2.19.2 (1979): 649–88; and Lee I. Levine, *The Rabbinic Class of Roman Palestine in Late Antiquity* (New York: Jewish Theological Seminary of America, 1989), chap. 4.

42. See *y. Yebam.* 12.7.13a; *Gen. Rab.* 81, p. 969; *y. Meg.* 4.5.75b; *y. Ta'an.* 4.2.681; *b. Ketub.* 103b; *b. Ber.* 55a.

43. Goodman, *State and Society in Roman Galilee*, 133–34, is a useful clarification on Levine, "Jewish Patriarch," 673, on this matter. See further the

arguments by Goodman, "The Roman State and the Jewish Patriarch in the Third Century," in *Galilee in Late Antiquity*, ed. Levine, 131–34.

44. Barbara Geller Nathanson, "Jews, Christians, and the Gallus Revolt in Fourth-Century Palestine," *BA* 79 (1986): esp. 30–34.

45. Aurelius Victor, *Liber de Caesaribus* 42.9–12.

46. On the cause of the destruction evident in mid-fourth-century Sepphoris archaeologists differ. James F. Strange, "Six Campaigns at Sepphoris: The University of South Florida Excavations at Sepphoris, 1983–89," in *Galilee in Late Antiquity*, ed. Levine, 352–53, points to the Gallus revolt, while Eric M. Meyers, Ehud Netzer, and Carol L. Meyers, *Sepphoris* (Winona Lake, Ind.: Eisenbrauns, 1992), 17, focuses on the earthquake of 363.

Chapter 2. Sepphoris and Tiberias

Epigraphs: Paul Zanker, *The Power of Images in the Age of Augustus* (Ann Arbor: University of Michigan Press, 1988), 324–26; Lee I. Levine, "R. Simeon b. Yohai and the Purification of Tiberias: History and Tradition," *Hebrew Union College Annual* 49 (1978) 173–74.

1. Sean Freyne, *Galilee, Jesus, and the Gospels* (Philadelphia: Fortress, 1988), 145. Freyne had drawn this same conclusion mainly on the basis of literary sources in the first attempt at a comprehensive view of Galilee in 1980 (*Galilee from Alexander the Great to Hadrian, 323 B.C.E. to 135 C.E.: A Study in Second Temple Judaism* [Wilmington, Del.: Michael Glazier, 1980]).

2. Eric M. Meyers and James F. Strange, *Archaeology, the Rabbis, and Early Christianity* (Nashville: Abingdon, 1981).

3. E.g., J. Andrew Overman, "Who Were the First Urban Christians? Urbanization in Galilee in the First Century," and Douglas R. Edwards, "First-Century Urban/Rural Relations in Lower Galilee: Exploring the Archaeological and Literary Evidence," both in *Society of Biblical Literature 1988 Seminar Papers*, ed. David J. Lull (Atlanta: Scholars Press, 1988), 160–68, 169–82. Cf. the earlier sketch of Lower Galilee in contrast with Upper Galilean villages in Eric M. Meyers, "The Cultural Setting of Galilee: The Case of Regionalism and Early Judaism," in *ANRW* 2.19.1 (1979): 686–702. Interestingly enough, the advocates of an urbanized Lower Galilee cited some of the same archaeological reports and Josephus references and used the same commercial economic model for Galilee as did Freyne.

4. E.g., F. G. Downing, *Christ and the Cynics*, JSOT Manuals 4 (Sheffield: JSOT Press, 1988); Burton L. Mack, *The Lost Gospel: The Book of Q and Christian Origins* (San Francisco: HarperCollins, 1993).

5. See Jonathan Reed, "The Population of Capernaum," *Occasional Papers of the Institute for Antiquity and Christianity* 24 (Claremont, Calif., 1992).

6. Magen Broshi, "The Population of Western Palestine in the Roman-Byzantine Period," *BASOR* 236 (1979): 1–10.

7. For critical review of methods of estimating ancient populations and their application to Palestine, see Reed, "The Population of Capernaum," and

J. Zorn, "Estimating the Population Size of Ancient Settlements: Methods, Problems, Solutions, and a Case Study," *BASOR* 295 (1994): 31–48.

8. Eric M. Meyers, Ehud Netzer, and Carol L. Meyers, *Sepphoris* (Winona Lake, Ind.: Eisenbrauns, 1992), 10.

9. There are some inaccuracies in ibid., 10–11.

10. Eric M. Meyers, "Roman Sepphoris in the Light of New Archaeological Evidence and Research," in *The Galilee in Late Antiquity*, ed. Lee I. Levine (New York: Jewish Theological Seminary, 1992), 330.

11. Since it is not at all clear that a "synagogue" was found at Masada, one can hardly argue that Herod may have "supported synagogue Judaism privately" (vs. Meyers and Strange, *Archaeology*, 24).

12. See further Richard A. Horsley with John S. Hanson, *Bandits, Prophets and Messiahs: Popular Movements at the Time of Jesus* (San Francisco: Harper and Row, 1985), chap. 3.

13. Meyers, "Roman Sepphoris," 323.

14. James F. Strange, "Six Campaigns at Sepphoris: The University of South Florida Excavations at Sepphoris, 1983–89," in *Galilee in Late Antiquity*, ed. Levine, 339–56.

15. Meyers, Netzer, and Meyers, *Sepphoris*, 33.

16. Strange, "Six Campaigns at Sepphoris," 342.

17. Josephus's account is that the Romans "burned the city and enslaved its inhabitants" (*B.J.* 2.68; *Ant.* 17.289). It is unclear why Meyers ("Roman Sepphoris," 323) says that Judas's attack on the royal palace/fortress "failed."

18. Meyers, "Roman Sepphoris," 322, 324–25; Meyers, Netzer, and Meyers, *Sepphoris*, 10. Meyers claims that the archaeological record "supports the picture of Sepphoris presented by Josephus and some of the rabbinic literature, i.e., that Sepphoris from the first century C.E. onward was a city inhabited by many well-to-do aristocratic Jews of a priestly background" ("Roman Sepphoris," 322). "There can be little doubt that... virtually all of the inhabitants of Sepphoris in the first century were Jewish.... The considerable first-century remains that have been uncovered... point to a Torah-true population" (324–25). But he cites very little by way of "first-century remains" and, as noted below, neither Josephus nor rabbinic literature provides evidence of priestly families in first-century Sepphoris.

19. Thomas R. W. Longstaff, "Nazareth and Sepphoris: Insights into Christian Origins," *ATR* 11 (1990): 12; Strange, "Six Campaigns at Sepphoris," 331–35.

20. The claim that the population of first-century Sepphoris was "Torah-true" places a great deal of weight on both the presence of ritual baths (*miqva'ot*) and burial customs (Meyers, "Roman Sepphoris," 325). Perhaps we could reach greater precision in our analysis by abandoning essentialist definitions in favor of a more realistic sense of mixed culture. One could imagine Sepphorites of Judean — even priestly — heritage continuing traditional burial customs and ritual bathing while participating fully in the life of

the administrative city of a Roman-sponsored client-ruler, which would likely have involved use of Greek.

21. Meyers, Netzer, and Meyers, *Sepphoris*, 10, cf. 12. Meyers himself does not locate the priestly clan of Yedaiah in Sepphoris until "the second half of the first century" and admits that "the extent of their influence on local leadership is not evident in the immediate post-70 period" (Meyers, "Roman Sepphoris," 326). Earlier scholarly arguments for priestly presence in first-century Sepphoris rely first on the lists of the twenty-four priestly courses (and their locations in Galilee) in medieval liturgical poems known as *piyyu-tim*, then take at face value the rabbinic tradition that included "the sons of Yedaiah," from the eighth-century Kohelet Rabbah. The earlier parallel in *y. Kil.* 9, 32b, however, lacks the crucial "sons of Yedaiah."

22. Stuart S. Miller, *Studies in the History and Tradition of Sepphoris* (Leiden: Brill, 1984), 62–88, 120–27.

23. It is even claimed, on the basis of a rabbinic tradition and a Josephus reference, that one priestly family in Sepphoris was so prominent that shortly before his death Herod bestowed the high priesthood on two of its members (*t. Yoma* 1.4; *y. Yoma* 1, 38d; *b. Yoma* 12b; and Josephus, *Ant.* 17.166; see, e.g., Menahem Stern, "Herod and the Herodian Dynasty," in *The Jewish People in the First Century*, CRINT 1.1, ed. S. Safrai and M. Stern (Assen: Van Gorcum, 1974), 272 n. 2. Stern and others, trusting these rabbinic traditions as good evidence for the prominence of the Sepphorean Joseph ben Ellim (who served as high priest for an hour!) at the time of Herod, then draws the conclusion that, because Josephus (in *Ant.* 17.166) describes Joseph as his "relative," the high priest Matthias was also from Galilee. See Freyne, *Galilee from Alexander the Great to Hadrian*, 165, 285, who takes the implications a logical step further, citing Joseph ben Ellim as an example of "priestly aristocratic landowners in Sepphoris," a step that Meyers appears to follow.

24. Miller, *Studies in Sepphoris*. Only one rabbinic text (*y. Ta'an.* 4, 68d) can be used to locate the priestly course of Yedaiah in Sepphoris, and that probably only in the fourth century, which fits with the dating of a fragmentary inscription of the priestly courses found at Caesarea. There is no evidence in the rabbinic traditions that Joseph ben Elim had any special social or political standing among the priestly aristocracy; and Josephus's reference to his "relative" Matthias does not place the latter in Sepphoris (Miller, *Studies in Sepphoris*, 62–88). There may also have been an influx of priests in the third and fourth centuries. It is curious, however, that these rabbinic traditions portray the legendary figure "ben Hamsan" and Joseph ben Elim as aggressive and self-interested (102). Similarly, the later tradition of Rabbi Berakhiah portrays the priestly course of Yedaiah as having been exiled to Sepphoris because of some wrongdoing. The rabbis were apparently critical, even somewhat hostile.

25. James F. Strange, "Some Implications of Archaeology for New Testament Studies," in *What Has Archaeology to Do With Faith?* ed. James H.

Charlesworth and Walter Weaver (Valley Forge, Pa.: Trinity Press International, 1992), 33.

26. So also Longstaff, "Nazareth and Sepphoris," 12.

27. When Strange, "Some Implications of Archaeology," 38, says that the relation of Jewish cultural elements would have varied with whichever element of the culture is under discussion he seems to imply that any given element can be discussed in abstraction from the overall context of the imperial situation in Roman Palestine.

28. On Herod's building projects, see now Peter Richardson, *Herod: King of the Jews and Friend of the Romans* (University of South Carolina Press, 1996), chapter 8.

29. Strange, "Some Implications of Archaeology," 32.

30. Vs. ibid.

31. Ibid., 39

32. Ibid., 34.

33. Thus the capacity of the Sepphoris theater at 5,000 may be another indication of the city's population in the first century. Cf. the 24,000 capacity at Ephesus, and the capacity of 10,000 for many medium-sized cities in the Roman empire: Mary T. Boatwright, "Theatres in the Roman Empire," *BA* 53 (1990): 185, 191.

34. Ibid., 185.

35. Meyers, "Cultural Setting of Galilee," 697–98.

36. It is difficult to discern how Cynic philosophers and their influence would fit the particular circumstances of Galilee in what must have been a transitional time as it adjusted to the new urban presence in its midst, both economically and culturally (see the conclusion). The mixed culture of Sepphoris and Tiberias should probably be viewed as somewhat similar to those of the cities of the Decapolis and other cities on the Eastern frontier of the Roman empire. The older view of these cities as islands of Hellenistic culture midst a Semitic sea is now changing to one characterized as a diverse population with a "veneer" or "all the external trappings" of Roman-Hellenistic urban culture. See, e.g., J. M. C. Bowsher, "Architecture and Religion in the Decapolis: A Numismatic Survey," *Palestine Exploration Quarterly* 119 (1987): 62; D. F. Graf, "The Nabataeans and the Decapolis," in *The Defense of the Roman and Byzantine East*, eds., P. Freeman and D. Kennedy (Oxford: BAR, 1986), 785–96; Glen W. Bowersock, *Hellenism in Late Antiquity* (Ann Arbor: University of Michigan Press, 1990), 7.

37. Meyers, "Roman Sepphoris," 326.

38. Michael Avi-Yonah, *A Gazetteer of Roman Palestine* (Jerusalem: Institute of Archaeology, Hebrew University, 1976), 95; Joan E. Taylor, *Christians and the Holy Places: The Myth of Jewish-Christian Origins* (Oxford: Clarendon Press, 1993), 53.

39. Y. Meshorer, *City-Coins of Eretz-Israel and the Decapolis in the Roman Period* (Jerusalem, 1985), 36–37. Meshorer reads the aniconic symbols on

the coins of Sepphoris during the previous reign of Trajan (palm tree, laurel wreath, ears of grain) as representative of the Jewish population in the city.

40. Started, although perhaps never completed, according to Taylor, *Christians and the Holy Places*, 53.

41. Michael Avi-Yonah, *The Jews under Roman and Byzantine Rule* (New York: Schocken, 1976). On the policy in general, Andrew Wallace-Hadrill, "Elites and Trade in the Roman Town," in *City and Country in the Ancient World*, ed. John Rich and Andrew Wallace-Hadrill (London: Routledge, 1992), 249: "Urbanisation is the unmistakable result of Roman control, and indeed without the self-governing mechanisms of the city-state Roman imperial government could scarcely have operated." See further, Peter Garnsey and Richard Saller, *The Roman Empire: Economy, Society, and Culture* (Berkeley: University of California Press, 1987), esp. 28–30.

42. Zeev Safrai, "The Roman Army in the Galilee," in *Galilee in Late Antiquity*, ed. Levine, 104–6.

43. Meyers believes that the priestly clan of Yedaiah relocated in Sepphoris either before or after the Bar Kokhba Revolt (Meyers, "Roman Sepphoris," 326; Meyers, Netzer, and Meyers, *Sepphoris*, 12). Miller (*Studies in Sepphoris*, 120–27) finds that only one rabbinic text (*y. Ta'an.* 4.68d) allows the location of the priestly clan of Yedaiah in Sepphoris, and that only in the fourth century.

44. Meyers, Netzer, and Meyers, *Sepphoris*, 21.

45. See further "Tiberias," in *NEAEHL* 1466–68.

46. See Lee I. Levine, "The Jewish Patriarch (Nasi) in Third-Century Palestine," *ANRW* 2.19.2 (1979): 649–88, and *The Rabbinic Class of Roman Palestine in Late Antiquity* (New York: Jewish Theological Seminary of America, 1989), chap. 4.

47. Just what can be deduced from the legend on the coin is a matter of dispute: see Y. Meshorer, "Sepphoris and Rome," in *Greek Numismatics and Archaeology — Essays in Honor of Margaret Thompson*, ed. O. Markholm and N. M. Waggoner (Wetteren, 1976); and C. M. Kraay, "Jewish Finds and Allies of Rome," *American Numismatic Society Museum Notes* 25 (1980): 53–57. What degree of Jewish prominence in Sepphorean politics, particularly membership on the city *boule*, can be inferred from *y. Pe'a* 1.1.16a; *y. Šabb.* 12.3.13c (*bouletai*) and *b. Sanh.* 8a (Jewish majority on the *boule?*) requires further critical examination of those rabbinic traditions, *pace* F. Manns, "An Important Jewish-Christian Center: Sepphoris," in *Essais sur le Judeo-Christianisme* (Jerusalem: Franciscan Printing Press, 1977), 165–90.

48. Meyers, "Roman Sepphoris," 329; Meyers, Netzer, and Meyers, *Sepphoris*, 21–29, 39–50.

49. E.g., Meyers, "Roman Sepphoris," 329; Meyers, Netzer, and Meyers, *Sepphoris*, 29.

50. Meyers, "Roman Sepphoris," 332; Strange, "Six Campaigns at Sepphoris," 345. Debate about what constitutes a *miqveh* or Jewish ritual bath and

how one can be identified will continue for some time before any helpful consensus will be reached. To date the discussion has yielded interpretative dominance to rabbinic literature. Moreover, it has proceeded largely in essentialist terms, with little or no attention to context and social location. The maximalist position, that nearly all stepped pools are *miqva'ot*, has been articulated largely by Ronnie Reich, with shorter treatments available in English: "More on Miqwa'ot," *BAR* 13 (1987): 59–60; "Four Notes on Jerusalem," *IEJ* 37 (1987): 158–67; "The Bath-House (Balneum), the Miqweh and the Jewish Community in the Second Temple Period," *JJS* 39 (1988): 102–7; and "The Great Mikveh Debate," *BAR* 19 (1993): 52–53. A somewhat cautionary position is articulated by Benjamin G. Wright, "Jewish Ritual Baths — Interpreting the Digs and the Texts," in *The Archaeology of Israel: Constructing the Past/Interpreting the Present,* ed. Neil Asher Silberman and David B. Small (Sheffield: Sheffield Academic Press, forthcoming 1997).

51. Meyers, "Roman Sepphoris," 329.

52. Vs. Goodman, *State and Society in Roman Galilee*, 88–89.

53. Meyers, Netzer, and Meyers, *Sepphoris*, 60.

54. Isaiah Gafni, "Reinterment in the Land of Israel: Notes on the Origin and Development of the Custom," *Jerusalem Cathedra* 1 (1981): 96–104; Zeev Weiss, "Social Aspects of Burial in Beth She'arim: Archaeological Finds and Talmudic Sources," in *Galilee in Late Antiquity,* ed. Levine 357–71.

55. Vs. Goodman, *State and Society in Roman Galilee*, 93, 177–78.

56. Shaye J. D. Cohen, "The Place of the Rabbi in Jewish Society of the Second Century," in *Galilee in Late Antiquity*, ed. Levine, 169, citing such tannaitic traditions as *t. Šabb.* 2.5, 13.2; *t.'Erub.* 1.2; 6.2; *t. Pesaḥ.* 10.12; *t. Sukk.* 1.9; *t. Ter.* 2.13; *t. Ḥag* 2.13; Levine, *Rabbinic Class of Palestine*, 69–71; Stuart S. Miller, "Intercity Relations in Roman Palestine: The Case of Sepphoris and Tiberias," *AJSRev* 12 (1987): 12–13.

57. Goodman, *State and Society in Roman Galilee*, chap. 7; Cohen, "Place of the Rabbi in Jewish Society." On the "synagogues" as village assemblies, see chapter 6 below. The rabbis did not take a leading role in the synagogues until the sixth or seventh century, according to Shaye J. D. Cohen, *From the Maccabees to the Mishnah* (Philadelphia: Westminster Press, 1987), 111–15, 219–21.

58. See A. Oppenheimer, *The Am ha-Aretz: A Study in the Social History of the Jewish People in the Hellenistic-Roman Period* (Leiden: Brill, 1977); Cohen, "Place of the Rabbi in Jewish Society."

59. Horsley, *Galilee*, 182–85.

Chapter 3. Trade, Tithes, Tribute, and Taxes

1. Eric M. Meyers, "Introduction," in Richard S. Hanson, *Tyrian Influence in the Upper Galilee: Meiron Excavation Project 2* (Cambridge, Mass.: ASOR, 1980), 1–2. Meyers insists that this should come as "a stunning piece of evi-

dence" for the biblical scholar, talmudist, and classicist who view Galilee as a cultural backwater out of the mainstream of Judaism.

2. Hanson, *Tyrian Influence in the Upper Galilee*, 53. The same conclusion that the presence of Tyrian coins means active trade with Tyre appears in previous publications, such as Eric M. Meyers, "The Cultural Setting of Galilee: The Case of Regionalism and Early Judaism," *ANRW* 2.19.1 (1979): 700; and "Galilean Regionalism: A Reappraisal," in *Approaches to Ancient Judaism*, vol. 5, ed. William S. Green (Atlanta: Scholars Press, 1985), 123. It is clear from the relative attention devoted to Tyrian history, politics, and culture, however, that the principal purpose of Hanson's monograph, as he comments just prior to the survey of the numismatic evidence, is to "gain further understanding of what was happening in Tyre itself," by "paying attention to the symbols on those coins" (54).

3. Meyers, "Introduction," 2–3.

4. Eric M. Meyers, James F. Strange, and Carol L. Meyers, *Excavations at Ancient Meiron* (Cambridge, Mass.: ASOR, 1981), 157–58.

5. Drawing on the critical historiographical treatments by Shaye J. D. Cohen, *Josephus in Galilee and Rome: His Vita and Development as a Historian* (Leiden: Brill, 1979); Tessa Rajak, *Josephus: The Historian and His Society* (London: Duckworth, 1983); and Per Bilde, *Flavius Josephus Between Jerusalem and Rome: His Life, His Works, and Their Importance*, JSOT SS 2 (Sheffield: JSOT Press, 1988).

6. Even the profiteering motive Josephus attributes to John appears more blatantly "rhetorical" in the *Life*. Anyone familiar with the cost of overland transport in antiquity (doubling the price with every ten miles) would be aware that John's margin of profit would have been a good deal less than implied by the simple comparison of price.

7. First of all, procedurally the coins found in Upper Galilee would need to be evaluated in the context of the provenance and use of coins generally from the Persian era through Byzantine times. As relevant information to that evaluation, the strata in which coins were found would have to be taken into consideration at every step of the evaluation.

8. See Meshorer, "Hoard of Coins from Migdal," 54–71. The archaeologists excavating in Upper Galilee would appear to have been aware of the extent to which Tyre supplied coinage to the whole Levant; as Hanson comments (*Tyrian Influence in the Upper Galilee*, 69 n. 5): "There may actually have been a larger supply of Tyrian coins in lower Galilee than previously supposed."

9. In a study published since the appearance of the work of Hanson et al., D. Barag, "Tyrian Currency in Galilee," *Israel Numismatic Journal* 6–7 (1982–83): 13, concludes that coins found in a number of excavations and hordes indicate that Tyrian coinage was more frequent than coins from other mints in Lower Galilee and further south. This probably means Tyre was authorized to produce coins on a larger scale than other mints.

10. Hanson, *Tyrian Influence in the Upper Galilee*, 67, citing Meyers's previous analysis, summarizes: Linguistically, moreover, the "population used Aramaic predominantly and Hebrew considerably," with much less Greek than in the rest of Galilee to the south.

11. "The peculiar features of Upper Galilean economy" would appear to distinguish it from the "cosmopolitan and pagan culture" of Tyre, little of which would appear to have "filtered back to the local [Galilean] villages," according to Meyers, "Introduction," 3.

12. David Adan-Bayewitz, *Common Pottery in Roman Galilee: A Study of Local Trade* (Ramat-Gan, Israel: Bar Ilan University Press, 1993), 246.

13. Ibid.; D. Adan-Bayewitz and Isadore Perlman, "The Local Trade of Sepphoris in the Roman Period," *IEJ* 40 (1990): 153–72.

14. Adan-Bayewitz, *Common Pottery in Roman Galilee*, 247: "In a rigorous sense, by determining the place of production and the recovery sites of common pottery we learn about trade in that one commodity." Yet, he hopes, "it is entirely possible that pottery . . . is only a symptom of more widespread commercial, and perhaps cultural, interaction which has left no other tangible trace."

15. Ibid., 19, citing the basic treatments of the Roman economy by A. H. M. Jones, R. MacMullen, and M. Finley, as confirmed by subsequent investigations by Garnsey, Hopkins, et al.

16. Ibid., 248.

17. Ibid., 229–30. The rabbinic passages refer to potters carrying or handling their pots, presumably to the buyers, but make no suggestion of a "market." The latter is supplied only by modern scholars.

18. Ibid., 232, referring to his study "The Itinerant Peddler in Roman Palestine," in *Jews in Economic Life*, ed. N. Gross (Jerusalem, 1985; in Hebrew).

19. Adan-Bayewitz, *Common Pottery in Roman Galilee*, 233 n. 7.

20. Keith Hopkins, "Economic Growth and Towns in Classical Antiquity," in *Towns and Societies*, ed. Philip Abrams and E. A. Wrigley (Cambridge: Cambridge University Press, 1978), 44. Cf. M. I. Finley's (*The Ancient Economy* [Berkeley: University of California Press, 1973], 137) curt critique of archaeologists and economic historians who follow Rostovtseff: "[pottery-manufacturing towns] flourish only in archaeological manuals." The distinguished classical archaeologist Anthony Snodgrass, "Archaeology," in *Sources for Ancient History*, ed. Michael Crawford (Cambridge: Cambridge University Press, 1983), 163, warns of "the 'positivist fallacy': pottery is nearly always the most plentiful and sometimes the only material evidence available — if we cannot use it, where else can we turn" (163), and points out that as "the economic significance of pottery exchanges has been scrutinised, many earlier conclusions about trade, economic policy and even political influence have been undermined" (169–70). With regard to ancient Greece, Athens in particular, archaeologist Robin Osborne, *Classical Landscape with Figures: The*

Ancient Greek City and Its Countryside (London: Sheridan House, 1987), 109, comments that "pottery can never have made a significant mark."

21. Hopkins, "Economic Growth and Towns in Classical Antiquity," 46. In contrast to the exaggeration of the system of roads in Galilee by archaeologists who emphasize trade, Mordechai Aviam offers a sobering, more realistic picture in "Galilee — Hellenistic to Byzantine Periods," *NEAEHL* 453–54.

22. Adan-Bayewitz and Perlman, "Local Trade of Sepphoris," 171–72, nn. 47 and 48, do not explain their claims and somewhat misrepresent the studies they cite.

23. These and the following phrases are taken from Martin Goodman, *State and Society in Roman Galilee, A.D. 132–212* (Totowa, N.J.: Rowman and Allanheld, 1983), 19, 54, 60–62; and Sean Freyne, *Galilee from Alexander the Great to Hadrian, 323 B.C.E. to 135 C.E.: A Study in Second Temple Judaism* (Wilmington, Del.: Michael Glazier, 1980), 170, 172, 175–77.

24. Goodman, *State and Society in Roman Galilee*, 54–60.

25. Ze'ev Safrai, *The Economy of Roman Palestine* (London: Routledge, 1994), 453, 430.

26. Ibid., 207–8, 390.

27. Daniel Sperber, "Objects of Trade between Palestine and Egypt in Roman Times," *JESHO* 19 (1976): 142–43.

28. Safrai, *Economy of Roman Palestine*, 126, 430. Nevertheless, that rabbinic traditions portray large-scale merchants as untrustworthy cheats (311) suggests that there were such merchants, at least in the cities.

29. Ibid., 237–38, 379–80. See further 399ff., 402 (coins).

30. Ibid., 115. The perhaps misleading statement on 365 is somewhat clarified on 368: "olives were undoubtedly also grown in Judaea and grapes also in the Galilee."

31. Ibid., 56, 58, 231, vs. 240–41.

32. Ibid., 239–41; Goodman, *State and Society in Roman Galilee*, 54.

33. Safrai, *Economy of Roman Palestine*, 231, 124.

34. Ibid., 353 (with illustrative examples), 200–201, 427–28, vs. the fragmenting statements on 352. It is thus highly doubtful that "village settlements . . . needed a trade network in order to market their surplus and buy necessary goods or commodities" (232).

35. Vs. ibid., 305–13.

36. Hopkins, "Economic Growth and Towns in Classical Antiquity," 57–58. With regard to ancient Greek farmers archaeologist Osborne, *Classical Landscape with Figures*, 23, 93, 103, 108: "Once farmers relied on the market on any scale they jeopardized their independence."

37. Safrai, *Economy of Roman Palestine*, 224–31. Safrai at first reads merchants into his texts (*m. B. Qam.* 3:4; *m. Tohar.* 7:1; etc.): "It would seem, then, that the potter brought his merchandise to market and sold it there to a shopkeeper or merchant." Then he corrects himself: "Even important

manufacturers such as those in Kefar Hananiah . . . , who produced their own pottery on a regional level, apparently sold their wares themselves" (229).

38. Lending and borrowing, mentioned frequently in rabbinic literature as well as in the Christian Gospels, should be understood as different from and perhaps more important in the village community than barter or trading. Cf. the comment of Osborne, *Classical Landscape with Figures*, 93: "Lending to neighbours, relatives and friends was part and parcel of everyday life."

39. Dean Arnold, *Ceramic Theory and Cultural Process* (Cambridge: Cambridge University Press, 1985), 193, 168.

40. Robert McC. Adams, *Heartland of Cities* (Chicago: University of Chicago Press, 1981); W. T. Sanders and B. J. Price, *The Basin of Mexico: Ecological Processes in the Evolution of a Civilization* (New York: Academic Press, 1979); Bruce Trigger, *A History of Archaeological Thought* (Cambridge: Cambridge University Press, 1989), 284.

41. See, e.g., the chapter on "Social Archaeology" in Colin Renfrew and Paul Bahn, *Archaeology: Theories, Methods, and Practice* (New York: Thames and Hudson, 1991).

42. Gerhard E. Lenski, *Power and Privilege: A Theory of Social Stratification* (New York: McGraw-Hill, 1966); Gideon Sjoberg, *The Preindustrial City* (Glencoe, Ill.: Free Press, 1964); G. E. M. de Ste. Croix, *The Class Struggle in the Ancient Greek World* (London: Duckworth, 1981).

43. Thomas F. Carney, *The Shape of the Past* (Lawrence, Kans.: Coronado, 1975).

44. Peter Garnsey and Richard Saller, *The Roman Empire: Economy, Society, and Culture* (Berkeley: University of California Press, 1987), 48. Kevin Greene, *The Archaeology of the Roman Economy* (London: Batsford, 1986), 14–16, provides a succinct review of research and theory on the "Roman Economy." That even the classical Greek city-states, basically agrarian and as self-sufficient as possible, also attempted to direct and control their economies politically is indicated by Osborne, *Classical Landscape with Figures*, 97–108; the grain supply was at the very center of the "politics" of the polis!

45. Renfrew and Bahn, *Archaeology*, 338; and Robert McC. Adams, "Anthropological Perspectives on Ancient Trade," *Current Anthropology* 15 (1974): 239–58.

46. Mireille Corbier, "City, Territory, and Taxation," in *City and Country in the Ancient World*, ed. John Rich and Andrew Wallace-Hadrill (London: Routledge, 1991), 219, notes the parallel with regard to the foundation of a city: "To give a territory — a *chora* — is in fact to confer a revenue."

47. Garnsey and Saller, *The Roman Empire*, 48.

48. Finley, "The Ancient City: From Fustel de Coulanges to Max Weber and Beyond," reprinted in *Economy and Society in Ancient Greece* (New York: Viking Press, 1981), 13.

49. Garnsey and Saller, *The Roman Empire*, 49.

50. On the problem of peasant indebtedness and its effects, see Martin Goodman, "The First Jewish Revolt: Social Conflict and the Problem of Debt," *JJS* 33 (1982): 418–27; and R. A. Horsley, *Sociology and the Jesus Movement* (New York: Crossroad/Continuum, 1989), 88–90.

51. Garnsey and Saller, *The Roman Empire*, 50.

52. Archaeological reports on the excavations at Jotapata/Yodfat will be forthcoming from Mordechai Aviam, who heads the project, and others.

53. Israel Shatzman, *The Armies of the Hasmoneans and Herod* (Tübingen: Mohr, 1991).

54. As often as not, the Hasmonean coins were found together with Roman coins of the fourth century c.e. Presumably this is why Hanson and Meyers, in *Tyrian Influence in Upper Galilee*, did not conclude that the volume of trade between Upper Galilee and Jerusalem in the early first century b.c.e. must have been far higher than that with neighboring Tyre in the third century c.e. But what about the 122 coins from pre-Hasmonean Tyre? In what strata were those earlier Tyrian coins found? Did Hanson take those as evidence of trade with Tyre, in contrast with the half of the Hasmonean coins not found with later Roman coins?

55. But why were virtually half of the Hasmonean coins found with fourth-century c.e. Roman coins? That with erosion many had simply washed into later strata below from earlier strata above may provide a partial explanation. But might it also have been because Upper Galilee was both a traditional agrarian economy with little local exchange and relatively isolated from commerce with the outside, such that the degree of monetary circulation was low and thus old coins were kept (in virtual nonusage, noncirculation) through several centuries?

56. See the rabbinic texts and other evidence cited in Goodman, *State and Society in Roman Galilee*, 130–34. Ironically, Goodman draws an inappropriate conclusion that "the role of the cities in the Galilean economy seems very slight" (133), not having discerned that the "economy" was not differentiated from the "purely [*sic*] administrative role" of the cities. But he has stated the important point in so many words, that "tax collection was the city's only important function," that the "*mokhsin* (tax collectors) were . . . most likely city officials," and that the city as "a market for goods . . . had comparatively little effect on its villages" (131–32). Political-economic relations in Galilee thus came to resemble those elsewhere in the Roman empire, as the Roman administration added tax collection to rents as means by which cities elsewhere exploited the countryside and as the tax-gathering functions resulted in Galilean peasant indebtedness, hence "rents" or "interest" owed to Sepphorean or Tiberian landlords. "Cities could live only by siphoning off the resources of the country, and this did not only take the form of rents. They derived profit from the collection of taxes and its inequalities" (Mireille Corbier, "City, Territory, and Taxation," in *City and Country in the Ancient World*, ed. Rich and Wallace-Hadrill, 234, 219).

57. See, e.g., Renfrew and Bahn, *Archaeology*, 307–11.

58. So also Safrai, *Economy of Roman Palestine*, 351.

59. Hopkins, "Economic Growth and Towns in Classical Antiquity," 59.

60. Adan-Bayewitz, *Common Pottery in Roman Galilee*, 236, speculates appropriately in this regard.

61. As suggested by Meyers, "Galilean Regionalism: A Reappraisal," 124.

62. See further "A Review of the History of Tyre," in Hanson, *Tyrian Influence in the Upper Galilee*, esp. 8–15.

63. Safrai, *Economy of Roman Palestine*, 349, notes that "taxes paid in kind ... were transferred directly from the producer to the consumer, viz. the Roman army." That, however, *was* the *government-administered* "business framework of the province."

64. Safrai, *Economy of Roman Palestine*, 267.

65. Vs. ibid., 115, we should not imagine that it was only "the surplus" that was "diverted" to the local markets and sold there. It is not only possible but certain "that the buying of wheat by these rabbis from the Galilee in Javneh does not represent regular trade."

66. James F. Strange, "First-Century Galilee from Archaeology and from the Texts," *Society of Biblical Literature 1994 Seminar Papers*, ed. Lovering (Atlanta: Scholars Press, 1994), 81.

67. Andrew Wallace-Hadrill, "Introduction," in *City and Country in the Ancient World*, ed. Rich and Wallace-Hadrill, x. Cf. Corbier, "City, Territory and Taxation," 222–23, who focuses on the images of the channeling of water (via aqueducts) and the stockpiling of grain as centripetal movements by which the cities siphoned off resources from their territories.

Chapter 4. Villages of Upper Galilee

Epigraph: Fernand Braudel, *The Mediterranean and the Mediterranean World in the Age of Philip II* (New York: Harper & Row, 1972), 1:33, 38.

1. The standard brief treatment of peasant society is Eric R. Wolf, *Peasants* (Englewood Cliffs, N.J.: Prentice-Hall, 1966). Cross-cultural historical studies such as the appropriate chapters of Gerhard Lenski, *Power and Privilege: A Theory of Social Stratification* (New York: McGraw-Hill, 1966); and John H. Kautsky, *The Politics of Aristocratic Empires* (Chapel Hill: University of North Carolina Press, 1982), require adaptation to the particular situation of Roman Galilee. On the latter see the more extensive analysis in Richard A. Horsley, *Galilee: History, Politics, People* (Valley Forge, Pa.: Trinity Press International, 1995), esp. chaps. 8–12.

2. Oral communication from Mordechai Aviam.

3. See further the discussion of household and village economy in chapter 3 above.

4. See further Horsley, *Galilee*, 189–93. Eric M. Meyers, "The Cultural Setting of Galilee: The Case of Regionalism and Early Judaism," *ANRW*

2.19.1 (1979): 700, estimates most villages in Upper Galilee at between 30 and 50 dunams (7.5–12.5 acres), which at 40 to 60 per acre would have these village populations at roughly 300–700 people each.

5. For a recent innovative (although still literarily problematic) attempt to combine archaeological and literary resources, see Ann Killibrew and Steven Fine, "Qatzrin: Reconstructing Village Life in Talmudic Times," *BAR* 17 (May/June 1991): 44–56.

6. See further D. H. K. Amiran, "Sites of Settlements in the Mountains of Lower Galilee," *IEJ* 6 (1956): 70–71.

7. Meyers, "Cultural Setting of Galilee," 689–90, 694–95.

8. Eric M. Meyers, "Galilean Regionalism as a Factor in Historical Reconstruction," *BASOR* 221 (1976): 97–99, and "Galilean Regionalism: A Reappraisal," in *Approaches to Ancient Judaism*, vol. 5, ed. W. S. Green (Atlanta: Scholars Press, 1985), 126; Eric M. Meyers and James F. Strange, *Archaeology, the Rabbis, and Early Christianity* (Nashville: Abingdon, 1981), 47.

9. Meyers, "Galilean Regionalism as a Factor in Historical Reconstruction," 101; Meyers and Strange, *Archaeology*, 43.

10. John Dominic Crossan, *The Historical Jesus: The Life of a Mediterranean Jewish Peasant* (San Francisco: HarperCollins, 1991), 15–19.

11. What are the criteria for the rather vague terms "Jewish" and "conservative" applied to Upper Galilean material culture? One suspects they have something to do with rabbinic literature. But we believe that the Mishnah itself was promulgated by Judah the Prince, friend of emperors, who produced this epitome of "Judaism" in the midst of that large urban center of cosmopolitan culture, Diocaesarea (Sepphoris).

12. Meyers and Strange, *Archaeology*, 43–44. But Beth-Shearim was not even clearly part of "Galilee" in the first century and was certainly not typical later.

13. See further chapter 7.

14. Ruth Vale, "Literary Sources in Archaeological Description: The Case of Galilee, Galilees, and Galileans," *JSJ* 18 (1987): 209-26; cf. Meyers, "Galilean Regionalism as a Factor in Historical Reconstruction," 99.

15. See further chapter 6.

16. As seen by Michael Avi-Yonah, *The Holy Land from the Persian to the Arab Conquest (536 B.C.E.–C.E. 640)* (Grand Rapids, Mich.: Baker, 1966), 112, who provided the basis for the regional hypothesis.

17. As might be implied from ibid.: "Greco-Roman culture...was regarded as a precondition of urban life" (112). As indicated in the epigraph to this chapter, Braudel is suggesting that there were structural obstacles to the "urbanization" of more rugged territories.

18. For example, in Meyers and Strange, *Archaeology*, 27, 32, 34, 38, 42, 141–43. Meyers and Strange find this resettlement of Judeans in Galilee to be an explanatory factor for a number of issues, from the lack of finds in the

early Roman period (34) to the eventual construction of synagogue buildings (141).

19. It may be significant that some standard histories of the Jews under Roman rule do not discuss such a migration: e.g., Michael Avi-Yonah, *The Jews under Roman and Byzantine Rule* (New York: Schocken, 1976), and E. Mary Smallwood, *The Jews under Roman Rule* (Leiden: Brill, 1976).

20. Admitting the lack of archaeological evidence for migration of Judeans to Galilee, Eric Meyers elsewhere refers somewhat vaguely to "the lists of priestly courses, Josephus, and the rabbinic literature" as literary evidence ("Cultural Setting of Galilee," 701; Meyers and Strange, *Archaeology*, 46). Josephus, of course, who wrote at the end of the first century, is an unlikely source.

21. Stuart S. Miller, *Studies in the History and Tradition of Sepphoris* (Leiden: Brill, 1984), 122–27.

22. Eric M. Meyers now admits that "archaeology can't really help us determine whether the priestly courses mentioned in the literature...are present" ("An Archaeological Response to a New Testament Scholar," *BASOR* 297 [1995]: 20). But the literary references are late and problematic. Little wonder then that "the question of the priestly courses and their settlement in Galilee remains a problem begging of solution" (20). Meyers, however, persists in the assumption of "the tremendous demographic shift after the Bar Kokhba war, which caused so many southerners to relocate to Galilee," despite the problematic literary evidence (21).

23. Michael Avi-Yonah, "The Caesarea Inscription of the Twenty-Four Priestly Courses," in *The Teacher's Yoke: Studies in Memory of Henry Trantham*, ed. E. J. Vardaman et al. (Waco, Tex.: Baylor University Press, 1964).

24. Argued from the limited evidence in Horsley, *Galilee*, chaps. 1–2.

25. Sean Freyne, *Galilee from Alexander the Great to Hadrian, 323 B.C.E. to 135 C.E.: A Study in Second Temple Judaism* (Wilmington, Del.: Michael Glazier, 1980), pictures the Galileans as having been "reunited" with their political and cultural "matrix" in Jerusalem.

26. On the dynamics of the "great tradition" vs. the "little tradition," see James C. Scott, "Protest and Profanation: Agrarian Revolt and the Little Tradition," *Theory and Society* 4 (1977): 1–38, 211–46.

27. The claim that "Josephus pictures Galilee as consisting mainly of Torah-true Jews" (Meyers, "Galilean Regionalism as a Factor in Historical Reconstruction," 93; "The Cultural Setting," 693, 701) is based solely on a 1973 dissertation written prior to much of the critical reading of Josephus's histories, such as Shaye J. D. Cohen, *Josephus in Galilee and Rome: His Vita and Development as a Historian* (Leiden: Brill, 1979); Tessa Rajak, *Josephus: The Historian and His Society* (London: Duckworth, 1983); and Per Bilde, *Flavius Josephus Between Jerusalem and Rome: His Life, His Works, and Their Importance* (Sheffield: JSOT Press, 1988).

28. Perhaps because Meiron became a holy site of pilgrimage later in the Middle Ages there has been a tendency to exaggerate its importance earlier in trade and communications. Even in the construction of the network of roadways between villages, we cannot infer that "Meiron lay on a major east-west route through upper Galilee," much less that it "straddled a major ancient crossroads and constituted the very heart of Jewish Galilee in all its conservatism" (Eric M. Meyers, James F. Strange, and Carol L. Meyers, *Excavations at Ancient Meiron* [Cambridge, Mass.: ASOR, 1981], 6, 4).

29. Ze'ev Safrai, *The Economy of Roman Palestine* (London: Routledge, 1994), 274–87, summarizes information on "the main road system" and "the local road system" with an apparatus far more elaborate than warranted by the importance of local networks for trade.

30. Eric M. Meyers, James F. Strange, Carol L. Meyers, and R. S. Hanson, "Preliminary Report on the 1977 and 1978 Seasons at Gush Halav," *BASOR* 233 (1979): 35–36. The formulation of a pottery typology as a basis for the stratigraphy of these village sites was a major contribution of these excavations.

31. With all this evidence for a fortress and garrison at Gush Halav, it is unclear why Meyers et al. conclude that there may also have been a garrison attached to the small community at Meiron, at such close proximity (*Excavations at Ancient Meiron*, 155).

32. Cf. ibid., 155–56; Meyers et al., "1977 and 1978 Seasons at Gush Halav," 36. Without citing particular evidence, Meyers asserts elsewhere that "on the basis of material culture alone, it would appear that Upper Galilean village life was firmly rooted, with its own distinctive elements, by the time the Second Temple was destroyed" ("Galilean Regionalism as a Factor in Historical Reconstruction," 101). Given that representatives of Jerusalem rule would have influenced the area for only a century prior to 4 B.C.E. and that the supposed influx of Judeans was later, Upper Galilean village life was presumably firmly rooted in traditional northern "Israelite" culture. That would have made it different from Jerusalem culture as well as from the Hellenistic-Roman "royal" cities of Lower Galilee.

33. Meyers, Strange, and Meyers, *Excavations at Ancient Meiron*, 156.

34. Meyers et al., "1977 and 1978 Seasons at Gush Halav," 55.

35. For fuller treatment of John and Gischala, see Horsley, *Galilee*, 81–83, and "Ancient Jewish Banditry and the Revolt against Rome, A.D. 66–70," *CBQ* 43 (1981): 409–32.

36. Although Meyers et al., "1977 and 1978 Seasons at Gush Halav," find no evidence of participation in the revolt of 66–67 in the villages themselves (except presumably the literary evidence for Gush Halav!), John of Gischala and others fled to Jerusalem. Does that suggest dedication to the Temple or simply a desperate flight from and continuation of resistance to the Roman reconquest?

37. Ibid., 55.

38. Cf. ibid., 36.

39. If, as the excavators admit, "stratigraphically speaking, a pre-70 C.E. community cannot be isolated from a post-70 C.E. community," then it is unclear what archaeological evidence they found in the Hellenistic and Early Roman strata (i.e., up to 135) that led them to claim a growth in the community's size or "a slow and gradual intensification of the Jewish character of Meiron" (Meyers, Strange, and Meyers, *Excavations at Ancient Meiron*, 156). Were the findings from earlier strata any less "aniconic" than those of that Late Roman stratum? Nor do they specify "the persistent reminders" from the Early Roman stratum that "despite Meiron's more priestly character" its material culture fits "within the mainstream of everyday life of first-century Palestine . . . strongly influenced . . . by outside influences, notably Hellenism" (156–57).

40. Meyers, Strange, and Meyers, *Excavations at Ancient Meiron*, 3, 156. In this connection the authors write that "it is this influx of new blood from Judea which enables the village to develop its distinctive character and its special sense of community"; and "archaeologically speaking they [the clan of Yehoiariv's] impact is readily discernible in the growth and building activity" of the Middle Roman period (135–250). However, they do not indicate what evidence leads them to these rather sweeping statements.

41. In their "preliminary observations" regarding the implications of neutron-activation analysis for pottery found at Meiron, Gush Halav, and Khirbet Shema', the excavators suggest that, despite their unknown provenance, certain vessels found at Meiron "have apparently been brought in from elsewhere in the Late Second Temple period," and claim that "surface sherding and survey in the area has tended to support the inference of a shift in population sometime in the Early Roman period" (Meyers, Strange, and Meyers, *Excavations at Ancient Meiron*, 145–46). Eric Meyers's more recent reaffirmation of the role of neutron-activation analysis appears to make the migration interpretation of the pottery findings dependent on the prior acceptance of the premise of "a major demographic shift . . . either after the first or second war with Rome" ("Archaeological Response," 20).

42. The medical report on the bones recovered in a tomb (spanning the second to the fourth centuries) at Meiron, indicating disease resulting from endogamy, or marriage among kin, may illustrate the problem of social conflict. The indigenous Galilean peasants and the conservative Judean priestly families would have found it difficult to assimilate to each other, with all the attendant issues of status and power. If endogamy is a credible hypothesis for the disease evident in the bones (Meyers, Strange, and Meyers, *Excavations at Ancient Meiron*, 110–18), then it would be consistent with the social conflict within the village that may have resulted from the influx of a priestly clan or other Judeans.

43. Ibid., 157. The hypothesis of a Roman-style town plan is based on only one "planned insula laid over [the Early Roman] remains" and is found

doubtful by Gideon Foerster, "Excavations at Ancient Meron," *IEJ* 37 (1987): 266. Unclear is how a decreasing number of coins somehow indicates a burgeoning population. Presumably the better indicators of population growth, an increase in space occupied or the density of occupation, were beyond the scope of a limited excavation. The excavators' parallel hypothesis of "expansion and modest wealth" for the nearby village of Nabratein is more credibly based on their finds in a villa that coincided with the construction of a synagogue building there (Eric M. Meyers, James F. Strange, and Carol L. Meyers, "Preliminary Report on the 1980 Excavations at en-Nabratein," *BASOR* 244 [1981]: 14). Of course, such construction might indicate less an expansion of population than the emergence of a modestly wealthy social stratum which spearheaded the mobilization of labor and economic resources for such major building projects.

44. Meyers, Strange, and Meyers, *Excavations at Ancient Meiron*, 36–38, 157–58. A fuller critique in Horsley, "Archaeology and the Villages of Upper Galilee: A Dialogue with Archaeologists," *BASOR* 297 (1995): 10–11.

45. Foerster, "Excavations at Ancient Meron," 266–67.

46. Meyers, Strange, and Meyers, *Excavations at Ancient Meiron*, 3 n. 23. With regard to the hypothesized barrels in which the oil was supposedly shipped, moreover, early rabbinic literature would presumably have been concerned about the purity of such vessels, making the presence/absence of such a topic in rabbinic literature an appropriate test of the hypothesis.

47. As noted in chapter 3, a consensus of ancient historians, such as M. I. Finley, *The Ancient Economy* (Berkeley: University of California Press, 1973), 95–149; A. H. M. Jones, *The Roman Economy* (Oxford: Blackwell, 1974), 29–60; Peter Garnsey and Richard Saller, *The Roman Empire: Economy, Society, and Culture* (Berkeley: University of California Press, 1987), 42–46.

48. So also Safrai, *Economy of Roman Palestine*, 387.

49. Meyers et al., "1977 and 1978 Seasons at Gush Halav," 56.

50. On the following, see Meyers, Strange, and Meyers, *Excavations at Ancient Meiron*, 41–44, 65–72; and Foerster, "Excavations at Ancient Meron," 267–68.

51. Meyers, Strange, and Meyers, *Excavations at Ancient Meiron*, 4.

52. Ibid., 4–5. For recent construction of the place of the rabbis in Galilean society based on critical analysis of rabbinic sources, see now Lee I. Levine, *The Rabbinic Class of Roman Palestine in Late Antiquity* (New York: Jewish Theological Seminary of America, 1989); and Shaye J. D. Cohen, "The Place of the Rabbi in Jewish Society of the Second Century," in *The Galilee in Late Antiquity*, ed. Lee I. Levine (New York: Jewish Theological Seminary of America, 1992).

53. *Pace* Meyers, "Archaeological Response," 19.

54. Cf. Levine, *Rabbinic Class of Roman Palestine*, 101.

Chapter 5. Villages of Lower Galilee

1. See now Joan E. Taylor, *Christians and the Holy Places: The Myth of Jewish Christian Origins* (Oxford: Clarendon Press, 1993).

2. Epiphanius, *Panarion* 30.11.10 (written 375–377); Taylor, *Christians and the Holy Places*, 227.

3. Bellarmino Bagatti, *Excavations in Nazareth*, vol. 1, *From the Beginning til the XII Century* (Jerusalem: Franciscan Printing House, 1969), 27, 29, 32, 35, 37, 52–59.

4. See further Taylor, *Christians and the Holy Places*, 244–50.

5. Eric M. Meyers and James F. Strange, *Archaeology, the Rabbis, and Early Christianity* (Nashville: Abingdon, 1981), 57.

6. As suggested by John Dominic Crossan, *The Historical Jesus: The Life of a Mediterranean Jewish Peasant* (San Francisco: HarperCollins, 1991), 17.

7. James F. Strange, "Nazareth," in *ABD* 4.1051.

8. Ibid., 1050; Bagatti, *Excavations at Nazareth*, 1:28.

9. Meyers and Strange, *Archaeology*, 57.

10. Colin Renfrew and Paul Bahn, *Archaeology: Theories, Methods, and Practice* (New York: Thames and Hudson, 1991).

11. Eric M. Meyers, "An Archaeological Response to a New Testament Scholar," *BASOR* 297 (1995): 21.

12. See the sketch in R. A. Horsley, "Popular Messianic Movements Around the Time of Jesus," *CBQ* 46 (1984): 471–95; and R. A. Horsley with John S. Hanson, *Bandits, Prophets, and Messiahs: Popular Movements at the Time of Jesus* (San Francisco: Harper and Row, 1985), chap. 3.

13. On the following, see the fuller analysis and argument by Taylor, *Christians and the Holy Places*, chap. 12.

14. Based on Taylor's critical reassessment, ibid., 274, 287.

15. V. C. Corbo, *The House of St. Peter at Capernaum* (Jerusalem: Franciscan Printing Press, 1969), 107–11; cf. James F. Strange, "The Capernaum and Herodium Publications (Part I)," *BASOR* 226 (1977): 69. The latter is an important critical review article on the publications by the Franciscan excavators of the western end of Capernaum.

16. The following is based on the close analysis of Taylor, *Christians and the Holy Places*, 278–84, 288–89.

17. Meyers and Strange, *Archaeology*, 58, apparently keying from Captain R. E. Wilson's 1871 estimate of the area covered by ruins.

18. Jonathan Reed, "The Population of Capernaum," *Occasional Papers of the Institute for Antiquity and Christianity* 24 (Claremont, Calif., 1992). With a still-generous estimate of the size of the first-century site and a realistic figure for the density of the population, Reed calculates Capernaum at 1,700, maximum.

19. S. Loffreda, "The Synagogue of Capernaum: Archaeological Evidence of Its Late Chronology," *LA* 20 (1972): 20; John C. H. Laughlin, "Caper-

naum: From Jesus' Time and After," *BAR* (Sept/Oct 1993): 57. This had been Strange's earlier estimate as well in 1976 (*IDB Suppl*), and it accords with Josephus's reference to "Kepharnocus" as an obscure "village" (*Vita* 403).

20. Corbo, *ABD* 1.866–68.

21. Corbo, *The House of St. Peter at Capernaum*, 37, 39.

22. Laughlin, "Capernaum," 57.

23. Ibid.

24. Ibid., 58, 59.

25. Meyers and Strange, *Archaeology*, 59.

26. In a portrayal that may owe something to the legends of the Maccabean martyrs and/or the story of Taxo in the *Assumption of Moses*, Josephus embellishes on the heroic resistance to the tyrant Herod:

> An old man who had been caught inside one of the caves with his wife and seven children...stood at the entrance and cut down each of his sons as they came to the mouth of the cave, and then his wife. After throwing their dead bodies down the steep slope, he threw himself down also, thus submitting to death rather than slavery. (*Ant.* 14.429–30)

27. The most extreme form of this line of interpretation is represented by Douglas R. Edwards, "The Socio-Economic and Cultural Ethos of the Lower Galilee in the First Century: Implications for the Nascent Jesus Movement," in *The Galilee in Late Antiquity*, ed. Lee I. Levine (New York: Jewish Theological Seminar, 1992), 53–73; and the earlier SBL seminar paper, "First-Century Urban/Rural Relations in Lower Galilee: Exploring the Archaeological and Literary Evidence," in *Society of Biblical Literature 1988 Seminar Papers*, ed. David J. Lull (Atlanta: Scholars Press, 1988), 169–82.

28. Eric M. Meyers, "The Cultural Setting of Galilee: The Case of Regionalism and Early Judaism," *ANRW* 2.19.1 (1979): 197–98.

29. James F. Strange, "Some Implications of Archaeology for New Testament Studies," in *What Has Archaeology to Do with Faith?* ed. James Charlesworth and Walter Weaver (Valley Forge, Pa.: Trinity Press International, 1993), 32, 41.

30. Eric M. Meyers, "Roman Sepphoris in Light of New Archaeological Evidence and Recent Research," in *Galilee in Late Antiquity*, ed. Levine, 333.

31. Ironically this passage is cited to illustrate how communities such as Nazareth were "dependent villages" in relation to Sepphoris.

32. Peter Garnsey, *Social Status and Legal Privilege in the Roman Empire* (Oxford: Clarendon Press, 1970).

33. Mary T. Boatwright, "Theatres in the Roman Empire," *BA* 53 (1990): 184–92.

34. Strange discusses a number of "urban features of Mark and Q" without discerning any serious tension between city and village life, in "Some Implications of Archaeology," 41–47.

35. Even if traditional Galilean culture had been under pressure for some time, we should not imagine it had simply disappeared. We believe that the Mishnah itself was promulgated by Judah the Prince in the midst of Diocaesarea (Sepphoris), by around 200 C.E. supposedly a large urban center of cosmopolitan culture. It seems clear that traditional rabbinic-Jewish and other Palestinian culture could survive, even thrive directly in the midst of (or is it over against?) cosmopolitan Greco-Roman culture. And if traditional culture could thrive in Diocaesarea, then how much more in the villages and towns?

36. See the analysis of these accounts by Josephus and conclusions drawn in R. A. Horsley, *Galilee: History, Politics, People* (Valley Forge, Pa.: Trinity Press International, 1995), 152–57.

37. E.g., Sean Freyne, *Galilee from Alexander the Great to Hadrian, 323 B.C.E. to 135 C.E.: A Study in Second Temple Judaism* (Wilmington, Del.: Michael Glazier, 1980), 309–18.

38. Josephus's accounts of Galilean hostility to Sepphoris fit both reconstructions of the political-cultural ethos of the city in the first century C.E., whether the Strange-Longstaff evidence of extensive (re-)building activity probably by Antipas (including the theater) or the Meyers et al. picture of a city dominated by aristocratic Jewish families. Although he believes it subsides by later in the second century, Meyers understands the "tensions between town and city," the "widespread opposition to the direct and indirect rule of the Roman administration . . . and to the urban elite" as an important factor in the first century ("Roman Sepphoris," 322–26).

39. James F. Strange, Dennis Groh, and Thomas R. W. Longstaff, "Excavations at Sepphoris: The Location and Identification of Shikhin," *IEJ* 44 (1994): 216–27.

40. Rabbinic references, results of neutron-activation analysis, and discussion in David Adan-Bayewitz, *Common Pottery in Roman Galilee: A Study of Local Trade* (Ramat Gan, Israel: Bar Ilan University Press, 1993), 23–41; and in Strange, Groh, and Longstaff, "Excavations at Sepphoris," 225.

41. These implications of Josephus's accounts make unlikely, at least for the early Roman period, the speculation that Shikhin may have functioned as the support village for a contingent of soldiers camped on Tell el-Badawiye further to the northwest (Strange, Groh, and Longstaff, "Excavations at Sepphoris" [last page in part II]). Josephus himself was able to exploit "Asochis's" independence of Sepphoris during the revolt, at points using the village as his own headquarters (*Vita* 384). Protected by his own mercenaries, he could thus keep a periodic watch on the disposition of Sepphoris while being ostensibly in alliance with "the Galileans" from the villages around Sepphoris.

42. The excavations are being headed by Mordechai Aviam, who has also recently published an extensive survey of village sites in Galilee (in Hebrew).

43. Perhaps it is partly because of his familiarity with the cliffs at Arbela that Josephus (intentionally?) misreads 1 Maccabees 9:1, which he is following at *Ant.* 12.421. See the explanation in Horsley, *Galilee*, 40.

Chapter 6. Before Synagogues Were Buildings

1. Expanded archaeological explorations have produced exciting new evidence for synagogue buildings and rich evidence at least for late antiquity. There are valuable updating of evidence and interpretive debate in the following collections of essays: *The Synagogue: Studies in Its Origins, Archaeology, and Architecture*, ed. Joseph Gutman (New York: KTAV, 1975); *Ancient Synagogues: The State of Research*, ed. Joseph Gutman, BJS 22 (Chico, Calif.: Scholars Press, 1981); *Ancient Synagogues Revealed*, ed. Lee I. Levine (Jerusalem: Israel Exploration Society, 1981); *The Synagogue in Late Antiquity*, ed. Lee I. Levine (Philadelphia: ASOR, 1987); *Ancient Synagogues: Historical Analysis and Archaeological Discovery*, ed. Dan Urman and Paul V. M. Flesher (Leiden: Brill, 1995).

2. Lee I. Levine, "The Second Temple Synagogue: The Formative Years," in *The Synagogue in Late Antiquity*, ed. Levine, 10–12, states that the evidence at Gamla remains inconclusive. Paul V. M. Flesher, "Palestinian Synagogues Before 70 C.E.: A Review of the Evidence," in *Approaches to Ancient Judaism*, vol. 6, ed. J. Neusner and E. Frerichs (Atlanta: Scholars Press, 1989), 75–80, along with other recent critics, decisively refutes the case that either of the rooms in the royal fortresses-palaces of Masada or Herodium were "synagogues." "None of these structures have any features that would identify them as specifically Jewish, let alone as synagogues." The attempt by Gideon Foerster ("The Synagogues at Masada and Herodion," *Journal of Jewish Art* 3/4 [1977]: 6–11) to argue for "a well-defined group of synagogues dated to the Second Temple Period" has been ably refuted by Marilyn J. Chiat, "First-Century Synagogue Architecture: Methodological Problems," in *Ancient Synagogues*, ed. Gutman, 50–58. It is unclear what was found at the "private house" in Magdala that would suggest that "the pious gathered [there] for prayer." So H. C. Kee, "The Transformation of the Synagogue after 70 C.E.: Its Import For Early Christianity," *NTS* 36 (1990): 8, following Eric M. Meyers and James F. Strange, *Archaeology, the Rabbis, and Early Christianity* (Nashville: Abingdon, 1981), 141. See also Lester L. Grabbe, "Synagogues in Pre-70 Palestine: A Re-Assessment," *JTS* 39 (1988): 401–10; and the candid admission by Yoram Tsafrir, "On the Source of the Architectural Design of the Ancient Synagogues in the Galilee: A New Appraisal," in *Ancient Synagogues*, ed. Urman and Flesher, 79.

3. Lee I. Levine, "Synagogues," in *NEAEHL* 4:1422.

4. Eric M. Meyers, "Synagogue," *ABD* 6:256. The excavations of Meyers et al. in Upper Galilee were instrumental in challenging the early typology.

5. Andrew R. Seager, "Ancient Synagogue Architecture: An Overview," in *Ancient Synagogues*, ed. Gutman, 42. So also Dennis E. Groh, "The Stratigraphic Chronology of the Galilean Synagogue from the Early Roman Period through the Early Byzantine Period," in *Ancient Synagogues*, ed. Urman

and Flesher, 51–69, who attempts to present a more complex typology of synagogues based only on carefully excavated and securely dated cases.

6. Ibid., 43.

7. Levine, "Synagogues," 1422.

8. Eric M. Meyers, James F. Strange, and Carol L. Meyers, *Excavations at Ancient Meiron* (Cambridge: ASOR, 1981), 157–58; cf. Richard A. Horsley, "Archaeology and the Villages of Upper Galilee: A Dialogue with Archaeologists," *BASOR* 297 (1995): 11–12.

9. See the various lists and summaries in Gideon Foerster, "The Ancient Synagogues of the Galilee," in *The Galilee in Late Antiquity*, ed. Lee I. Levine (New York: Jewish Theological Seminary of America, 1992), 289–319; and Z. Ilan, *Synagogues in the Galilee and Golan* (Jerusalem, 1987) (in Hebrew).

10. Eric M. Meyers, James F. Strange, Carol L. Meyers, and R. S. Hanson, "Preliminary Report on the 1977 and 1978 Seasons at Gush Halav," *BASOR* 233 (1979); Meyers, "Giscala," in *ABD* 2:1029–30; Meyers, "Ancient Gush Halav (Gishala), Palestinian Synagogues and the Eastern Diaspora," in *Ancient Synagogues*, ed. Gutman, 61–77.

11. Meyers says in his *ABD* "Synagogue" article that the *bema* dates to the second phase or fourth century, whereas in the *ABD* "Giscala" article, he dates the large *bema* to the Period I building, with a lesser, rebuilt *bema* in the Period II building.

12. Meyers, "Ancient Gush Halav," 70.

13. Ibid., 69.

14. Eric M. Meyers, "The Synagogue at Horvat Shema'," and Lee I. Levine, "Ancient Synagogues: A Historical Introduction," both in *Ancient Synagogues Revealed*, ed. Levine, 70–74, 6.

15. Foerster, "Ancient Synagogues of the Galilee," 294–95, says it faced east, like pagan temples.

16. Lee I. Levine, "Excavations at Horvat ha-'Amudim," in *Ancient Synagogues Revealed*, ed. Levine, 78–81.

17. Meyers, "Ancient Gush Halav," 71.

18. Eric M. Meyers, "Ancient Synagogues in Galilee: Their Religious and Cultural Setting," *BA* (Spring 1980): 106.

19. E.g., Foerster, "Ancient Synagogues of the Galilee," 295–96.

20. Levine, "Ancient Synagogues," 7.

21. Foerster, "Ancient Synagogues of the Galilee," 300.

22. Levine, "Ancient Synagogues," 7. This would appear to pose a problem for the argument that synagogue buildings are evidence for the relocation of numbers of Judeans to Galilee after the Bar Kokhba Revolt: it is unclear what would identify these buildings as Judean. How can interpreters sort out what would indicate Judean rather than indigenous (Israelite) Galilean — or for that matter, non-Israelite — culture?

23. Was this at least in part a response to the sudden presence of Chris-

tian pilgrims and pilgrimage churches in the fourth century, evoking among Jewish Galileans a need for their own unique symbols?

24. Foerster, "Ancient Synagogues of the Galilee," 294–95, 299.

25. Seager, "Ancient Synagogue Architecture," 41.

26. Meyers, *ABD* 6:255; yet he also claims that a fixed Torah shrine was found in the third-century basilica at Nabratein, in *NEAEHL* 1077–79.

27. Levine, "Ancient Synagogues," 5.

28. Meyers, *ABD* 6:255–56.

29. Dan Urman, "The House of Assembly and the House of Study: Are They One and the Same?" *JJS* 44 (1993): 249 n. 100.

30. L. Y. Rahmani, "Stone Synagogue Chairs: Their Identification, Use, and Significance," *IEJ* 40 (1990): 192–214, analyzes all the available archaeological and literary evidence, has sorted critically through the previous suggestions and proposed a highly suggestive alternative. Cf. Levine, "Ancient Synagogues," 5.

31. Vs. I. Renov, "The Seat of Moses," *IEJ* 5 (1955): 262.

32. Rahmani, "Stone Synagogue Chairs," 198.

33. Ibid., 205 n. 67.

34. Ibid., 206–7.

35. Seager, "Ancient Synagogue Architecture," 43.

36. Chiat, "First-Century Synagogue Architecture," 52.

37. Urman, "House of Assembly," 240–41; and Ze'ev Safrai, "The Communal Functions of the Synagogue in the Land of Israel in the Rabbinic Period," in *Ancient Synagogues*, ed. Urman and Flesher, 181–204, and the literature in Hebrew cited in both.

38. Richard E. Oster, "Supposed Anachronism in Luke-Acts' Use of *SYNAGOGE*," *NTS* 39 (1993): 178–208, illustrates the procedural problem. Precisely in response to challenges about both the meaning of terms and the standard synthetic concept, he persists in *assuming* an unstated definition of "the synagogue" and its artifactual manifestations so that then one can "identify" a building of Second Temple times as "a synagogue." He insists upon reversing the usage of Early Roman times, referring to the buildings rather than to the congregation as "synagogues," as in the statement that: "the word used most frequently in the period of Second Temple to refer to the synagogue [!] was the Greek word *proseuche*" (183).

39. Martin Hengel, "*Proseuche* und *Synagoge:* Juedische Gemeinde, Gotteshaus, und Gottesdienst in der Diaspora und in Palaestine," in *Festschrift fuer K. G. Kuhn*, ed. G. Jeremias, H. W. Kuhn, and H. Stegemann (Göttingen: Vandenhoeck and Ruprecht, 1971), now in *The Synagogue*, ed. Gutman; Howard C. Kee, "The Transformation of the Synagogue after 70 C.E.: Its Import For Early Christianity," *NTS* 36 (1990): 1–24; and R. A. Horsley, *Galilee: History, Politics, People* (Valley Forge, Pa.: Trinity Press International, 1995), chap. 10.

40. Hengel, *"Proseuche* und *Synagoge,"* 169, 172, 181; H. J. Leon, *The Jews of Ancient Rome* (Philadelphia: Jewish Publication Society of America, 1960), 139; W. Schrage, *"Synagōgē,"* *TDNT* 7:806ff; A. T. Kraabel, "The Diaspora Synagogue: Archaeological and Epigraphic Evidence since 'Sukenik,'" in *ANRW* 2.19.1 (1979): 185. Oster, "Supposed Anachronism," 185, demonstrates this point in a chart that lists *proseuche* as the dominant term used for a meeting place.

41. A. T. Kraabel, "Unity and Diversity among Diaspore Synagogues," in *Synagogue in Late Antiquity*, ed. Levine, 51–55, points out that the associations which the Jewish *synagogai* resemble socially were not particularly "of a religious nature," even though they usually had a patron deity. As Kraabel's own discussion indicates, moreover, these Jewish communities were far more than a "voluntary association." That point seems to pass unrecognized in Ze'ev Safrai, "The Communal Functions of the Synagogue," although he does draw the important distinction between "small communities" and "large communities." Clearly in Sepphoris/Diocaesarea and Tiberias, which were governed by city councils, the several "assemblies" would have functioned more like those in diaspora cities than those in villages.

42. It is therefore important to become both more precise and more comprehensive with regard to "synagogues" in first-century Galilee than recent standard handbook treatments. For example, it is not historically warranted to say that "during Second Temple times the term 'synagogue' referred both to a group of people and/or a building or institution," and it is too narrow to suggest that "synagogues" only "met together for worship and religious purposes," as does Meyers, "Synagogue," 251–52.

43. S. Safrai, "The Synagogue," in *The Jewish People in the First Century*, CRINT I.2, ed. S. Safrai and M. Stern (Assen: Van Gorcum, 1976), 933.

44. Ibid., 919. Ze'ev Safrai, *The Economy of Roman Palestine* (London: Routledge, 1994), 239–40, cites several passages from the Mishnah, Tosefta, and Talmuds that refer to the "days of assembly" and the prayers, Torah reading, fasts, and court-sessions that take place then — ironically in a section entitled "Regional Markets and Fairs."

45. Presumably, since local charity was no more monetarized than the local economy in general (see chap. 3 above), such collection was of goods, not money, vs. Martin Goodman, *State and Society in Roman Galilee, A.D. 132–212* (Totowa, N.J.: Rowman and Allanheld, 1983), 121–22.

46. *Discoveries in the Judaean Desert*, vol. 2, *Les grottes de Murabba'at. Texte*, ed. P. Benoit, J. T. Milik, and R. de Vaux (Oxford: Clarendon, 1961), 2:124, no. 24B, and 155–59, no. 42.

47. So also Goodman, *State and Society in Roman Galilee*, 122–23; and Safrai, "The Communal Functions of the Synagogue," 181, 189, 193.

48. The Book of Judith portrays the local assembly (*ekklēsia;* which includes the young women as well as young men) as headed by an apparently indeterminate number of "elders" among whom two or three "magistrates"

take leading roles (6:14–16, 8:10, 35; 10:6; 13:12). The story of Susanna has two "elders" from the people appointed as "judges" but then overruled and executed "by the whole synagogue" (Susanna 5, 41, 60).

49. G. McL. Harper, *Village Administration in the Roman Province of Syria* (Princeton, N.J.: Princeton University Press, 1928), 27–38.

50. See further Goodman, *State and Society in Roman Galilee*, 124, and Horsley, *Galilee*, 231–32.

51. Kee, "Transformation of the Synagogue," 12–14, even argues that the Pharisees led the development of the synagogues as worshipping communities. Sean Freyne, *Galilee, Jesus, and the Gospels: Literary Approaches and Historical Investigations* (Philadelphia: Fortress Press, 1988), esp. 202–10, proceeds on the assumption that the synagogue was the "natural focal point" for the activity of "the scribe with his torah scroll," who supposedly controlled "the various media of education, including the synagogue."

52. Shaye J. D. Cohen, "The Place of the Rabbi in Jewish Society of the Second Century," and Lee I. Levine, "The Sages and the Synagogue in Late Antiquity: The Evidence of the Galilee," in *Galilee in Late Antiquity*, ed. Levine, 157–73 and 201–22, respectively. Safrai, "The Communal Functions of the Synagogue," 183–85, 201–3, offers evidence that leads to this conclusion, but does not draw it.

53. Cohen, "Place of the Rabbi," 157; Levine, "The Sages and the Synagogue," 203.

54. Cohen, "Place of the Rabbi," 161.

55. Ibid., 167–68.

56. On the following see Levine, "The Sages and the Synagogue," 206–19. Levine at first claims that "there was a marked increase in rabbinic involvement in synagogue affairs from the mid-third century on" (206), but by the conclusion of his examination of the evidence states that "rabbinic influence was indeed peripheral to the actual operation of the ancient synagogue" (219).

57. *Codex Theodosianus* 16.8.4; 8; 13; 15. See A. Linder, *The Jews in Roman Imperial Legislation* (Detroit: Wayne State University Press, 1987), 186–89, 201–4, 220–22. Cohen, "Place of the Rabbi," 169, points out that before Judah the Patriarch the rabbis were not communal functionaries. They would not appear to have become such very soon after Judah either.

58. Levine, "The Sages and the Synagogue," 220.

59. The most developed and systematic discussion of the social role of the Pharisees as that of "retainers" is Anthony J. Saldarini, *Pharisees, Scribes, and Sadducees* (Wilmington, Del.: Michael Glazier, 1988).

60. Recently, e.g., Kee, "Transformation of the Synagogue," esp. 14–16.

Chapter 7. Languages and Cultural Traditions

Epigraphs: Claude Lévi-Strauss, *Tristes Tropiques* (London: Cape, 1973); W. V. Harris, *Ancient Literacy* (Cambridge: Harvard University Press, 1989), 176.

1. Glen W. Bowersock, *Hellenism in Late Antiquity* (Ann Arbor, Mich.: University of Michigan Press, 1990), 7.

2. W. W. Tarn and G. T. Griffith, *Hellenistic Civilisation*, 3rd ed. (London: Arnold, 1952), 268.

3. Harris, *Ancient Literacy;* Rosalind Thomas, *Oral Tradition and Written Record in Classical Athens* (Cambridge: Cambridge University Press, 1989); Paul J. Achtemeier, "*Omne verbum sonat.* The New Testament and the Oral Environment of Late Western Antiquity," *JBL* 109 (1990): 3–27; Pieter J. J. Botha, "Greco-Roman Literacy as Setting for New Testament Writings," *Neotestamentica* 26 (1992): 195–215, with helpful bibliography.

4. Harris, *Ancient Literacy*, 110. The figures for Pompeii, of course, will be on the high side for literacy, as Harris points out later (202): "Both the Italians of Pompeii and the Greeks of Egypt undoubtedly used writing much more than the inhabitants of some backward parts of the Empire, and the information which they give us about the functions of writing cannot be applied to other populations."

5. On inscriptions in the Roman empire, key studies are Ramsay Mac-Mullen, "The Epigraphic Habit in the Roman Empire," *AJP* 103 (1982): 233–46; Fergus Millar, "Epigraphy," in *Sources for Ancient History*, ed. M. Crawford (Cambridge: Cambridge University Press, 1983), 80–136; and William V. Harris, "Literacy and Epigraphy, I," *Zeitschrift fuer Papyrologie und Epigraphie* 52 (1983): 87–111; on inscriptions in ancient Athens, see Thomas, *Oral Tradition and Written Record*, 286.

6. On public inscriptions and other ways the imperial government imposed itself psychologically as well as administratively, see Harris, *Ancient Literacy*, 206–13, 232. "It was above all coins which, potentially at least, could bring politically significant phrases before the eyes of the population at large." See also Richard Oster, "Numismatic Windows in the Social World of Early Christianity: A Methodological Inquiry," *JBL* 101 (1982): 195–223.

7. Harris, *Ancient Literacy*, 261–65.

8. See S. F. Bonner, *Education in Ancient Rome: From the Elder Cato to the Younger Pliny* (London: Methuen, 1977), 37–38.

9. Fergus Millar, *The Emperor in the Roman World* (London: Duckworth, 1977), 313–41; Harvey J. Graff, *The Legacies of Literacy: Continuities and Contradictions in Western Culture and Society* (Bloomington, Ind.: Indiana University Press, 1987), 12; and Harris, *Ancient Literacy,* 333–35: "There cannot be the least doubt that writing was an indispensable instrument of imperial domination.... The empires of Greek and Roman antiquity all depended heavily on writing and documents."

10. Carl J. Couch, "Oral Technologies: A Cornerstone of Ancient Civilizations?" *Sociological Quarterly* 30 (1989): 587–602, citation from 589.

11. For example, the comment, in connection with Judea in the first century C.E., that "writing was an essential accompaniment of life at almost all levels," by C. H. Roberts, "Books in the Graeco-Roman World and in the

New Testament," in *Cambridge History of the Bible* (Cambridge: Cambridge University Press, 1970), 1:48.

12. See, e.g., the note in the standard translation by Herbert Danby, *The Mishnah* (London: Oxford, 1933), 177 n. 6.

13. Vs. Martin Goodman, *State and Society in Roman Galilee, A.D. 132–212* (Totowa, N.J.: Rowman and Allanheld, 1983), 72, who assumes that "the general rabbinic tendency [is] to assume literacy." Yet the fact that "all tannaitic texts assume a division of Jewish society into *haverim*, who keep the purity and tithing laws, and *amme haaretz* ('people of the land'), who do not" (77) suggests that much of Goodman's discussion of "education" (71–81) does not pertain to village culture.

14. Among the treatments of languages in Roman Palestine, Chaim Rabin, "Hebrew and Aramaic in the First Century," in *The Jewish People in the First Century*, CRINT I.2, ed. S. Safrai and M. Stern (Assen: Van Gorcum, 1974–76), 1007–39; and G. H. R. Horsley, "The Fiction of 'Jewish Greek,'" in *New Documents Illustrating Early Christianity*, vol. 5, *Linguistic Essays*, ed. G. H. R. Horsley (Sydney, Australia: Macquarrie University Press, 1989), esp. 23–25, take sociolinguistics into consideration.

15. Among the recent surveys of languages in Roman Palestine are Joseph A. Fitzmyer, "The Languages of Palestine in the First Century A.D.," *CBQ* 32 (1970): 501–31; Rabin, "Hebrew and Aramaic in the First Century," 1007–39, and G. Mussies, "Greek in Palestine and the Diaspora," in *The Jewish People in the First Century*, ed. Safrai and Stern, 1040–64; Eric M. Meyers and James F. Strange, *Archaeology, the Rabbis, and Early Christianity* (Nashville: Abingdon, 1981), 62–91; Horsley, "The Fiction of 'Jewish Greek,'" 5–40.

16. See further Rabin, "Hebrew and Aramaic in the First Century," 1012–13.

17. J. T. Milik, "Textes hebreux et arameens," in *Discoveries in the Judaean Desert*, vol. 2, *Les grottes de Murabba'at. Texte*, ed. P. Benoit, J. T. Milik, and R. de Vaux (Oxford: Clarendon, 1961), 62–205.

18. John J. Collins, *Between Athens and Jerusalem* (New York: Crossroad, 1983), provides a survey of Jewish literature in Greek.

19. Martin Hengel, *The "Hellenization" of Judaea in the First Century after Christ* (Philadelphia: Trinity Press International, 1989), 88–102.

20. Ibid., 8–10.

21. *Discoveries in the Judaean Desert of Jordan*, vol. 2, *Les grottes de Murabba'at*, ed. Benoit, Milik, and de Vaux.

22. Yigael Yadin, *Bar-Kokhba: The Rediscovery of the Legendary Hero of the Last Jewish Revolt against Imperial Rome* (London: Wiedenfeld and Nicolson, 1971), 130.

23. Rabin, "Hebrew and Aramaic in the First Century," 1033.

24. E.g., ibid., 1036.

25. Lawrence T. Geraty, "Khirbet el-Kom Bilingual Ostracon," *BASOR* 220 (1975): 55–62.

26. *EAEHL* 2, nos. 8, 12 (1975): 634–35.

27. Yadin, *Bar-Kokhba*, 181.

28. Ibid., 222–53.

29. Eric M. Meyers, "Galilean Regionalism as a Factor in Historical Reconstruction," *BASOR* 221 (1986): 97, citing a survey reported in a paper by James F. Strange, "New Evidences for the Language of Galilee/Golan: First-Fifth Centuries."

30. Ibid. Note the cautionary comments of Harris, *Ancient Literacy*, 177: "The difficulties of inferring from epigraphical evidence which languages were spoken in given areas at given periods are extreme.... Spoken languages often left no epigraphic trace."

31. Despite his statement that Greek "could become a first language for many, even unlettered people" (141), Sean Freyne, *Galilee from Alexander the Great to Hadrian, 323 B.C.E. to 135 C.E.: A Study in Second Temple Judaism* (Wilmington, Del.: Michael Glazier, 1980), concludes that "Aramaic remained the most commonly spoken language of the vast majority of the inhabitants of Galilee throughout the whole period" (144). Hence, despite Meyers's protests about his ignoring the regional differences within Galilee ("Galilean Regionalism: A Reappraisal," in *Approaches to Ancient Judaism*, vol. 5, ed. William S. Green [Atlanta: Scholars Press, 1985], 119–21), Freyne's overall discussion (141-44) seems implicitly more sensitive to the likely variations between the cities and the Galilean villages generally.

32. Rabin, "Hebrew and Aramaic in the First Century," 1035–36: "For the sake of argument we may assume ... "

33. Meyers and Strange, *Archaeology*, 68.

34. As Meyers and Strange themselves note in ibid., 68. On epitaphs, see further Harris, *Ancient Literacy*, 221–22, 275.

35. Contra Meyers and Strange, *Archaeology*, 69–72.

36. G. Mussies, "Greek as the Vehicle of Early Christianity," *NTS* 29 (1983): 362–64; Horsley, "The Fiction of 'Jewish Greek,'" 20.

37. Gary A. Rendsburg, "The Galilean Background of Mishnaic Hebrew," in *The Galilee in Late Antiquity*, ed. Lee I. Levine (New York: Jewish Theological Seminary of America, 1992), 225–39. Previous arguments that Hebrew was spoken in Galilee can be found in H. Birkeland, *The Language of Jesus* (Oslo: I Komisjon Hos J Dybwad, 1954); and J. A. Emerton, "The Problem of Vernacular Hebrew in the First Century A.D. and the Language of Jesus," *JTS* 24 (1973): 1–23.

38. Cf. Meyers and Strange, *Archaeology*, 72–73.

39. Jack Finegan, *The Archaeology of the New Testament* (Princeton, N.J.: Princeton University Press, 1969), 119–20.

40. Cf. Hengel, *Judaism and Hellenism*, 104: "Between Herod and the destruction of A.D. 70 [Jerusalem] must have had a quite considerable minority who spoke Greek as their mother tongue, as Greek inscriptions show." Saul Lieberman, *Greek in Jewish Palestine*, 2nd ed. (New York: Feldheim, 1965),

30, concluded that "the very poverty and vulgarity of the [Greek] language inscriptions [in Palestine] shows that it was spoken by the people and not written by learned men only." We might rather conclude that such poverty and vulgarity show that whoever wrote such inscriptions just knew little Greek and that poorly. Given the historical development of Greek in Jerusalem, if a minority could speak Greek it consisted largely of the upper class.

41. Cf. Meyers and Strange, *Archaeology*, 82: "These [Greek ossuary inscriptions] prove beyond any reasonable doubt that the majority of Jewish families could read and write Greek and did so even for strictly family business." J. N. Sevenster, *Do You Know Greek? How Much Greek Could First-Century Christians Have Known?* NovTSup 19 (Leiden: Brill, 1968), 115–28, also based his argument that knowledge of Greek was widespread on funerary inscriptions. In an important recent critical response to such arguments, G. H. R. Horsley, in *New Documents Illustrating Early Christianity*, ed. Horsley, 5:21, counters that "in the main, the Greek epitaphs surviving in Palestine from this period reveal only a rudimentary ability in written Greek. Yet the rudimentary facility in *speaking* the language is not thereby proved." Harris, "Literacy and Epigraphy, I," 87–111, even questions whether epigraphy can yield us much tangible data concerning the percentage of literates in society. More specifically, Harris, *Ancient Literacy*, 221–22, explains the role that status played in epitaphs among partially Romanized provincials, and (275) indicates that epitaphs in Greek rarely appear among peasants.

42. E.g., Meyers and Strange, *Archaeology*, 84–86; Strange, "Archaeology and the Religion of Judaism in Palestine," *ANRW* 2.19.1 (1979): 661: "The surprise is that almost two-thirds [of the ossuary inscriptions from ancient Palestine] are in Greek alone. Clearly, then, Greek is the dominant language of family life even at the point of burial customs."

43. Isaiah Gafni, "Reinterment in the Land of Israel: Notes on the Origin and Development of the Custom," *Jerusalem Cathedra* 1 (1981): 96–104.

44. For the inscriptions found in Beth Shearim, see M. Schwabe and B. Lifshitz, *Beth She'arim*, vol. 2, *The Greek Inscriptions* (Jerusalem: Israel Exploration Society, 1974), and N. Avigad, *Beth She'arim*, vol. 3, *Catacombs 12–23* (Jerusalem: Israel Exploration Society, 1976).

45. The conclusions of Harris, *Ancient Literacy*, 187, for Syria and Judea generally is worth noting:

> Greek occupies a fairly definite place. It is one of the languages of provincial and city government. It is the language of immigrants and their descendants, and of partially Hellenized social and commercial elites, whose members...simultaneously hold on to one or more local languages. It is not the language of the streets except in a few places, and it is not the language of ordinary villages.

The situation in Galilee would appear to have been the same as in Egypt:

"In the villages most Egyptians spoke their own language and had little or no reason to learn Greek" (190; cf. 276–78).

46. Rabin, "Hebrew and Aramaic in the First Century," 1032, beginning with the assumption: "Normally, a language is also the bearer of a culture. If this is evidently true of national languages, it applies with even greater force to the upper language of a *diglossia* situation." Ironically he cites Judah the Prince's statement about "either the holy tongue or Greek" as evidence — which, of course, points in the opposite direction: people were loyal to their Aramaic language!

47. The deity "Zeus Atabyrios" appears in widely scattered sites of Sicily, Rhodes, and Crimea, even prior to Hellenistic times as well. See Martin Hengel, *Judaism and Hellenism* (Philadelphia: Fortress, 1974), 2:172 n. 27, 198 n. 245.

48. Moshe Fischer, Asher Ovadiah, and Israel Roll, "The Roman Temple at Kedesh, Upper Galilee: A Preliminary Study," *Tel Aviv* 11 (1984): 168–71; Jody Magness, "Some Observations on the Roman Temple at Kedesh," *IEJ* 40 (1990): 173–81.

49. A pertinent substantive as well as theoretical discussion of the "great" and "little" traditions is James C. Scott, "Protest and Profanation: Agrarian Revolt and the Little Tradition," *Theory and Society* 4 (1977): 1–38, 211–46. It has often been pointed out in recent discussions of literacy and orality (e.g., Harris, *Ancient Literacy*, 30) that memories of a people's traditions are much stronger among oral cultures than among highly literate societies — something that must be considered in historical and archaeological analysis.

50. Argued as the most satisfactory hypothesis to explain the fragmentary evidence for the identity of the Galileans in R. A. Horsley, *Galilee: History, Politics, People* (Valley Forge, Pa.: Trinity Press International, 1995), esp. chaps. 1–2.

51. Originally argued in R. A. Horsley, "Popular Messianic Movements around the Time of Jesus," *CBQ* 46 (1984): 471–95; see also with John Hanson, *Bandits, Prophets, and Messiahs: Popular Movements at the Time of Jesus* (San Francisco: Harper and Row, 1985), chap. 3.

Conclusion

1. I.e., in ways not yet clear in Richard Horsley, *Galilee: History, Politics, People* (Valley Forge, Pa.: Trinity Press International, 1995), or other previous publications.

2. E.g., Gunther Bornkamm, *Jesus of Nazareth* (New York: Harper, 1960); Norman Perrin, *Rediscovering the Teachings of Jesus* (New York: Harper and Row, 1967); John Riches, *Jesus and the Transformation of Judaism* (London: Darton, Longman, and Todd, 1980).

3. E.g., Richard A. Horsley with John S. Hanson, *Bandits, Prophets, and Messiahs: Popular Movements at the Time of Jesus* (Minneapolis: Winston, 1985);

R. A. Horsley, *Jesus and the Spiral of Violence: Popular Jewish Resistance in Roman Palestine* (San Francisco: Harper and Row, 1987); John Dominic Crossan, *The Historical Jesus: The Life of a Mediterranean Jewish Peasant* (San Francisco: HarperCollins, 1991).

4. The usual failure to consider Galilee itself, in distinction from the rest of "greater Judea" or "Jewish Palestine," can be illustrated from my own *Jesus and the Spiral of Violence;* only with *Sociology and the Jesus Movement* (New York: Crossroad, 1989) did I finally begin to consider the possible regional differences between Galilee and Judea/Jerusalem.

5. Burton L. Mack, *A Myth of Innocence* (Philadelphia: Fortress, 1988) 53–98; *The Lost Gospel: The Book of Q and Christian Origins* (San Francisco: HarperCollins, 1993); Crossan, *The Historical Jesus.*

6. Gerd Theissen, *The Sociology of Early Palestinian Christianity* (Philadelphia: Fortress, 1978). Both Mack's and Crossan's representation of Jesus as a (Jewish) Cynic presupposes Theissen's itinerant individualism; cf. the critique of and alternative to Theissen in Horsley, *Sociology and the Jesus Movement.*

7. Regardless of whether we opt for vagabonds or debtors as the more important for the activity of Jesus, this debate points to a centrally important issue that archaeologists might be capable of addressing: the cost and likely relative impact on Galilee and Perea of Antipas's building projects. The cost of Solomon's building projects was a major issue for the Deuteronomic historians, with major impact on subsequent historical events (see 1 Kings 4–11). The cost of Herod the Great's building projects and of his lavish gifts to Hellenistic cities and to the Roman imperial family looms prominently in Josephus's accounts. What was likely the extent and the time-frame of Antipas's expansion of Sepphoris and founding of Tiberias and what would have been the cost in terms of labor and support? How was that cost financed or managed? With all the archaeological explorations of major building programs in classical antiquity along with other comparative archaeology, it should be possible to estimate the cost of such building programs and the impact on a ruler's economic base if spread over a limited period of time.

8. E. P. Sanders, *Jesus and Judaism* (Philadelphia: Fortress, 1985), combines an incisive critique of certain forms of "Jesus versus Judaism" while continuing to abstract Jesus from the concrete historical situation into a synthetic construction of "Judaism."

9. Frequently encountered, for example, among scholars of Q, such as John S. Kloppenborg, *The Formation of Q* (Philadelphia: Fortress, 1987).

10. See the analysis in *Jesus and the Spiral of Violence*, 199–208.

11. Argued more fully in R. A. Horsley, "Q and Jesus: Assumptions, Approaches, and Analyses," *Semeia* 55 (1992): 175–209; "Social Conflict in the Synoptic Sayings Source Q," in *Conflict and Invention: Literary, Rhetorical, and Social Studies on the Sayings Gospel Q*, ed. John S. Kloppenborg (Valley Forge, Pa.: Trinity Press International, 1995), 37–52; and *Jesus and the Spiral of Violence*, chap. 10.

12. Used in connection with the distinctive Israelite/Jewish popular movements mentioned by Josephus in R. A. Horsley, "Popular Messianic Movements around the Time of Jesus," *CBQ* 46 (1984): 471–95; and "'Like One of the Prophets of Old': Two Types of Popular Prophets at the Time of Jesus," *CBQ* 47 (1985): 435–63; and for the wisdom of Jesus over against that of professional literate sages in Crossan, *Historical Jesus.*

13. Eric M. Meyers, "Roman Sepphoris in Light of New Archaeological Evidence and Recent Research," in *The Galilee in Late Antiquity*, ed. Lee I. Levine (New York: Jewish Theological Seminary of America, 1992), 331, 333–34.

14. Joan E. Taylor, *Christians and the Holy Places: The Myth of Jewish Christian Origins* (Oxford: Clarendon Press, 1993), 56–64.

15. Ibid., 321, 340.

16. The two ends of the spectrum are represented by Gedalihu Alon, *Jews, Judaism, and the Classical World*, trans. I. Abrahams (Jerusalem: Magnes, 1977), to Erwin R. Goodenough, *Jewish Symbols in the Greco-Roman World*, 13 vols. (New York: Pantheon, 1953–68), 12:184–98.

17. Continued in Martin Goodman, *State and Society in Roman Galilee, 135–212 A.D.* (Totowa, N.J.: Rowman and Allanheld, 1983).

18. See esp. Lee I. Levine, *The Rabbinic Class of Roman Palestine in Late Antiquity* (New York: Jewish Theological Seminary of America, 1989); Levine, "The Sages and the Synagogue in Late Antiquity: The Evidence of the Galilee," and Shaye J. D. Cohen, "The Place of the Rabbi in Jewish Society of the Second Century," *The Galilee in Late Antiquity*, ed. Levine, 201–22, 157–73, based on a larger study to appear in *Cambridge History of Judaism*, vol. 4. The following sketch is heavily dependent on these studies.

19. Vs. Goodman, *State and Society*, 93, 177–78.

20. Cohen, "Place of the Rabbi," 169, citing such tannaitic traditions as *t. Šabb.* 2.5, 13.2; *t. 'Erub.* 1.2, 6.2; *t. Pesaḥ.* 10.12; *t. Sukk.* 1.9; *t. Ter.* 2.13; *t. Ḥag* 2.13; Levine, *The Rabbinic Class*, 69–71; Stuart S. Miller, "Intercity Relations in Roman Palestine: The Case of Sepphoris and Tiberias," *AJSRev* 12 (1987): 12–13.

21. Levine, *Rabbinic Class of Roman Palestine*, 47–55; Levine, "Social Aspects of Burial in Beth She'arim: Archaeological Finds and Talmudic Sources," in *Galilee in Late Antiquity*, ed. Levine, 367.

22. Cohen, "Place of the Rabbi," 159–60, adds statistics on the places assigned to the legal decisions, with one-third or nineteen to cities (but only eight to Galilean cities) and thirty-eight to villages or towns (but only a few to Galilean villages). Assuming that more than two-thirds of the populace lived in towns and villages, however, that tilts the statistics slightly to the cities. It is unclear also whether the legal decisions pertained to particular places and whether the sages were (temporarily) located there. Does the assignment of a legal decision to a particular place indicate "followers" of the rabbis in that place?

23. R. El'azar, a colleague of R. Yohanan, had moved to Tiberias from Sepphoris, along with R. Ami, R. Asi, R. Hiyya, and R. Zera, according to Lee I. Levine, "R. Simeon b. Yohai and the Purification of Tiberias: History and Tradition," *HUCA* 49 (1978): 173–74.

24. Goodman, *State and Society*, chapter 7; Cohen, "Place of the Rabbi," with more rigorous criteria for cases, makes the point even more convincingly.

25. Shaye J. D. Cohen, *From the Maccabees to the Mishnah* (Philadelphia: Westminster Press, 1987), 111–15, 219–21.

26. Cohen, "Place of the Rabbi," 157. The rabbis "were neither agents of the state nor communal leaders. In sum, the rabbis did not control the religious and civil life of second-century Palestinian Jewry" (164).

27. Such divisions among the rabbis that correspond to their agreement with the patriarch cannot be dissolved into the supposed continuing rivalry between Sepphoris and Tiberias, as now demonstrated by Miller, "Intercity Relations in Roman Palestine," 1–24.

28. A basic thesis of Levine, *The Rabbinic Class of Roman Palestine.*

29. Horsley, *Galilee*, 182–85.

30. See the many works of Jacob Neusner, e.g., *Judaism: The Evidence of the Mishnah* (Chicago: University of Chicago Press, 1981), chaps. 4 and 5.

31. Although the Temple is long since destroyed, portions of the crops are still reserved for the priests. The rabbis did apparently attempt to place themselves in the place of the priests as recipients of the tithes. Evidence in Levine, *Rabbinic Class of Roman Palestine*, 71, 172. Neither the Mishnah nor any other source indicates, however, whether any systematized gathering and distribution of tithes was set up in Galilee once the Temple was gone.

INDEX